AF412114

The Legacy of Language

THE LEGACY OF

Language

A TRIBUTE TO CHARLTON

Laird

EDITED BY PHILLIP C. BOARDMAN

UNIVERSITY OF NEVADA PRESS

RENO AND LAS VEGAS

1987

Publication of this book has been partially funded by a grant from the Nevada Humanities Committee.

The paper used in this book meets the requirements of American National Standard for Information Sciences—Permanence of Paper for Printed Library Materials, ANSI Z39.48-1984. Binding materials were chosen for strength and durability.

Library of Congress Cataloging in Publication Data

The Legacy of language.

   Bibliography: p.
   Includes index.
   1. Language and languages.   2. Sociolinguistics.
3. Laird, Charlton Grant, 1901–   . I. Laird,
Charlton Grant, 1901–   . II. Boardman, Phillip C.
P26.L29L44   1987   401'.9   86-30840
ISBN 0-87417-121-0 (alk. paper)

University of Nevada Press, Reno, Nevada 89557 USA

Book and jacket design by Richard Hendel

Printed in the United States of America

FRONTISPIECE: Charlton Laird, 1901–1984. *Ahmed Essa.*

Contents

vi | Contents

Preface

Robert Gorrell

O N E afternoon in the fall of 1945 the doorbell interrupted my preparation for my first classes at the University of Nevada. Charlton Laird, who had returned a few days before from a year as a postdoctoral fellow at Yale, was on the porch. He was holding in his left hand, rather awkwardly, a five-foot-long board. "I'm sorry to trouble you," he said very quietly, "but do you happen to have a hatchet or a small axe?"

And then he pointed to the board. "I can't seem to get this off." A nail at the end of the board was driven completely through his thumb. I found a hatchet and managed to split the board from the nail without hurting him, and we got to the hospital, where a surgeon finally removed the nail with no serious long-range damage.

He had been unpacking a crate; a tough elm slat had slipped as he was pulling it loose and had sprung back with enough force to drive the nail. He had calmly walked the three blocks to our house, carrying the board nailed to his throbbing thumb, to get a practical solution for his problem.

Although this is a preface to a book dedicated to Larry's writing, I find myself recalling incidents like this—or that Larry was a varsity fencer at Iowa, or that as a young man he was a farm worker following the wheat harvest through the Middle West, or that he worked three or four hours a day for ten years building his house south of town. I suppose that in some vague way they make me think of the ingenuity and imagination and versatility and integrity and also modesty behind the writing that provided the reason for the essays that follow.

That writing was extensive and varied, and it occupied Larry all his life. He did newspaper work and university publicity in Iowa. He

---

R O B E R T G O R R E L L, former vice president of the University of Nevada, Reno, is widely known as a writer and lecturer on rhetoric and composition. With Charlton Laird he co-authored several books, including the successful *Modern English Handbook*.

wrote poetry through most of his life, although little of it was published. One of his two novels won an *Atlantic Monthly* prize. He even wrote some sermons during a summer college vacation when he had a job as an itinerant country preacher.

He wrote fast, and he put in long hours, and some of his books never got edited down as much as they should have been. He had difficulty refusing any proposal, and he often was working on three or four projects at the same time, not always without confusion. The edited manuscript for a series of lectures disappeared in his stacks of papers sometime in 1980 and was lost for a year. Larry searched frantically, at home and in his office and in his friends' briefcases. He finally found it in a box in his garage where he had put it for safekeeping, and it was published in 1981 as *Walter Van Tilburg Clark: Critiques.*

When Laird was doing his graduate work at Iowa, Columbia, and Stanford, notions about the proper role of a scholar were pretty clear. The scholar was to find a topic specific enough that investigating it could produce new knowledge and to become the world authority on this narrow topic. Laird respected this traditional view of scholarship and research, and he produced important research studies on medieval literature and later on Noah Webster and Horne Tooke.

His early scholarly interests were broad, however, and his studies in world literature prompted him in the 1950s to accept editorship of the *Guide to Comparative Literature,* an ambitious project sponsored by the American Library Association, the National Council of Teachers of English, and several other groups. The *Guide* was a comprehensive annotated bibliography, including translations of basic texts in many languages, criticism with a comparative approach, important works in general disciplines like folklore or semantics, and studies of relations between literature and other disciplines like psychology or the law. Two or three hundred established scholars contributed bibliographies over the years. But the project was plagued by delays and changes in sponsorship. Laird produced completed and edited manuscripts on two occasions, but each time the texts were outdated before details of publication could be worked out, and the unpublished manuscript, with some 13,000 entries, is still floating around somewhere.

Even though he had been working on a series of specialized studies, including the book that is still in wide use as *Webster's New World Thesaurus,* Laird was seriously concerned about general topics, especially about problems of teaching. He was for forty years an enthusiastic and innovative teacher. And again when I think of his teaching, I think of a tenuously relevant incident. The Lairds, or their daughter, had acquired a mainly cocker spaniel pup named Taffy. Taffy was a car chaser, and none of the recommended educational procedures had discouraged her from attacking the rear tire of any passing vehicle. Larry had worked out, logically, a new procedure. Punishment, either after or during the event, didn't work; Taffy didn't relate the punishment to the car chasing. What was needed was some way of making Taffy find chasing cars unpleasant. We had an old Ford pickup truck. The plan was that I drive the truck as temptingly as possible past the Laird house, with Larry concealed prone in the truck bed with a long whip. When Taffy attacked the rear wheel, Larry could nick her with the whip without being seen. Taffy would have to associate the pain with the attack on the car. We completed two treatments. Amazingly to me, though not to Larry, the procedure worked, and Taffy resorted to cultivating her other bad habits.

Larry did not use a whip in class—he tended to be gentle and amusing—but he did approach teaching creatively. In the early 1950s, for example, when we were faced with a surge in enrollment and a shortage of staff, he worked out a system of peer instruction, with student-run conferences and criticism, to manage the composition courses. It worked—for him, at least, and in experiments he conducted as a visiting professor at the University of Oregon—and articles explaining it attracted a good deal of national attention.

Laird was active in the National Council of Teachers of English and a popular speaker to teachers' groups. Some of his lectures to teachers were collected in 1970 as *And Gladly Teche*. Many of them still seem revolutionary: they emphasize his devices for trying to get students to think, to find the big questions, and to realize that questions can be more important than answers. His enthusiasm, I suspect, sometimes deceived him into overestimating the achievements of his students, but students in his classes never lacked a challenge.

One of Laird's early academic concerns was that students in English departments throughout the country, many of whom were going to be teachers, typically had almost no courses in language along with their courses in literary history. He introduced an "Introduction to Language," which became a required course for majors in English. It was an attempt to acquaint students with major topics in language study and thereby to give them some understanding of how language works.

Partly from his experiences with the course, Laird wrote *The Miracle of Language*. In the preface to the book he says: "I tried to ask myself all the most important questions about language, answering those for which the present state of our scholarship provides answers and guessing at the rest."

Both Laird's writer-editor wife, Helene, and I were a little skeptical about the book's approach, which the preface admits "probably lacks a becoming decorum." Chapter headings like "English's Shrinking Grammatical Pants" or "The Speech That Blooms on the Tongue, Tra-la" seemed perhaps frivolous. But Laird was right, and the tone of the book was part of its success and set a pattern for Laird's method of presenting sound scholarship in generally readable form.

Laird turned his attention to popularization with his eyes open. He was aware that the academy suspected the generalist, and he knew about the risks of superficiality or glibness. But he also recognized the value of his approach.

He saw, in the first place, a real need, in a society depending more and more on communication, to make more people knowledgeable about language. He believed that teaching should not be limited to the classroom. He wrote textbooks, and he lectured to the public as well as to teachers, always zealous to expose errors about the nature of language and to encourage understanding of what he more than once called the most important tool of civilization.

He set out therefore to make his books readable. "I have deliberately tried to make this book engaging," he says in the preface to *The Word,* although he recognizes that "many prospective users will feel that an amusing book cannot be serious." But the information in the books is serious. And even though in its preface he says that *Language in America* "is not mainly original research," the book—which I consider his best—contains a great deal of original research.

There is another advantage to Laird's approach. It allows a writer to consider the big questions. Laird knew the importance of tracing a single etymology or editing an obscure manuscript. But he was more concerned with broader topics—where some American dialects originated, how languages migrate, how language affects society, where the language is going, where language came from, how language works. These are not the safest kinds of topics for a linguist, but they are usually the most interesting, and sometimes they produce the most significant insights.

The essays in this book deal with big topics, mainly discussing some of the ways in which language and society are related, how they influence each other. And they attempt, as Laird did, to make scholarly information about language available to the general reader.

Introduction

Phillip C. Boardman

Tʜᴇ belief in language as the source of human power has an unbroken tradition. Genesis shows Adam naming the animals spontaneously as they are paraded before him, a sign of his "knowing" their natures. Cultures around the world have invoked the efficacy of curses, the inviolability of oaths, and the magical power of spells. Personal names, too, have magical power, as thousands of new parents attest when they choose baby names from books giving their significance. A changed identity brings a new name, as when the covenant with God is marked in Abram's becoming Abraham, or when Saul adopts a new mission and the new name Paul. Car salesmen and mail-order computers invoke a person's name at every turn, teasingly redefining the character around the need for the product.

Words are the coins in the barter we call communication, and they have therefore become treasured possessions. The Jewish historian, to show us the high esteem in which Samuel the seer was held, says that "none of his words did fall to the ground." When Beowulf boasts of his intention to defeat the monster Grendel to a troop of terrified Danish retainers, he does so by "unlocking his word-hoard." The thesaurus, one of our collections of words, comes from a Greek word meaning 'treasury'. The ancient Hebrews perceived the nature of this barter in their story of the Tower of Babel: success comes to humans when they communicate, even if their purposes are perverse, but the confusion of tongues brings defeat, even as we today blame our own setbacks on "the failure to communicate."

In this century, linguists have concerned themselves increasingly with language structure, manifested in vernacular oral performance and in "speech acts." While this concern with the oral marks a shift away from the historical and written and seems to value language at

Pʜɪʟʟɪᴘ ᴄ. Bᴏᴀʀᴅᴍᴀɴ is a former editor of the medieval newsletter *Chronica*. He teaches at the University of Nevada, Reno, where he has published on language, on Chaucer, and on the Arthurian legends.

its most transient and ephemeral, modern philosophers and critics have, at the same time, become "obsessed with language," in the words of one scholar. Contemporary French critics have attacked the emphasis on spoken language as creating a false validation based on the authority or "presence" of the speaker. Philosophers have discovered that language is arbitrary, that words refer not to objects but to concepts in the mind, and therefore that words ("signifiers") are more real or have more substance than the concepts they signify.

Nobody appreciated the mystery and power of language more than Charlton Laird. Laird was born in 1901; his life spanned our century's often heated discussions about the nature of language. Attending college and graduate school in Iowa, he worked as an editor on the *Des Moines Register and Tribune,* going on to teach journalism at Drake University. This early experience undoubtedly lay behind Laird's word-smithery, his knowledge of the ins and outs of language at a practical level, and his ability to write fluently and with style. Doctoral and postdoctoral studies at Columbia, Stanford, and Yale cemented another quality of Laird's writing, his great learning and scholarship, tempered by a finely honed critical sense. Finally, his personal qualities, not the least of them humor, shine through his words, and contribute to the distinctive quality of his great popular successes *The Miracle of Language* and *Language in America.* (There is a list of Laird's major writings at the end of this book.) These works came as only part of a distinguished academic career at the University of Nevada, Reno, where Laird went as professor of English in 1943 (he had earlier taught in Pocatello and at Purdue). Admired widely as a teacher and lecturer, Laird also built his own house, published two novels, and took an active role in curricular and political struggles during some turbulent university years.

Late in 1983, fifteen years into Laird's very active retirement, Robert Gorrell, who had collaborated with Laird on many projects, and Elmer Cole, then director of the Nevada Humanities Committee, discussed the notion of a symposium in honor of Laird. Because of the range of his accomplishments, there were a number of forms such a tribute might take. A committee of his colleagues and friends enthusiastically supported the idea and through the early months of 1984 settled on a program of widely known speakers in the field of language and linguistics. Sponsored by the Department of English at the University of Nevada, Reno, and generously funded by the Nevada Humanities Committee and the University of Nevada Foundation, the program was set for November 1984. Laird himself, it must be added, was very pleased when told of plans for the conference, especially since he hoped to draw participants into a critique of his latest book on language, *The Word.*

Laird's sudden death in May 1984 saddened his many friends and admirers. The conference, now changed to a memorial, remained nevertheless a celebration, a tribute to his life and work. Early on, it had been decided that the papers should embody some of Laird's own spirit, attempting to present generous amounts of the most recent scholarship to a general audience. The decision to publish the papers, undertaken with support from the Nevada Humanities Committee, partakes of that same spirit, for it is hoped that this volume will give the ordinary reader new insight into the workings of language and into the discoveries of linguistic scholarship.

The first two papers, by Harry Brent and William Jacobsen, will appear in some ways the most difficult, for they are more specialized in their subject and approach than the others. They grow, however, directly out of Laird's primary interests. His ready background in etymology, in the history of the English language, and in the historical and structural place of English in the larger scheme of human languages developed naturally from his training in philology. On my shelf I have Laird's own copy of *Handlyng Sinne,* a long medieval penitential treatise. The book, some four inches thick, is marked, page after page, with Laird's margin-filled annotations in different colored inks, virtually a word-for-word gloss on this little-known Middle English text. The book exemplifies Laird's close attention to the details of language, his later tracing of the histories of words, and his lifelong relishing of the work of the word-wise, whether Geoffrey Chaucer or W. S. Gilbert. It also reminds us of his early role as a medieval scholar and teacher, recreated in Harry Brent's depiction of Laird's classes in Old English.

Through comparison with Laird as teacher, Brent's essay characterizes Chaucer's "ideal" teacher, the Clerk of Oxford. The Clerk's Tale is one of the problems in the *Canterbury Tales,* for although the story of the patient Grisilde was much admired by Chaucer's contemporaries, modern readers are stunned by the cruelty of the lord Walter and therefore reject the self-defacing passivity of his wife, the saintly peasant Grisilde. Most readers find in the story much to deplore, with contradictory signals from the Clerk as to Chaucer's own attitude toward the material. Brent, picking up some clues from Chaucer's portrait of the Clerk, urges us to reconsider Walter's behavior in the light of medieval notions of sovereignty and the related virtue of steadfastness.

Etymology was another of Laird's specialties, and his books bristle with interesting points about the history of words, both their inner structure and their meanings in society. Etymology is in many ways a paradoxical field of study. Its basic tools are quite esoteric, requiring a wide-ranging familiarity with dead languages, a masterly ability to organize data and to perceive patterns, and a mind that delights in code-cracking guesses. Yet, perhaps even because of this odd array of habits, etymology has long been the playground of amateurs, home to clown as well as shaman. Medieval monks were devilishly clever at inventing spurious etymologies to justify or create desired implications in names. A long tradition of books promises to delight with the ingenious stories behind words and phrases (*A Hog on Ice, Brewer's Dictionary of Phrase and Fable*), and just as many offer "increased word power" through the learning of important Latin and Greek roots. A pundit and poet like John Ciardi could make a tidy living on the radio-writing-lecture circuit with clever hunches about the labyrinthine histories of words. And pop-grammarians, eager to justify their usage preferences, often argue from etymology that a word's meaning can only and always properly be the sum of its roots (this is the reason they argue that *hopefully*—an adverbial form of 'full of hope'—cannot introduce and modify a whole sentence with the meaning 'it is to be hoped'). While Laird, too, had an ear for the whimsical in these games, he grounded his etymological work in scholarship, culminating in his last book on language, *The Word*.

Linguist William Jacobsen looks more closely at the sources most of us rely on for our etymologies—the dictionaries. By presenting us with the data of some very specific and carefully chosen examples, Jacobsen is able to show that there is considerable variation in the kind of material actually presented in the etymologies of different dictionaries—that, in fact, the kind of information we find is largely determined by the source we consult. As in family trees, there are two directions in which etymologies can trace histories; one discovers the ancestors of our words, the other the descendants of the old roots. By testing their treatment of these histories, Jacobsen evaluates the comparative usefulness of a group of standard reference dictionaries. The results should prove especially interesting to the many readers whose eyes tend to move first to the bottom of dictionary entries.

While Jacobsen sees in words their ancient constituent histories, how meanings are reflected in the very bones of words, David Guralnik's essay is concerned with the outer garments, the appearance that words take in society, the ways words adopt and betray the style of a culture. That Guralnik, like Jacobsen, turns to the dictionary as his source is a reminder to us of the treasures contained in our common desk dictionaries.

Although lexicographers may be "harmless drudges," as Samuel Johnson joked, Guralnik shows how their work enshrines the "current value" of words, "in terms of either price or status," giving dictionaries some of the usefulness for cultural studies that old Sears catalogs have. After tracing some of the foibles of early lexicographers, Guralnik shows how scientific modern dictionary-making has become: "The modern lexicographer is the beneficiary, if not the slave, of the science of linguistics." As a modern science, linguistics has attempted to describe language rather than to change or control it, and modern dictionary-makers have followed this descriptive program. Since the revolutionary *Webster's Third,* dictionaries have increasingly sought "to state meanings in which words are in fact used, not to give editorial opinion on what their meanings should be."[1] This means that dictionaries are now more inclusive in the reflection of contemporary usage and quicker to adopt changes occurring in the language. Writing elsewhere, Guralnik says, "Change, even change through error, has been a natural process in our language from its very beginnings, and nature is not to be denied."[2] The dictionary is a mirror, not a model, of language.

What seems natural to Guralnik and other lexicographers has not been enthusiastically accepted by all the public, and Guralnik's essay here describes some of the pressures applied in a competitive marketplace. Nowhere are these pressures more complex than in relation to taboo words, where any decision can bring charges of cowardice, permissiveness, or racism. In his essay, Guralnik accounts for the decision to exclude taboo words from the Second College Edition of the *New World Dictionary,* a decision called "mistaken" by a rival lexicographer.[3] Looking more closely at this troubled area now, Guralnik sees reason for hope. A count of his citation slips shows a movement away from the use of racial slurs, and Guralnik speaks of the wonder if, for once in our history, "the truly obscene became unspeakable."

Another contribution of descriptive linguistics has been to examine nonstandard dialects. Demonstrating that different dialects are always complete languages, adequate to accomplish the communicative needs of the culture, linguists have gone far to dispel the myths attaching to dialects previously labeled "substandard." The recognition of the linguistic integrity of all human languages has not blunted the social and political problems attaching to the use of dialects, however, especially in our schools. The essays by Robert Bentley and James Sledd deal with these problems, Bentley in terms of race, Sledd in terms of social class.

Though political ends may differ, ironically there is wide agreement that one goal of language teaching should be literacy in the standard or majority dialect. Monroe K. Spears puts it bluntly: "Anyone who encourages students to believe Black English is acceptable at the top levels of our society is perpetrating a cruel hoax."[4] Jim Quinn, as much a linguistic relativist as anyone, puts the case more generally in *American Tongue and Cheek:*

> The fact remains that there is a way of writing that is necessary to success, just as there are rules about which fork to use at an expensive restaurant. And preparing children for success means preparing them to manipulate those rules. . . . There is really no argument about teaching children to read and write Standard English—only about how it is to be done.[5]

Both Bentley and Sledd agree with this argument in their essays, acknowledging the importance of giving the opportunities that *may* arise with mastery of the standard dialect. But for both, that *may* is a nearly prohibitive word.

Bentley sees that even advances in the study of dialects have not led to a uniformly successful approach to teaching speakers of Black English (and by extension other linguistic minorities) in the schools. In fact, arguments about theories of "linguistic deprivation" and "dialect interference," he claims, continue to blind educators to the real problem in minority education, "attitude interference." Bentley argues strongly for what was Laird's primary concern, making genuine linguistic knowledge available to educators and the general public.

James Sledd sees in the battle of dialects the nemesis of social class. For many Americans, especially outside New England and the South, class, if it exists at all, is hardly an important issue. It is common in London, where I am writing this, to encounter Americans who have discovered the "class system" for the first time. Although we are sensitive to status, our patriotic notions of the melting pot have traditionally kept us from seeing evidence of a class system in America. But as Paul Fussell points out in his recent book *Caste Marks:*

> Actually, just *because* the country's a democracy, class distinctions have developed with greater rigor than elsewhere, and language, far from coalescing into one great central mass without social distinctions, has developed even more egregious class signals than anyone could have expected.[6]

The recognition that language reinforces class distinctions is not new, of course, as even Shakespeare's plays show us. But in this century there has been increased understanding of the complicity of language in the manipulation of people by those with prestige and power, both individual and corporate. Language does not just reflect social class; it helps create the distinctions that serve class exploitation. In Sledd's view, the standard language insulates the powerful from encroachment by those below them even while it teases their illusions of upward mobility. For almost unconsciously Americans give assent to the optimistic satiric premise of Shaw's *Pygmalion*. As Quinn suggests, "there is hardly a person reading this who has not changed his speech in some way, to eliminate some 'lower-class' or 'illiterate' feature of his native dialect, whether it is ethnic or regional."[7] The social reality, however, is closer to Fussell's conclusion:

> Linguistic class lines are crossed only rarely and with great difficulty. . . . The sad thing is that by the time one's an adult, these stigmata are virtually unalterable and ineffaceable. We're pretty well stuck for life in the class we're raised in. Even adopting all the suggestions implied in this chapter, embracing all the high-class locutions and abjuring the low ones, won't help much.[8]

Thus pressure is on the schools, following the great leveling program of democracy, to erase those class marks *before* adulthood. The schools fail because, as Sledd argues, education has generally been made to serve the interests of class distinctions. Contrasting with the patrician irony of Fussell's examination of the structure of the classes and their comic preoccupations is Sledd's sense of urgency. Sledd knows the dangers of manipulation and wants teachers to be aware of the true nature of the struggle they engage when they teach language and writing.

Sledd describes the boardroom or the War Office, a world of political power with language as one of the tools. William Lutz takes us to the ad agency or the Ministry of Information, where this language of control is created. Deceitful manipulation by the masters of language has come to be called *doublespeak*. Rhetorical incantations—some known at least as long ago as Aristotle, many used daily by four-year-olds confronting parents or teachers, others depending on new technologies and recent theories of psychology—are the everyday stock of language hoping to influence people's choices, to cover a mistake or scandal, or to turn thin ice into thick. Language can be made to serve falsehood as well as truth, sin and salvation alike. But as in all propaganda, what is salvation to one is damnation to another,[9] so the awareness and judgment of the audience are crucial defenses, as Lutz, Sledd, and Walker Gibson all emphasize.

The education of that audience is taken seriously by the National Council of Teachers of English. Its Committee on Public Doublespeak annually holds up to public ridicule and abuse the most striking examples of the deliberate misuse of language, sometimes because they are unintentionally funny in their self-puncturing pretension, but more often because they represent a sinister threat of deception. Lutz speaks authoritatively of doublespeak from his experience as chair of this committee. In his essay he offers an analysis of the varieties of doublespeak, the types made vivid by a large number of recent examples. To these can be added, in the essay by Walker Gibson, the examples of linguistic creativity from the 1984 election campaign, which, while they are more comic than sinister, remind us of the continual pressure politics puts on language.

George Orwell's "Politics and the English Language" is probably the central text in the modern study of doublespeak. The implications of the essay are made dramatically real in Orwell's novel *Nineteen Eighty-Four,* which Lutz examines closely in his essay. Orwell believed that innocent or ignorant people can be enslaved through the agency of language, that language can be made first to frame, then to narrow, finally simply to comprise available human experience. This deeply political meaning arises from the main argument of Orwell's essay, that "if thought corrupts language, language can also corrupt thought."[10] While we are made the victims of deceitful rhetoric, the language, our chief weapon of defense, is itself weakened. The deliberate misuse of language then becomes a form of thought control. Lutz offers this warning: "Doublespeak is insidious because it can infect and ultimately destroy the function of language, which is communication between people and social groups."

The solution is education: "only by using language well will we come to appreciate the perversion inherent in doublespeak," Lutz says. It is a deep irony of this business that those who are educated to use language well can themselves become manipulators of others, given the class dynamics that Sledd describes. Nevertheless, the warning and arming of potential victims seems the best answer. To this end Orwell finally urges a simple list of six rules of diction and style, ending with the thunderer, "Break any of these rules sooner than say anything outright barbarous."[11] The prominent position of these rules and the ease with which any list can be turned to the task of writing instruction have made Orwell seem to serve not only the prescriptive rhetoricians, but also the prescriptive grammarians. As a rhetorician, Lutz recognizes that "doublespeak is not the product of careless language or sloppy thinking. Indeed, most doublespeak is the product of clear thinking." In contrast, Orwell's restatement of his thesis is broader and takes less account of deceitful intent: the English language "becomes ugly and inaccurate because our thoughts are foolish, but the slovenliness of our language makes it easier for us to have foolish thoughts."[12] This view of the nature of our language and Orwell's doom-laden sense that "the English language is in a bad way"[13] are part of the traditional laments of all the well-known pop-grammarians, including John Simon, Edwin Newman, William Safire, and Richard Mitchell.

So influential are the views of these prescriptivists and so heated their long-standing debate with the descriptive linguists that a whole session at the conference was devoted to the controversy. Papers by John Algeo, Thomas Clark, and Edward Finegan weigh the assumptions of both sides and take the measure of the arguments. These essays can best be understood in the larger context of the usage conflict. Clark looks at Edwin Newman rather closely, so here I use examples chiefly from John Simon.

The besetting tone of the pop-grammarians is authority: "Although *long-lived* is hyphenated, the comparative *longer lived* and the superlative *longest lived* are not when they follow a verb—implied or stated."[14] This seems a harmless enough example, but it precisely typifies the mind-set of the prescriptivists, the sense of absolute certainty, the quality of legalistic scriptural quotation. One would never guess from the tone that such a statement rests on a thread of inherited custom, by no means unanimous. Anyone who has sat in an English Department office for any length of time will be aware of the large number of calls that come in asking for rulings on points of grammar and usage. A surprising number of these are on vexed, unclear questions, matters calling for judgment between balanced alternatives. Is John Simon really correct above—more correct, that is, than the poor writer who innocently set him off by hyphenating *longer-lived*? "'Connotations are what evaporate in translations' is wrong, *what*, being synonymous with 'that which,' is singular—hence 'what evaporates,'" Simon says.[15] What if I say that *what* is synonymous with 'those things which'? Who is right? Who is to say who is right?

Writers like Simon and Newman are admired because of their certainty, because they promise clear answers to doubtful questions. Their pronouncements save time for busy editors and journalists, and they offer the reassurance that there *are* right answers for those who write only occasionally. Furthermore, as we noted with dialects, the desire for social acceptance works in their favor. As Geoffrey Nunberg puts it, "There is a clear risk of irresponsibility in counseling others to disregard rules that they may be judged by."[16] Still, an examination of the principles of the prescriptivists is revealing. In his essay, John Algeo identifies ten assumptions underlying the traditional arguments of the prescriptivists and exposes the fallacies on which they are founded. The conclusion is clear: the mansion-house of language built by the prescriptivists, though it attracts many visitors and makes fortunes for the proprietors, rests on weak foundations, for these lords of language have little real understanding of the grammar or of the history of the language. As popular writers, however, they have a remarkable sense of what's hot.

What's hot is grammar. The descriptive revolution in the thirties, the transformational restructurings beginning in the late fifties, the difficulty in finding a pedagogical model for introducing descriptive views of language into school curricula, and, related, the rapid and isolating professionalization of academic linguistics—all these have made grammar an area of great controversy. Scholars like Laird have worked hard to make the advances of linguistics available to a general public. But only rarely is language brought into consciousness as a public issue, as when, for instance, Noam Chomsky and B. F. Skinner debate behaviorism, or when sexism in language or bilingualism in schools erupts into a policy issue. Such discussions, and the "feature stories" that feed upon them, are staged in the political arena and do not often advance linguistic understanding.

By comparison the "nightly news" about language seems far more prosaic and forever the same, carried through the newspaper columns, magazine articles, bestselling books and lectures of the prescriptivists. But we should recognize that the message is apocalyptic, brought by righteous emissaries from the wilderness who cry out against our gross assault on our language and attack our illiteracy.

Those who style themselves thus as prophets are often called popgrammarians, but their program has little to do with the scholarly tradition of grammar mentioned above. Clark, who prefers to call them "usageasters," demonstrates in his essay their relation to the different understandings of the grammatical tradition. Even when a true point of grammar is being discussed, the issue is often not grammatical. In the angry arguments over *everyone . . . they* (what pronoun should be used with the indefinite singular antecedent), for instance, traditional grammar is actually quite clear that the pronoun should be singular, and traditional English usage selects *he* as the approved form. But the dispute is not over grammar. Geoffrey Nunberg puts the issue succinctly:

> There will always be points of usage on which grammar and political principle find themselves at odds, such as the *everyone . . . he* business. But debates in these cases are not over which usage is grammatically preferable; rather they are over the relative strength of the claims that grammatical and other principles have on us. Grammarians should no more decide these issues for all than physicists should decide whether we ought to have a space program.[17]

This was the choice some years ago when the NCTE voted a formal policy of preference for the ungrammatical *everyone . . . they*. The vote provoked a storm of negative reaction:

> The National Council of Teachers of English [is] a body so shot through with irresponsible radicalism, guilt-ridden liberalism,

and asinine trendiness as to be, in my opinion, one of the major culprits—right up there with television—in the sabotaging of linguistic standards.[18]

But, even while they betrayed John Simon's "linguistic standards" in a decidedly political decision, the English teachers simply ratified what had been a common resort of English speakers and writers for centuries. Even without the pressure of feminist awareness, speakers of English often felt the inappropriateness of *everyone . . . he* and overrode the grammar in favor of the more precise meaning. George Orwell, who as we noticed eschewed the "outright barbarous," states the principle perfectly: "The defence of the English language . . . has nothing to do with correct grammar and syntax, which are of no importance so long as one makes one's meaning clear."[19]

Orwell's ethic of clarity is decidedly *not* the chief interest of the prescriptivists. What they are really talking about can be seen in some further examples from John Simon, who, handily for our purposes here, seldom weasels his words. "*Anymore* in one word is offensive to good taste even though the worthy *American Heritage Dictionary* condones it."[20] This sentence says nearly everything. There is no question here of grammar or of clarity. Simon is not being ironic about the worthiness of the *American Heritage Dictionary,* for it is his favorite. But as a standard of authority, it, too, is disposed of in the face of the criterion of taste. *De gustibus non est disputandum:* the only true arbiters of taste are, ahem, those with undoubted good taste. Those who know, simply know. "Bad grammar is rather like bad manners: someone picking his nose at a party will still be recognized as a minimal human being and not a literal four-footed pig; but there are cases where the minimal is not enough."[21] The purpose of Simon's "linguistic standards"—implicit in the very word *standards*—is to measure people by their habits of speech and find them wanting. It is no accident that many of the traditionally disputed "problems of usage" are also markers of class and regional dialects. They are, as Clark points out, "shibboleths that serve as labels of social class, education, and parentage."

The vexed argument about usage arises ultimately from the central social paradox about language, spelled out in Laird's *Miracle of Language:*

First we noticed that language relies upon a body of human agreement bewildering in its complexity. Human beings can speak, and be understood, only because they have at their call millions of meanings and countless ways of putting these meanings together. . . . These meanings . . . rest upon an agreement unconsciously entered into, signed, and sealed by all of us. Language is language only because it has currency . . . and understandable only if studied as the commonality of many minds over many generations. On the other hand we have seen that language as it exists is always the possession of individuals. . . . Looked at from this point of view, language becomes a pattern of infinitely blending dialects.[22]

Laird describes here the double pull of language, the movement toward individual creativity and anarchy resisted by the constraining force of normalization and social standards.

As Laird implies, communication depends upon the "currency" of language. The nearly unconscious continuing decision by individual speakers to conform to the collective judgments of a speech community maintains the critical mass of uniformity necessary for communication within the group. In *The Philosophy of Composition*, E. D. Hirsch puts the general case: "The normalization of language serves to enlarge its range of communicability over space and time."[23] In practice—perhaps because of human nature, as Algeo implies—normalization has often meant the imposition and enforcement of standards. Theorists who favor the written language, like Hirsch, argue the necessary existence of these standards as the preservers of written tradition. The conservatism informing the teaching of standards, says Hirsch, "is absolutely essential to the persistence of the written language as an intelligible oral medium."[24] The assumption beneath this view, one denied by most linguists, is that the force for anarchy, represented for Hirsch in unrestrained human speech, is potentially stronger than the social agreement that validates the continuing tradition of the written language. A similar assumption, favoring linguistic corruption, underlies the view of Paul Robinson: "Language exists in a kind of tension, and if there are no forces to resist the inevitable process of evolution, the result will be linguistic incoherence. . . . Conservatives, therefore, should think of themselves as performing an essential role in an historical drama."[25] Hirsch enlarges this role: "Linguistic conservatism in all the modern national languages probably belongs now to the sphere of historical inevitability."[26]

The pressure of orthodoxy, on the other hand, has undoubted

dangers, expressed by British writer Angela Carter as she summarizes one strongly feminist view of language:

> Sisterhood, therefore, has a certain self-confidence about dismissing structured, patriarchal, authoritarian devices like syntax, grammar, and artistic form with a supercilious smile; they are part of the conspiracy to stifle Women's Voice in its uniqueness. (In a sense, they are part of a wider conspiracy to stifle everybody's voice in its uniqueness for the sake of our understanding one another more easily, if less profoundly, but that's another story.)[27]

This view, which sees social conformity as stifling and the structure of language itself as authoritarian, nevertheless recognizes the playoff between uniqueness and understanding. The use of "unique" begs a question, for the singular "Women's Voice" masks a social community with quite varied voices. As a community, women are capable of establishing norms and standards fully as stifling as those of any other linguistic community. But Carter also draws attention to our complicity in the "wider conspiracy" that aims, after all, at what many see as the chief good of language, "our understanding one another more easily." Out of this tension between the freedom of the individual voice and the conformity necessary to social communication, poets draw the great power of their language; James Joyce is a striking example of the exploitation of this tension.

Nowhere is this paradox more compellingly expressed than in Alice's argument with Humpty Dumpty in *Through the Looking Glass*. Although the exchange is well known, it is so much to the point that I offer it here:

> ". . . There's glory for you!"
>
> "I don't know what you mean by 'glory,'" Alice said.
>
> Humpty Dumpty smiled contemptuously. "Of course you don't—till I tell you. I meant 'there's a nice knock-down argument for you!'"
>
> "But 'glory' doesn't mean 'a nice knock-down argument,'" Alice objected.
>
> "When *I* use a word," Humpty Dumpty said in rather a scornful tone, "it means just what I choose it to mean—neither more nor less."

"The question is," said Alice, "whether you *can* make words mean different things."

"The question is," said Humpty Dumpty, "which is to be master—that's all."[28]

Alice and Humpty Dumpty tug on the language from different directions, Alice speaking for society and the larger communicative function of language and Humpty for the great creative freedom individuals can exercise over language. If they also sound a bit like a pop-grammarian taking offense at a somewhat populist linguist, we can begin to sense the deep roots of the so-called Grammar Wars. Finegan, noting the tradition of hostility between the guardians and the linguists, seeks a truce based on the greater understanding that can come from new studies of the linguistic data.

Finegan recasts the tension just described in new terms, which he calls "centripetal" and "centrifugal," neatly avoiding the usual associations of "left" and "right." The centrifugal force, representing society's need for clear and unambiguous communication, is a pull toward a one-to-one relationship between form and meaning and thus toward a fullness of expression. The centripetal, representing the individual speaker's freedom and efficiency, collapses meanings and abbreviates forms, often enhancing them for clarity with other, nonverbal signals.

Finegan uses this physics of language to argue two controversial propositions: first, that prescriptivists' preferences have not been arbitrary but have rather consistently favored one-to-one correspondence of form and meaning; and second, that current studies seem to show that the dialects of elite, educated classes differ from other nonprestige dialects systematically (not arbitrarily), again by favoring fuller expression and tending toward a one-to-one correspondence between form and meaning. By comparison, nonprestige dialects are marked by "telescoping" of forms, simplification, vowel shifts, and efficiency of expression—characteristics of the centripetal force in language.

The great triumph of this centripetal force is identified in the essay by Walker Gibson, presented as a talk at the closing luncheon for the conference. After characterizing the new language of an election year, Gibson casts a congenial eye on 1066 and discovers the revolution that occurred in English when the prestige dialect was another language—French. For several centuries, Gibson notes, while people of quality and authority turned their attention elsewhere, an illiterate peasantry unconsciously transformed the English language, especially its grammar and syntax. Gibson reminds us how startling a development this was: "The most profound reform movement in our language took place without benefit of professionals, writers, scholars, professors—who in any case would have opposed it. It was a folk operation." Yet the result of this folk operation was the great English language, invoked in the yearnings of those who decry our recent falls from grace. It was the language of all the great writers in the Anglo-American tradition. It was, indeed, the subtle language with which Chaucer in the fourteenth century created the Clerk and his problematic tale, the subject of our first essay.

The essays in this book engage issues of lasting interest in the study of language. As such, they contribute to discussions long enlivened by the distinctive voice of Larry Laird, who believed that "promoting the popular understanding of language is a worthy endeavor." In that spirit, and in his memory, they are presented here.

Notes

1. Philip B. Gove, preface to *Webster's Third New International Dictionary of the English Language* (Springfield, Mass.: G and C. Merriam, 1961), p. 6a.

2. *New York Times Magazine,* August 26, 1977; cited in John Simon, *Paradigms Lost* (New York: Potter, 1980), p. xvi.

3. Robert Burchfield, "Dictionaries and Ethnic Sensibilities," in *The State of the Language,* ed. Leonard Michaels and Christopher Ricks (Berkeley: University of California Press, 1980), p. 21.

4. "Black English," in *State of the Language,* p. 177.

5. *American Tongue and Cheek: A Populist Guide to Our Language* (New York: Pantheon, 1980), p. 161.

6. *Caste Marks: Style and Status in the U.S.A.* (London: Heinemann, 1984), p. 152.

7. Quinn, *American Tongue and Cheek,* p. 154.

8. Fussell, *Caste Marks,* p. 169.

9. See P. C. Boardman, "'Beware the Semantic Trap': Language and Propaganda," *Etc.* 35 (1978): 78–85.

10. In *The Collected Essays, Journalism and Letters of George Orwell,* ed. Sonia Orwell and Ian Angus, 4 vols. (Berkeley: University of California Press, 1976), 4:137.

11. Ibid., 4:139.

12. Ibid., 4:128.

13. Ibid., 4:127.

14. Simon, *Paradigms Lost,* p. 88.

15. Ibid., p. 47.

16. "The Decline of Grammar," *Atlantic* (December 1983), p. 46.

17. Ibid., p. 46.

18. Simon, *Paradigms Lost,* p. 45.

19. Orwell, *Collected Essays,* 4:138; it is instructive to compare John Simon on this point: "But we cannot and must not let 'one' become plural. That way madness lies" (*Paradigms Lost,* p. 41).

20. Simon, *Paradigms Lost,* p. 46.

21. Ibid., p. 111.

22. *Miracle of Language* (Cleveland and New York: World, 1953), pp. 15–16.

23. *The Philosophy of Composition* (Chicago: University of Chicago Press, 1977), p. 40.

24. Ibid., p. 39.

25. "Lost Causes," *New Republic,* January 26, 1980, p. 27.

26. Hirsch, *Philosophy of Composition,* p. 39.

27. "The Language of Sisterhood," in *State of the Language,* p. 233.

28. Lewis Carroll, *Through the Looking Glass* (London: Macmillan, 1904), pp. 113–14.

Acknowledgments

THAT these essays have become a book is due to the help and support of many people. The contributors of essays and other participants in the original conference are identified on the following page. The planning committee who devised the commissioning of these essays included, besides myself, Elmer Cole, Catherine Fowler, Robert Gorrell, William Jacobsen, Joanne Kimball, Mary Ellen McMullen, Wilbur Shepperson and Judith Winzeler. Publication was aided by a grant from the Nevada Humanities Committee and I thank the members of that committee for their support of the project. I am especially grateful to Judith Winzeler, Dina Titus and Wilbur Shepperson for their guidance and encouragement. To President Joseph Crowley and to the Board of Regents of the University of Nevada, I owe gratitude for the sabbatical leave during which the book took shape. Particular help with details of the manuscript came from Haig Bosmajian, Thomas Clark, Robert Gorrell, William Jacobsen, Michael Linn, and Thomas Nickles. The contributors themselves responded with cooperation and good humor at all stages of the project. Finally, I owe a lasting debt to Anne Phillips, Cameron Sutherland, and Kathleen Boardman for their generous expenditures of time, energy and intelligence in support of this book.

P.C.B.

Participants in the "Miracle of Language" Symposium
November 1984

John Algeo, University of Georgia, Athens, GA
Robert H. Bentley, Lansing Community College, Lansing, MI
Bruce Bledsoe, *Nevada State Journal,* Reno, NV
Phillip C. Boardman, University of Nevada, Reno, NV
Harry Brent, Baruch College, The City University of New York, NY
Robert Clark, Montana Historical Society, Helena, MT
Thomas L. Clark, University of Nevada, Las Vegas, NV
Edward Finegan, University of Southern California, Los Angeles, CA
Fred Fogo, Wadsworth Publishing, Salt Lake City, UT
Allen Gardner, University of Nevada, Reno, NV
Beatrix Gardner, University of Nevada, Reno, NV
Walker Gibson, University of Massachusetts, Amherst, MA
Robert Gorrell, Emeritus, University of Nevada, Reno, NV
Charles Greenhaw, Northern Nevada Community College, Elko, NV
David B. Guralnik, Simon & Schuster, Cleveland, OH
Edward Hancock, Truckee Meadows Community College, Reno, NV
James Hulse, University of Nevada, Reno, NV
William H. Jacobsen, Jr., University of Nevada, Reno, NV
Sven Liljeblad, Hilliard Professor, University of Nevada, Reno, NV
William D. Lutz, Rutgers University, Camden, NJ
Allen Walker Read, Emeritus, Columbia University, New York, NY
Nelson Rojas, University of Nevada, Reno, NV
James Sledd, University of Texas, Austin, TX

And Gladly Teche
"Stedfastnesse" in the Clerk's Tale and in the Pedagogy of Charlton Laird

Harry Brent

CHARLTON LAIRD is principally known to the academic world for his work with language. But Laird's interest in language grew out of his early writings in medieval studies. It is to Charlton Laird the medievalist that this essay on Chaucer is dedicated.

As most of you know, the title of this essay is also the title of one of Professor Laird's books. So I am stealing it from him. But he in turn stole it from Chaucer, who used the phrase "and gladly teche" to describe one of the pilgrims of the *Canterbury Tales,* the student or "Clerk" of Oxford:

> A clerk ther was of Oxenford also,
> That unto logyk hadde long ygo.
> As lenne was his hors as is a rake,
> And he nas nat right fat, I undertake,
> But looked holwe, and therto sobrely.
> Full thredbare was his overeste courtepy,
> For he hadde geten hym yet no benefice,
> Ne was so worldly for to have office.
> For hym was levere have at his beddes heed
> Twenty bookes, clad in blak or reed,
> Of Aristotle and his philosophie,
> Than robes riche, or fithele, or gay sautrie.
> But al be that he was a philosophre,
> Yet hadde he but little gold in cofre.

HARRY BRENT of Baruch College (The City University of New York) in New York City is a specialist in medieval literature. He has published textbooks on writing and teaching and has served as an officer of the National Council of Teachers of English.

> But al that he myghte of his freendes hente,
> On bookes and on lernynge he it spente,
> And bisily gan for the soules preye
> Of hem that yaf hym wherwith to scoleye.
> Of studie took he most cure and most heede.
> Nought o word spak he more than was neede,
> And that was seyd in forme and reverence,
> And short and quyk and ful of hy sentence.
> Sownynge in moral vertu was his speche,
> And gladly would he lerne and gladly teche.[1]

Here we have the prototypically "good" student of the late fourteenth century, the kind of fellow who would rather have at his bedside the collected works of Aristotle than the medieval equivalent of a laser stereo system. This student does not spend his money on designer jeans—his clothes are "threadbare." In the tradition of Boethius, he is a true devotee of Lady Philosophy and has no interest in acquiring the medieval equivalent of an M.B.A. with its attendant perquisites of a six-figure income, urban condo, summer beach house, Mercedes or Porsche: modern parallels of the medieval "benefice" or clerical benefice.

The Clerk of Oxford seems the paragon of medieval virtue. But he is not the usual figure in Chaucer's portrait gallery,[2] and thus his perfection gives us pause. Chaucer does not regularly draw perfect pictures, at least not in the *Canterbury Tales*. His vision is charged with irony and sarcasm directed in varying degrees toward the lusty Monk, the supercilious Prioress, the unscrupulous Friar, and the utterly corrupt Summoner and Pardoner.

One might take the generally accepted view that against these imperfect characters is set an array of righteous individuals, exemplars of the best in the Chaucerian world: the Parson who teaches his parishioners by example instead of through rhetoric, his brother the Plowman who labors in the vineyard, the Knight who represents Christian virtue taken to heroic proportions, the Knight's dutiful son, the Squire, who would "carf beforn his fader at the table" (GP, 1. 100) and indeed our Clerk, the perfect student. According to this view, Chaucer's world is balanced—the less perfect among us juxtaposed against the more perfect.

But, we might ask, would the brilliant and playful Geoffrey Chaucer create a world in which things are so predictable and obvious?

Would not the sophisticated members of English royal courts of the late fourteenth century, to whom Chaucer read his poetry, expect more than moral parallelism? Does Chaucer's irony embrace a wider ground than most criticism has led us to believe?

Recently some holes have been poked in the traditional, balanced picture of the *Canterbury Tales*. Among the iconoclasts is Terry Jones, whose book *Chaucer's Knight: The Portrait of a Medieval Mercenary* presents the case that this "worthy man" (GP, 1. 43), this "parfit gentil knyght" (GP, 1. 72) was an unscrupulous soldier of fortune who took part in the medieval equivalent of the My Lai massacre (the siege of Alexandria), that he lent his arms to the highest bidder, Christian or infidel, that he worked for the medieval equivalent of organized crime (the Visconti of Milan), and that in tournaments he unnecessarily killed his opponents.[3]

There is no question in my mind that Jones often overstates his case. However, I tend to favor his general approach even though early reactions from my colleagues have not been entirely positive—a critical reception that Jones's supporters attribute to the man's notorious background: he is one of the creators of the "Monty Python" series for BBC, a pedigree that has caused his views on Chaucer to become known, at least by word of mouth, as "The Monty Python Theory of the *Canterbury Tales*."

Be that as it may, I bring Jones's analysis of the Knight into this discussion because his position, even if only partially correct, necessarily alters our view of Chaucer as artist and demands that we look anew at Chaucer's "exemplary" characters. This is not to say that I expect to discover in the Plowman an anarchist or in the Parson a closet atheist, but that we might expect to find Chaucer's best characters less ideal than critics have previously thought. We might expect them to be more complex, drawn with more deliberate irony, than the traditional criticism would suggest. To my mind Jones's major contribution is not that he demolishes Chaucer's Knight, but that he calls into question the conventional wisdom according to which Chaucer's characters are neatly pigeonholed. In so doing, Jones, whatever one may finally think of his attack upon the Knight, demonstrates that Chaucer's irony extends even to his most positive characters.

In redefining the range of Chaucer's irony, there are many directions in which we might start out. I am tempted to take the hardest road and uncover the "real" Parson. But despite the suggestion in the

Epilogue to the Man of Law's Tale that the Parson is a stuffed shirt and perhaps a Lollard, there seems little basis for a Jonesian case against the man. It does seem that the Parson really is the model of charity that Chaucer makes him out to be in the General Prologue. On the other hand, perhaps Chaucer may have intended to do more with the Parson. If, to use Donald Howard's phrase, the *Canterbury Tales* is "unfinished but complete,"[4] perhaps the knock at the Parson by Harry Bailey may have been Chaucer's first stroke in a revision of the Parson's portrait. Perhaps the magnitude, indeed the near impossibility, of extending an ironic voice to the long and moral Parson's Tale proved a task too great even for Chaucer, or one that he put off until too late.

With the Clerk such is not the case. In that tale, Chaucer's bitingly ironic undercurrents are all too obvious. We may tend to see human behavior in the Clerk's Tale as overdrawn or even absurd. On the other hand, we cannot forget that the Clerk's veneration of order in his tale echoes Boethian doctrine, or that Petrarch, from whom Chaucer took the story,[5] saw great beauty in its message.

What is the Clerk up to in his tale? Without doubt we hear a voice that mocks Walter's behavior. But I think there is a voice in counterpoint that speaks for the beauty associated with symmetry and order—virtues of which Walter, in his marriage, would be the champion. Is it possible to resolve these conflicting appreciations? We will make some headway in our attempt, I think, if we give our Clerk credit for not merely stating the obvious. Obviously his tale is about marriage, but it is about other things, too, specifically the nature of order and authority in society—for which order and authority in marriage stand as an emblem. An examination of the Clerk's Tale that takes political authority, rather than simply authority in marriage, as the subject reveals a more complex and ironic agenda for both Chaucer and his Clerk. That reading also suggests that the Clerk is a more complex man than we may think. A review of the Clerk's Tale with an eye toward political authority rather than simply authority in marriage bears this conclusion out.[6]

At the center of the Clerk's Tale are the Markys Walter and his patient-beyond-belief wife Grisilde, a woman of humble origin who is tormented by her husband to an extent well beyond the heroines of today's most heart-rending accounts of battered wives. Grisilde endures the apparent abduction and murder of her two children, a summary divorce in which she is stripped nearly naked (she must beg for her underwear) before being sent into the streets of the town, and finally the humiliation of having to prepare the bridal bed for her husband's new wife. Throughout her tribulations, Grisilde keeps telling us how happy she is to serve her lord and husband. She, in contrast to the Wife of Bath, is patient and obedient in the extreme.

Of course, all the tribulations inflicted upon Grisilde by her husband are merely devices to test the patient wife's constancy. The children, we learn at the tale's end, have not really been murdered. The divorce is a loyalty test, and the supposed new bride is Grisilde and Walter's now-grown daughter. The couple are reunited in a typical happily-ever-after ending.

The Clerk's announced purpose in telling the tale is first of all to echo Petrarch's call for uxorial loyalty. His second and more immediate purpose is to comment upon the Wife of Bath's notorious lack of loyalty in her relationships with her five husbands. The Clerk's direct reference to the Wife of Bath and "hir secte" (1. 1171) indicates Chaucer's desire to allow the real scholar (the Clerk) and the scholar pretendant (the Wife of Bath) to argue in a mockedly learned way about the nature of authority in marriage.

This argument constitutes one of the great interlacings of the *Canterbury Tales*. But the delight it evokes may obscure the emphasis in the Clerk's Tale that Chaucer places on a larger and broader species of loyalty, one parallel to the uxorial variety, a virtue Chaucer calls "stedfastnesse." To explore Chaucer's treatment of this theme, we might first focus on a fact usually glossed over in typical appreciations of the description of the Clerk in the General Prologue—that at his "beddes heed" he would have not just any books, but the works of Aristotle.

Among the works of Aristotle is his *Politics*, in which Aristotle (and here I risk oversimplifying his views) indicates his preference for systems of government that are neither tyrannical nor democratic.[7] That Chaucer chooses the works of Aristotle for the Clerk's library should not seem surprising since the themes of order and obedience operate at the heart of the Clerk's Tale. What *is* surprising is the degree of authoritarian sentiment that a careful reading of the Clerk's Tale conveys.

Walter's subjects do not seem capable of rationally or effectively dealing with their own legitimate political concerns. They form their political opinions on the basis of rumor and partially real, partially imaginary, fears. Their anxiety begins to surface early in the tale when a representative of the people petitions that Walter, who to this time has been content to "hauke and hunte," leave his pleasures for the responsibilities of marriage:

> Boweth youre nekke under that blisful yok
> Of soveraynetee, noght of servyse,
> Which that men clepe spousaille or wedlok. (II. 113–15)

The representative tells Walter that the people are happy but nervous. They fear that the day of Walter's death will leave them without prince and protector, an image that evokes the Old English word *aldorleasse*, 'lordless'—the worst state that could befall one—cast out to wander the earth with no lord to depend upon for sustenance and protection.

This fear is legitimate. The "straunge successour" (I. 138) who might follow Walter could upset the social order and do the people ill, and it is not unreasonable, therefore, for the people to fear such an eventuality. But is it reasonable, in the "faire cheyne of love," for subjects to make such demands of a prince? Who are Walter's subjects that they should tell him to bow his head, to marriage or anything else? The rhetoric of Walter's response reflects his thoughts on the dual nature of the request—the legitimate appeal that there be a successor and the unwarranted demands by the common people upon a prince. He will marry but he will bow to no choice of wife but his own:

> Wherfore of my free wyl I wole assente
> To wedde me as soone as ever I may.
> But ther as ye han profred me today
> To chese me a wyf, I you relesse
> That choys, and prey you of that profre cesse.
>
> (II. 150–54)

Walter continues with the theme that the choice of a wife must be left to him. And, in yielding to the people's request, he adds the caveat that they must agree to yield their obedience to his wife:

> But I you preye, and charge upon youre lyf,
> What wyf that I take, ye me assure
> To worshipe hire whil that hir lyf may dure,
> In word and werk, bothe heere and everywheere,
> As she an emperoures doghter weere. (II. 164–68)

Those familiar with the story immediately see the point of the final line, the central irony on which the tale turns. In seeming to bow to the will of the people, Walter sets in motion a course of events that ultimately increases their anxiety about the succession. In seeming to bow he remains firmly unbent.

There is another passage, often overlooked, in Walter's answer that adds a larger dimension to his view of the world as contrasted with that of his subjects:

> For God it woot that children ofte been
> Unlyk hir worthy eldres hem bifore;
> Bountee comth al of God, nat of the stren
> Of which they been engendred and ybore.
> I truste in Goddes bountee. . . . (II. 155–59)

Seen in the scope of the story, these words constitute an ironic comment on Grisilde's parentage. In another and larger sense, however, they are a rebuke to Walter's subjects who have wrongly assumed that in begetting an heir Walter will necessarily ensure their future happiness. That, Walter tells them, is something only God can ensure. Residing below their prince and below their God in the medieval hierarchy, Walter's subjects are not as capable as they pretend in ordering their future happiness. They, in short, do not have the right notion of sovereignty.

As is well known, medieval notions of sovereignty did not place the king as subordinate to the collective will of the people. Despite changes in notions of sovereignty from the thirteenth through the sixteenth centuries, the king remained sovereign of all but God, a theme reflected over and over again in representational art, the most well known example perhaps being the Wilton Diptych in London's National Gallery. There Chaucer's king, Richard II, is depicted as receiving his authority from the Christchild held in the arms of Mary. This relationship between Christ and king was not unique to this particular painting but was present in contemporary representational art, especially in the abundance of nativity paintings depicting the adoration of the magi. From the twelfth century through the sixteenth, political poets who questioned royal sovereignty were hanged, drawn, and quartered. In essence they did no more than Art Buchwald does today.[8]

In this context, the political implications of the Clerk's Tale are not difficult to see, nor are they particularly appealing to our age. The Clerk tells us that the people should know their place. In making the request that their prince marry, the people have lost sight of that place. They exhibit a lack of "stedfastnesse" in and to the order of things created by God—the "faire cheyne of love." Their prince's station in life demands that he bow not to their demands, but to those of God. Walter's response, and, ironically, the entirety of the Grisilde episode, can thus be read as a defense of hierarchy. In this context Walter is to his subjects as Richard was to the peasants at Mile End, the scene of the apex event of the Peasants' Revolt of 1381, where the king was confronted by an angry group of his subjects, an episode of which Chaucer was certainly aware. In Chaucer's view, "stedfastnesse" demands of the sovereign that he be firm but merciful to his people. That same virtue demands of the people that they be loyal to their lord's will.

In the second part of the tale, Walter determines to marry the "faire ynough to sighte" (1. 209) Grisilde, daughter of the impoverished Janicula. Although the immediate cause of Walter's decision to marry is the demand of his subjects, the ultimate decision, in keeping with his princely station, is his own. His determination does not in truth spring from the imprecations of his subjects:

> For thogh the peple have no greet insight
> In vertu, he considered ful right
> Hir bountee and disposed that he wolde
> Wedde hire oonly, if evere he wedde sholde.
>
> (II. 242–45)

Two independent lines of chance converge (as in the Knight's Tale) in Walter's selection of Grisilde: the people's pressure on Walter and Walter's own desire. If marry he will, which as prince he recognizes he eventually must, then he already has his eye set. Much as in the setting of a pastourelle, Walter's vision of Grisilde is described by the Clerk:

> Upon Grisilde, this poure creature,
> Ful ofte sithe this markys caste his eye
> As he on huntyng rood, paraventure . . . (II. 232–34)

Walter does what he had wanted to do in the first place. His apprehension of Grisilde is part of his old hunting ways, the occupation appropriate to a nobleman. It is not the people who are in control, but the prince.

The initial reaction of Walter's subjects to the marriage is in some sense surprising. At first they seem pleased:

> And for he saugh that under low degree
> Was ofte vertu hid, the peple hym heelde
> A prudent man, and that is seyn ful seelde. (II. 425–27)

But their tune quickly changes. Soon enough the people, bored with the memory of the royal wedding, again begin to wonder about their future ruler, Walter's heir:

> Now sey they thus, "Whan Walter is agon,
> Thanne shal the blood of Janicle succede
> And been oure lord, for oother have we noon." (II. 631–33)

Walter is moved to editorialize on the grumbling of the populace:

> Swiche wordes seith my peple, out of drede.
> Wel oughte I of swich murmur taken heede,
> For certeinly I drede swich sentence,
> Though they nat pleyn speke in myn audience. (II. 634–37)

Again the people change their minds. When Walter's horrendous behavior toward Grisilde becomes rumored about, the gossip turns against him:

> For which, where as his peple therbifore
> Hadde loved hym wel, the sclaundre of his diffame
> Made hem that they hym hatede therfore—
> To been a mordrere is an hateful name. (II. 729–32)

But, of course, Walter is not a murderer. The people thrive on rumor. Yesterday's just ruler becomes today's sadistic killer, and is tomorrow transformed to Solomon. When Walter announces that he has the Pope's permission to divorce Grisilde and to marry a new wife, the people are happy. Ironically, it is because of them that the Pope grants his permission:

> To stynte rancour and dissencioun
> Bitwixe his peple and hym; thus seyde the bulle. . . .
>
> (II. 747–48)

The subjects, who just a short time ago put pressure on their prince to marry, now have become jealous of the "blood of Janicle" and press this "mordrere" of children to divorce a loyal wife and mother:

> The rude peple, as it no wonder is,
> Wenden ful wel that it hadde be right so. . . .
>
> (ll. 750–51)

Walter's explanation to Grisilde concerning the divorce is often seen as a transparent attempt on his part to excuse himself. However, given the changeable nature of his subjects' opinions, it has the ring of truth:

> I may nat doon as every plowman may.
> My peple me constreyneth for to take
> Another wyf, and crien day to day;
> And eek the pope, rancour for to slake,
> Consenteth it, that dar I undertake. (ll. 799–803)

Walter could, of course, bluntly exercise his authority, and thus silence his subjects. But their mood is bound to shift in any case, so it is pointless for him either to accede to or to thwart their demands at any given time. Like the tournament participants in the Knight's Tale, Walter's subjects have no clear view of the real order of causality. Their vision, as opposed to Walter's, or that of the gods in the Knight's Tale, is "as through a glass darkly." In the tale of the Clerk, as in that of the Knight, order comes through the agency with the widest and most far-reaching view.

It is because their view is extremely limited that the people keep changing their attitudes. One moment they accept Grisilde; the next they reject her. When Walter rejects her, they accept her again. As she leaves the palace they lament with her:

> The folk hire folwe, wepynge in hir weye,
> And Fortune ay they cursen as they goon. (ll. 897–98)

Yet at the coming of Walter's new wife, the mob, true to capricious form, changes attitude again. They say of the new bride:

> For she is fairer, as they deemen alle,
> Than is Grisilde, and moore tendre of age,
> And fairer fruyt bitwene hem sholde falle,
> And moore plesant, for hire heigh lynage . . .

> For they were glad right for the noveltee
> To have a newe lady of thir toun. (ll. 988–91, 1002–3)

With such "lak of stedfastnesse" in his subjects, what is Walter to do? He faces the perennial problem of any ruler or government attempting to deal with the changing and shortsighted feelings of subjects or citizens—imagine the shifting public reactions if Prince Charles divorced Princess Diana and announced his upcoming marriage to a cocktail waitress.

Walter's highest duty as prince is to preserve the order of his realm. Grisilde's legendary patience must be viewed in this light as well. Were she to thwart Walter's will, she would risk a fundamental disruption of the social order. Chaucer draws her so thinly, however, that it is impossible to tell whether she is consciously aware of her political role. However, even cursory awareness of medieval marriage relationships among the nobility suggests that she must see her position in political terms. Certainly Chaucer's audience would. In this light, Grisilde's predicament and her seemingly obsequious and masochistic behavior are endured for larger social good. The central evil that must be avoided is mob rule, and it is to this principle that Walter's vision and Grisilde's submission point.

Walter's subjects certainly are not fit to control the direction of the polis. As I have argued here, they are quite possibly the root of Walter's cruel and deceptive game. Chaucer, in the words of the Clerk, views the mob for what it is:

> O stormy peple, unsad and evere untrewe!
> Ay undiscreet and chaungynge as a vane,
> Delitynge evere in rumbul that is newe,
> For lyk the moone ay wexe ye and wane!
> Ay ful of clappyng, deere ynogh a jane,
> Youre doom is fals, youre constance yvele preeveth,
> A ful greet fool is he that on you leeveth. (ll. 995–1001)

The Clerk's theme is one of Chaucer's favorites: loyalty, or "stedfastnesse." The theme of "stedfastnesse" held great interest for Chaucer, especially in relation to the loyalty of the people to their sovereign, and of the sovereign to them. Chaucer's intense concern for this idea is also developed in his short poem "Lak of Stedfastnesse."[9] In that poem, he laments the lack of loyalty of individuals to their prince and recommends justice, sometimes a retributive and severe justice, in the prince's relations with unsteadfast subjects, themes markedly similar to those operating in the Clerk's Tale.[10] Yet "Lak of Stedfastnesse" also contains an injunction to the prince to be merciful, to exhibit charity, the highest of the medieval virtues, something Walter ultimately does in restoring Grisilde to her wifely position.

The tale of the Clerk, like Chaucer's attitude toward contemporary political events as reflected in "Lak of Stedfastnesse," is informed by complex attitudes toward the nature of authority, the scope of politics, and the meaning of loyalty. Some of those attitudes, it turns out, may not fit very easily with twentieth-century commonplaces regarding egalitarian social relationships, the position of women in society, the meaning of cruelty, and the nature of justice. Nor do they fit immediately with commonplace medieval notions. One would not expect a warm reception for this tale among most of Chaucer's pilgrims. Only a Petrarch, a Chaucer, or a learned man such as the Clerk would see the wisdom housed in the baseness of Grisilde's treatment. For the Clerk and for Chaucer, "stedfastnesse" is all, and ultimately Walter and Grisilde do live in "stedfastnesse" to each other in a steadfast realm.

Twentieth-century critical concern for the Clerk's Tale is thus misfocused. The story is not properly about Grisilde, whom we see little of, but about her husband the markys. It is a story about power, its uses and misuses, and its theme is the dangers of power misplaced, in this instance in Walter's subjects. Chaucer's point in the stories of both the Knight and the Clerk is that stability in the political realm is necessary for the good of the social order, even though the maintenance of that stability may require cruelty. These are hard tales told by hard men.

Our Clerk is thus not simply a naive schoolboy with a great love of learning, an easy subject for analogy with our favorite teachers. If we take the tale at all seriously,[11] we are forced to deal with the problem of having to attribute hard attitudes to the Clerk, and very likely to Chaucer himself. The universe of the *Canterbury Tales*, seen in this way, is not one of ever-recurring spring, but the real world through which Chaucer traveled, filled with the likes of the Visconti—and the highwaymen who thrice assaulted Chaucer himself. Our Clerk, like Terry Jones's Knight, does not fit so easily with our own conceptions of the way the world ought to work, or with the attractive simple pastoralism of the opening lines of the General Prologue. One of the great dramatic ironies of the *Canterbury Tales* is that through the vernal Kentish landscape ride people with dark but necessary lessons.

Were we to go to school to the Clerk, and listen to him "gladly teche," we would certainly learn lessons at odds with pastoral or youthful idealism. We might, as in the story of Walter, learn lessons seemingly at odds with some of our own values. Our Clerk's examples would be pointed, sometimes extreme. He might be glad to teach, but his students might not immediately be glad to learn—and the challenge might gladden his heart all the more. This Clerk has not merely kept Aristotle at his bed's head. He has read him and passed his lessons on, as arguable or as difficult as they may be.

Terry Jones may have been too harsh with Chaucer's Knight, but in that harshness he has at least rescued the Knight from the banal respectability to which a century of Chaucer criticism had assigned him. Taking a cue from Jones, this essay will, I hope, spark some interest in further discussion of the Clerk as the complex character he is.

I have a purpose in undermining the easy, perfect picture of the Clerk, and I think you can guess what it is. There are many rites of passage in the academic world, but none of us wants to go through the last one. That's when we die and when, if we have been distinguished enough, somebody puts together a *Festschrift* in our honor with our picture inside the front cover. These pictures, incidentally, are never taken from the vigorous prime of life, but from old age—when all the lines are there and show only too well in facial closeups. Such pictures are supposed to convey a sense of profundity and wisdom. One is supposed to marvel at them as Goldsmith did about the vicar of Wakefield "that one small head could carry all he knew."

With a *Festschrift,* or with a memorial conference—and we should all remember that this conference is a memorial only through sad accident—there comes the temptation to view the person being honored as someone more than human—which is to say, as someone also other, and thus perhaps less, than human. As somebody wise, old, kind, and understanding, but not possessed of qualities to temper, and thus strengthen, those virtues—such as pride in and dedication to one's work—that, when combined with generosity of spirit, often make that generosity all the stronger.

I think that Larry Laird would be sorely displeased if this conference were merely to celebrate his apotheosis. I think he would much rather be remembered as the man he truly was. I did not know him well in his personal life, but I knew him as well as any of his graduate students, I think, in his life as a teacher. I witnessed his teaching in three graduate courses, in his direction of my master's thesis, and in the most harrowing oral examination I ever took.

And this brings me back to the theme of this paper: "And gladly teche." Chaucer's phrase is misleading. It suggests a picture of the monkish scholar sacrificing himself for his students and enjoying it. It leaves out the part of teaching that is hard: dealing with under-prepared or willfully ill-prepared students—creatures not unlike the Markys Walter's "stormy people," chasing after fads and fancies while neglecting the hard part of learning, the mastering of the central core of a discipline. This view forgets that teaching is full of frustration and that sooner or later in every teacher's life there comes the awful recognition that perhaps one has made an unwise career choice, that it would have been better to pursue the Mercedes, the summer home in Devonshire, perhaps even the private plane, rather than "twenty bookes, clad in blak or reed, / Of Aristotle." It forgets that teachers are human and that a big part of teaching is the communication of that humanity to one's students.

During my first semester as graduate student at the University of Nevada in 1965 I took Larry Laird's course in Old English. At that time every graduate student in English was required to take one se-mester of Old English and one semester of *Beowulf*. This was one of the good old rites of passage.

I had no idea of what to expect of Laird, then director of the graduate program, who even that long ago was viewed as the grand old man of the English department. He had a great shock of white hair. I thought he resembled a picture of Martin Van Buren that I remembered from a high school history text.

Nor did I have any idea of what to expect from the course, since there was no syllabus. The dozen or so students met in a seminar room the first day. We already knew that it would be folly to show up without the required texts. And we were right. Laird already had our names listed in his grade book. He took attendance and then imme-diately instructed us to open to the Anglo Saxon version of Genesis.

With my last-name initial *B,* I was the first to be called upon. Laird said, "Mr. Brent, would you please read and translate the first sen-tence." I had never read Old English before that day, and I struggled through a pretty bad version of "*On angine god gesceop heofan and eorthan.*"

In that class we read a very large chunk of the extant corpus of Anglo Saxon prose and poetry. It was thus a relief that in the second semester we were required to read only one poem: *Beowulf*. *Beowulf* was shorter, but Laird got harder. No longer did we simply translate and make some fledgling comments on the philology. We translated, and commented on the philology and the criticism in detail. Several students quit.

In the next Laird course I took, the name of which I forget, we read the following books, one a week:

1. Wellek and Warren, *Theory of Literature*
2. Northrop Frye, *Anatomy of Criticism*
3. Arthur Lovejoy, *The Great Chain of Being*
4. Erich Auerbach, *Mimesis*
5. E. R. Curtius, *European Literature and the Latin Middle Ages*
6. Johann Huizinga, *The Waning of the Middle Ages*
7. Basil Willey, *The Seventeenth Century Background*
8. Paul Hazard, *The European Mind*
9. M. H. Abrams, *The Mirror and the Lamp*
10. John Livingston Lowes, *The Road to Xanadu*
11. Northrop Frye, *Fearful Symmetry*
12. Cleanth Brooks, *Modern Poetry and the Tradition*

This list is but a paltry indication of the wealth of Charlton Laird's scholarly interests. I gave this reading list my best, but, like any good graduate student, I knew that one had to read selectively in courses like Laird's. There was not time in a week *really* to read *Fearful Symmetry*. I was lucky that Laird did not find me out, or, if he did, that he let it go. Some others were not so lucky. And this brings me to one of the incidents that first came to mind when I began writing this paper.

In the third course I took from Laird, the one with all the critical books, we all had to read our seminar papers in class. There was an individual in the class who had written a paper on a topic not related in the remotest sense to the subject matter of the course. This paper had something to do with the history of the American West. It was a well-composed journalistic essay that in another context might have merited much applause. But, along with other students in the seminar, I sensed what was coming as the paper was read. About halfway through, Laird interrupted and said quietly, and very firmly, "Excuse me, please stop, this is not a seminar paper." The class ended early.

After the class, I found myself walking beside Laird. I didn't plan to say anything about what had just happened, but, almost as though I were someone else listening to myself, the words came out: "Did you really have to do that?" He gave me a very stern look that was at the same time somehow sad and replied, "What else could I do? The rest of the class?" He made no effort to continue the conversation. Nor did I. He walked on ahead. I saw his point: to have let the person go on would have been bad teaching. And Charlton Laird, who was always the perfect gentleman, did not flinch from doing what he knew to be best for his class. I could tell that it pained him to be hard, but in that instance he knew he had to be.

This was the same man who took a great personal interest in his students, who, as director of graduate studies, willingly taught undergraduate composition courses and volunteered to coach writing to underprepared freshmen. This was a man immersed in intense, far-reaching, and extremely time-consuming scholarship, who took the time to comment in detail on theses and dissertations—to guide my own thesis through four revisions, each of them badly needed.

This is the man who constructed individually tailored master's and doctoral exams for every one of his students. This is the man who was so sensitive to students' needs and fears that instead of setting a specific time and place for those exams, he would leave the questions with his secretary. You could pick them up any time in the space of a week, pick an empty classroom, and write your answers. You were on your honor. If you had gotten this far with Laird, you knew that you had won his trust.

Laird also served as a model for his students outside the classroom. I remember him showing up, six-pack in hand, at a teaching assistants' BYOB party. He melded into the various discussions, listening and smiling mostly, never attempting to steal center stage. He came to the party to enjoy himself, not to have his ego stroked. I remember visiting his home on several occasions and always being welcomed with a glass of ale—Larry would not drink "weak" American beers. I also always found in Larry's home a genuine concern for the little triumphs and disasters in my career and personal life.

Like many others, I also learned something of courage from Charlton Laird. The annals of the American Association of University Professors record how he and his colleagues risked their professional lives in the 1950s in defense of academic freedom—and did it with good humor.

I am still learning from Laird through his writings. Prolific and entertaining to the end, he himself more than met the standards of scholarship he set for others.

Charlton Laird, like Chaucer's Clerk, was a much more complex man than many of us may take him to have been. From him I have learned something of understanding and compassion for students. And from him I have learned to be sometimes hard and demanding. I have not yet learned, precisely, how to mix those attitudes. He knew that mixture, and it was in this sense that Charlton Laird would "gladly lerne and gladly teche."

Notes

1. Geoffrey Chaucer, *The Canterbury Tales,* in *The Complete Poetry and Prose of Geoffrey Chaucer,* ed. John H. Fisher (New York: Holt, Rinehart and Winston, 1977), p. 15.

2. See Thomas A. Kirby, "The General Prologue," in *Companion to Chaucer Studies,* ed. Beryl Rowland (New York: Oxford, 1968), pp. 208–28, for a comprehensive review of scholarship on Chaucer as literary portrait painter. See also J. Burke Severs, "Chaucer's Clerks," in *Chaucer and Middle English Studies in Honour of Rossel Hope Robbins,* ed. Beryl Rowland (London: Allen and Unwin, 1974), pp. 140–52, for a continuation of this discussion with particular reference to the Clerk.

3. Terry Jones, *Chaucer's Knight: The Portrait of a Medieval Mercenary* (London: Eyre Methuen, 1982).

4. Donald R. Howard, *The Idea of the Canterbury Tales* (Berkeley: University of California Press, 1976), p. 1.

5. Chaucer's source is Petrarch's *De Obedientia ac Fide Uxoria Mythologia,* and indirectly, through Petrarch, Boccaccio's *Decameron.*

6. For references to the themes of order and obedience in the Clerk's Tale, see S. K. Henninger, Jr., "The Concept of Order in Chaucer's *Clerk's Tale,*" *JEGP* 56 (1957): 382–95; John P. McCall, "The *Clerk's Tale* and the Theme of Obedience," *Modern Language Quarterly* 27 (1966): 260–69; and Irving N. Rothman, "Humility and Obedience in the *Clerk's Tale,* with the Envoy Considered as an Ironic Affirmation," *PLL* 9 (1973): 115–27.

7. See book IV of Aristotle, *The Politics,* trans. T. A. Sinclair (New York: Penguin, 1962), pp. 235–94.

8. V. J. Scattergood, *Politics and Poetry in the Fifteenth Century* (New York: Barnes and Noble, 1972), p. 21.

9.   Sumtyme the worlde was so steadfast and stable
     That mannes worde was obligacion

And nowe it is so false and deseiuable
That worde and dede as in conclusion
Is not thing lyke   for turned vp so doun
Is all this worlde for mede and wilfulnesse
That al is lost for lak of stedfastnesse

What maketh this worlde to be so veriable
But lust that folke haue in discencion
For amonge vs now a man is holde vnable
But yif he can by som collusion
Do his neyghburgh wrong or oppression
What causeth this but wilfull wrechidnesse
That all is lost for lake of stedfastnesse

Trouthe is putte doun   resoun is holden fable
Vertu hath now no domynacion
Pite exiled no man is merciable
Through couetise is blent discrescioun
The world hath made a permutacion
Fro right to wrong fro trought to fikelnesse
That all is lost for lak of stedfastnesse

ENVOY

O prince desire to be honurable
Cherice thi folk and hate extorcioun
Suffre no thing that may be repreuable
To thine estaat doen in thi regioun
Shewe forth thy swerde of Castigacioun
Drede god do law   loue truthe and worthynesse
And wed thi folk ayen to stedfastnesse   Explicit

"Lak of Stedfastnesse," in *The Minor Poems of Geoffrey Chaucer,* ed. George B. Pace and Alfred David, *A Variorum Edition of the Works of Geoffrey Chaucer* (Norman: University of Oklahoma Press, 1982), pp. 85–89.

10. It should be pointed out that there has been much discussion regarding Chaucer's sentiments in this short poem. The dating of the poem, and thus the object of the line "Shewe forth thy swerde of Castigacioun," remains unclear. Some analyses (see Pace and David, *Variorum Edition,* pp. 77–79) favor a date of composition near the end of Richard's reign (and Chaucer's life). In this case, Chaucer would be indirectly criticizing actions of Richard himself, or of those close to him. An earlier date, in the late 1380s, would more logically point the finger at Richard's uncles. The earlier date might also bring into consideration Chaucer's attitudes toward the Peasant's Revolt of 1381, in which case the poem suggests a desire that Richard firmly

suppress remnants of the rebellion but in a just and merciful way. In either case, the poem shows Chaucer's disenchantment with the lack of order and just reciprocity in social relations following the revolt.

11. See James Sledd, "The *Clerk's Tale:* The Monsters and the Critics," *Modern Philology* 51 (1953): 73–82, for the major statement on this point. See also Delores W. Frese, "Chaucer's *Clerk's Tale:* The Monsters and the Critics Reconsidered," *Chaucer Review* 8 (1973): 133–46.

The Root of the Matter
Reflections on English Etymological Dictionaries

William H. Jacobsen, Jr.

Y paper stands apart in being about etymologies and etymological dictionaries. Yet this is a subject that was very close to the heart of Charlton Laird. Already in his book *The Miracle of Language* (1953) he devoted considerable space to the idea that a very few roots or bases of Indo-European have multiplied themselves into some half-million words of English. This centers on chapter 6, "Both a Borrower and a Lender Be," with its memorable subtitles "Blessed Are the Greedy for Words, for They Shall Have Vocabulary" and, concerning so-called loanwords, "Forgive Us Our Debts, for We Shall Not Pay Them," with this general thesis epitomized by "And All from Grandma Indo-European." This interest is even more pronounced in his last book, *The Word* (1981), especially in chapter 3, entitled "The Roots of English," which at its end (pp. 65–68) presents a selected list of eighty-nine Proto-Indo-European roots along with half a dozen English words stemming from each. An interest in dictionaries is also demonstrated by chapter 12 of this work, entitled "A Tool Kit for Studying English Words," which outlines the history of English dictionaries and guides the reader through sample entries from dictionaries and thesauri; he also includes (pp. 323–27) an annotated guide to dictionaries and other word and usage books, and recommends (p. 114, fn. 8) certain etymological dictionaries.

In thinking on these matters I have focused on two questions. First, what exactly is a root? And second, if you look up the same word in different etymological dictionaries, do you get the same information? I will return to the first question near the end of the pa-

WILLIAM H. JACOBSEN, JR., a linguist at the University of Nevada, Reno, has published extensively in descriptive and historical linguistics and is an authority on American Indian languages. He recently received the university's Outstanding Researcher Award.

per. In order to answer the second I looked up many words in many dictionaries and kept score. A sampling of the results is given here.

Appendix A lists a baker's dozen of etymological dictionaries that I am reporting on. These are probably most of those that would be consulted nowadays by an American seriously interested in determining the etymology of a word. The listing is arranged alphabetically by labels that I use to refer to the individual works. I give the bibliographical references, leaving out in several cases a more complicated history of earlier or later editions, and each work is provided with a characterization involving the aspects that I am discussing.

These dictionaries fall into a few broad types. Intended for general-purpose consultation and thus giving a variety of information about each word are American Heritage, Random House, Universal, and the three Webster's. Of explicitly etymological orientation are the relatively recent works of Klein, Oxford, Partridge, and Shipley, to which I add the older but still commercially available works of Skeat and Weekley. (Indo-European Roots is a recent etymological off-shoot of American Heritage that is not separately exemplified.) The OED or Oxford English Dictionary is unique in its detailed treatment of words within the historically documented stages of English; its etymologies are thorough as regards Germanic relationships, but limited for deeper connections. Three of these must also be singled out for important innovations in their organization: Partridge groups together numerous related words under one English head word, with cross-references to this consolidated entry. American Heritage features an appendix arranged under headings of Indo-European roots, where the relationships connecting words of different languages are made clear by a series of reconstructions; connections among English words are established by references between the main body of the work and this appendix. The recent book by Shipley conversely arranges the main body of its entries under simplified Indo-European roots; one is then led to the appropriate entry by the index of English words.

Appendix B lists some other dictionaries of interest, although they are not among those I am systematically sampling. Four of them are general-purpose dictionaries. Both Funk and Wagnalls and Webster's New Twentieth Century are unfortunate examples of large general-purpose dictionaries that are deliberately circumscribed in their etymologies: most native words are traced back only to Old English. New Century is less readily available nowadays. It is comparable in its etymological treatments to the weakest members of my sample, Random House and Weekley, but has even fewer cross-references to doublets. The citing of cognates in the Shorter OED has been systematically curtailed from that of the OED so that Indo-European cognates are usually limited to Latin, Greek, and Sanskrit, and Germanic cognates are seldom shown. Holthausen is a compact, specifically etymological dictionary that is less apt to be consulted since it is written in German. Although it is convenient for quickly finding the immediate sources of words of the core vocabulary, it is weak in the aspects sampled in the following pages: few reconstructions are given, few cognates are cited, and cross-references to other English words are sporadic. In these respects it is also comparable to Random House and Weekley, but the latter are stronger when it comes to citing Germanic cognates. The other entries in appendix B are useful resources other than English etymological dictionaries, and are characterized below.

To give an idea of the kinds of etymological information provided by these dictionaries, I present extracts from the entries for a few English words. I have arbitrarily limited these to words beginning with *f,* which comes from Proto-Indo-European **p* in words of native Germanic stock. In this I am following what seems to be a subliminally agreed upon tendency in many sources to favor these labial sounds. Thus Laird's presentation of Indo-European relationships and of dictionary formats in *The Word* features the words *foot* and *full* (pp. 62–65, 152–53, 281–91, 293–94); in an introductory list of English-Latin cognates (p. 57), half of them have this initial consonant. Proto-Indo-European **p* remains in Latin, Greek, and Sanskrit, so that the most commonly mentioned cognates or doublets of native English words beginning with *f* begin with *p*.[1]

I start with the simplest case I have come across, the word *fen,* meaning 'low, flat, swampy land; a bog; a marsh' (American Heritage), from Old English *fenn, fen,* a word which has no related words within English and few cognates elsewhere.

These are the Indo-European reconstructions offered, given by only three of the thirteen dictionaries:

American Heritage: pen-. Swamp. Suffixed o-grade form
   *pon-yo-.
Webster's New World: IE. base *pen-, wet, slime, mire.
Shipley: pen: swamp.

These all show at least the root *pen-*. Exactly these three dictionaries are the ones that can be counted on to give such reconstructions, although, as we will see, several others also give them on occasion. Since roots are used as headings for entries, this is inevitable for American Heritage and Shipley, although the latter sometimes does enter words elsewhere than under their actual roots. Webster's New World uses the English words as headings, but usually shows the Indo-European roots (labeled *bases*) as a matter of policy. Here only American Heritage shows the actual stem derived from the root, **pon-yo-*, on which the Germanic words rest, which has an *o* rather than the *e* in the first syllable, in accordance with vowel alternations that are called *ablaut*—a point of some importance, since the reader might otherwise assume that the *e* came directly down to English.

Some dictionaries show cognates in other Indo-European languages outside of Germanic:[2]

> Universal 4/3: M.Ir. an, 'water'; Gaul. anam, 'marsh' (fr. *pan-);
>   O Prussian pannean, 'ditch'; also w. suff. -k-, Scrt. pankaš,
>   'slime'.
> Klein 3/2: Gaul. anam, MIr. an 'water', OI. páṅkaḥ 'bog, marsh,
>   mud'.
> Webster's Second 2/2: MIr. an water, Skr. paṅka mud.
> Webster's Third 1/1: Skt. paṅka 'mud, mire'.
> Partridge 1/1: Skt. paṅka 'mud'.

It will be seen that only five of the thirteen dictionaries give these; moreover, the three that give the reconstructions are other than the five that give this evidence on which the reconstructions are based. Following the label for each source, I indicate the number of languages represented followed by the number of branches of the Indo-European family that they come from, out of a possible eleven.

All of these sources recognize a relationship to Sanskrit *paṅka* 'mud' (this labeled Old Indic by Klein); in addition, the first three listed bring into account Celtic words for 'water' (Middle Irish *an* and Gaulish *anam*). We are thereby reminded that Proto-Indo-European **p* has been lost in Celtic. And Universal uniquely compares in addition an Old Prussian word. Thus the three branches of Indo-European in question here are Indic, Celtic, and Baltic.[3]

Next we can note the Proto-Germanic reconstructions presented by three of these dictionaries:

> American Heritage: Germanic *fanja- swamp, marsh.
> Skeat: Teut. type *fanjom, n.
> OED: OTeut. *fanjo(m (-jo-z, -jâ).

Only one of these dictionaries, American Heritage, gives either of the previously discussed kinds of information. These three dictionaries, along with Oxford, are the ones that routinely give reconstructions at this level; Oxford, however, uniquely lacks an entry for *fen*. These reconstructions provide, not merely a root, but either a stem or a completely inflected word in the nominative case.

We can now see more clearly the circuitous trajectory leading from the *e* of the root *pen-* to the *e* of English *fen*. This *e* of the root reflects a tradition of normalizing with this vowel when citing roots in isolation, whereas the actual underlying stem, as shown by American Heritage, had a variant with *o*. The regular change of Proto-Indo-European *o to Proto-Germanic *a, along with the regular change of initial *p to *f and the purely orthographic replacement of *y* by *j* lead to the Proto-Germanic stem as shown by American Heritage. (The reconstruction of *o in the second syllable by the other two dictionaries is now regarded as old-fashioned.) Subsequent to this, the following *y* affected the first vowel in North and West Germanic, causing it to change to *e* as part of the pattern of changes labeled *umlaut*. Thus the *e* of *pen-*, far from coming down unchanged to that of *fen*, as the user of Webster's New World or Shipley might understandably assume, was replaced by *o* according to the alternation pattern called *ablaut*, which became Proto-Germanic *a* by regular sound change, which in turn became West Germanic *e* by the conditioned sound change called *umlaut*.[4]

Finally, we can review the cognate words in other Germanic languages that are cited by works in our sample:

> OED 8/3: OFris. fenne, fene masc. (MDu., MLG. venne, Du. ven fem., Du. veen neut.) water-meadow, bog, OHG. fenna fem., fenni neut. (Ger. fenne neut., fehn fem.) marsh, ON fen neut., quagmire, Goth fani neut., mud.
> Klein 7/3: OS. feni, ON. fen, OFris. fenne, fene, Du. veen, OHG. fenna, G. Fenn 'marsh', Goth. fani 'mud'.
> Partridge 6/3: OFris. fene or fenne, OS fen, OHG fenna, G Fenn, ON fen 'marsh', Go. fani 'mud'.

Webster's Second 6/3: D. veen, OFris. fenne, fene, OHG. fenna,
  G. fenn, ON. fen, Goth. fani mud.
Universal 4/3: O.N. fen, O.Fris. fenne, O.H.G. fenni, 'fen';
  Goth. fani, 'mud, clay'. Cp. also O.H.G., O.E. fūht, 'damp'
  (fr. *fuŋχt-).
Weekley 4/3: Du. veen, LG. fenne, ON. fen, Goth. fani.
  Orig. mud.
Random House 4/3: Icel. fen 'quagmire', Goth. fani 'mud',
  D. ven, G. Fenn 'fen, bog'.
Skeat 3/3: Du. veen, Icel. fen, Goth. fani.
Webster's Third 3/3: OHG fenna 'marsh', ON fen, Goth. fani
  'clay'.
Webster's New World 2/2: G. fenne marsh, feucht damp, Goth
  fani mud.

The three dictionaries not represented here are Oxford, which lacks
an entry for *fen,* although it would otherwise give this information;
Shipley, which does not give Germanic cognates; and American Heritage, which cites cognates only if they have been borrowed to give
English words. After the label for each source, the two numbers indicate the number of languages represented followed by the number of
branches of Germanic that they represent, out of three. Here only
Gothic represents East Germanic, and only Old Norse or Icelandic
represents North Germanic; the remaining languages are West Germanic like English. All three branches are represented except in
Webster's New World, which lacks the Old Norse; minimally cover-
ing these three branches seems to be a conscious principle of selection for Universal, Weekley, Random House, Skeat, and Webster's
Third. Those citing more than four languages add older West Germanic languages, Old Frisian and Old Saxon, or show more than one
chronological stage of a language, such as Old High German beside
German or Middle Dutch beside Dutch. Looking at these forms we
can see the retained *a* in Gothic *fani,* reminding us that East Germanic does not display umlaut, and we can see the double or long *nn*
in some West Germanic languages, coming from the *ny* (*nj*) cluster.

We take up next the word *fish,* from Old English *fisc,* which is only
a little less limited in the distribution of recognized cognates and in
related English words, but in ways that may be instructive. Five of the
dictionaries give Indo-European (or at least pre-Germanic) recon-

structions (in addition to which reconstructions applying to Celtic are given by Klein, Partridge, and Universal):

American Heritage: peisk-. Also pisk. Fish.
Webster's New World: IE base *pisk-.
Shipley: peisk: fish.
OED: pre-Teut. *pisko-s (OIr. < *peiskos).
Oxford: *piskos (Ir., Gael. < *peiskos).

Here again there is something of a problem concerning the vowel of the root: American Heritage and Shipley show a normalized shape with -*ei*-, which indeed underlies the Celtic forms, whereas the Germanic and Latin words clearly point to a so-called zero grade form with just -*i*-, which is mentioned by American Heritage, OED, and Oxford. It is probably just this difference that called forth the reconstructions in OED and Oxford.

Here are the Indo-European cognates of *fish* given by our sources:

Klein 3/3: L. piscis, OIr. īasc, gen. ēisc (for *piska) 'fish', Russ. piskar' 'groundling'.

Partridge 7/2: OIr iasc (for *piska) or aesc, with gen éisc, Ga iasg (gen éisg), Cor pisc, pisk, pysc, pysk, Br pisk, pesk, W pysc, Mx eeast, eease, OC *eiskos for *peiskos.

Oxford 5/2: L. piscis, Ir. iasc, Gael. iasg, (W. pysg, Corn. pisc are < Lat.) There is no CIE word for 'fish'.

Skeat 4/2: L. piscis, Irish and Gael. iasg. O.Ir. iasc (with loss of initial *p*).

Universal 3/2: Lat. piscis, O.Ir. iasc for *pisc-. W. pysg &c. is a fresh borrowing from Lat.

Weekley 2/2: L. piscis, OIr. iasc.

OED 2/2: L. piscis and OIr. iasc.

Webster's Second 2/2: L. piscis, OIr. iasc.

Webster's Third 2/2: L. piscis, OIr. īasc.

Random House 2/2: L. piscis, Ir. iasc.

American Heritage 1/1: Latin piscis.

Webster's New World 1/1: L. piscis.

Shipley 1/1: L. piscis.

These are limited to the westerly branches of the family, Germanic, Celtic, and Italic (i.e., Latin), and perhaps Slavic, thus making it unlikely that its ancestor was already present in Proto-Indo-European. Other words show a similar geographical distribution, as, for example, the set containing English *mere* 'lake', formerly also 'sea'. Here only Oxford warns of this limitation.[5] All thirteen of our dictionaries cite at least one cognate, and all show the Latin word. All but three show additionally a Celtic cognate, which for six is limited to Old Irish. Partridge, Oxford, and Universal list forms from the Brythonic Celtic languages, Cornish, Breton, and Welsh, but Partridge fails to warn that they are probably borrowings from Latin, accounting thereby for the initial *p*. Only Klein lists a potential cognate from a third, Slavic, branch of Indo-European.[6] American Heritage and Shipley give clear evidence here of their policy of citing Indo-European cognates only when they have led to English borrowings, since we have taken in the Latin, but not the Irish, word.

The Proto-Germanic reconstructions for 'fish' are from the same four works that usually give these, and teach us nothing new:

American Heritage: Germanic *fiska-.
Oxford: CGerm. *fiskaz.
Skeat: Teut. type *fiskoz.
OED: OTeut. *fisko-z.

The listing of Germanic cognates for this word is fuller than for *fen*:

Klein 11/3: OS., OFris., OHG. fisc, ON. fiskr, Dan., Swed. fisk, MDu. visc, Du. vis, MHG. visc, visch, G. Fisch, Goth. fisks 'fish'.
OED 10/3: OFris. fisk, OS. fisc (Du. visch), OHG. fisc (MHG. visch, Ger. fisch), ON. fiskr (Sw. and Da. fisk), Goth. fisks.
Partridge 9/3: OFris and OS fisk or fisc, OHG fisc, MHG visch, G Fisch, MD visc, (as in D) visch, Go fisks, ON fiskr.
Oxford 7/3: OFris. fisk, OS., OHG. fisc (Du. visch, G. fisch), ON. fiskr, Goth. fisks.
Skeat 6/3: Du. visch, Icel. fiskr, Dan. and Swed. fisk, G. fisch; Goth. fisks.
Universal 5/3: O.S., O.H.G. fisc, Mod. Germ. fisch, Goth. fisks, O.N. fiskr.
Webster's Second 5/3: D. visch, OHG. fisc, G. fisch, ON. fiskr, Goth. fisks.
Weekley 4/3: Du. visch, Ger. fisch, ON. fiskr (whence name Fisk), Goth. fisks.
Random House 4/3: D. vis, G. Fisch, Icel. fiskr, Goth. fisks.

Webster's Third 3/3: OHG. fisc, ON. fiskr, Goth. fisks.
American Heritage 1/1: Middle Dutch vische, vis [in English
weakfish].
Webster's New World 1/1: G. fisch.

All works except Shipley give such cognates, and the number of languages represented is in several cases higher than for *fen*. Only two dictionaries give words from fewer than the three branches of Germanic: American Heritage under its policy of limitation to donor languages, giving only the Middle Dutch form that shows up in English *weakfish;* Webster's New World under a policy of sharp limitation favoring German.

There are a few doublets of *fish* in English, borrowed words coming ultimately from Latin *piscis* or its derivatives. The following listing indicates the number and identification of dictionaries which give a cross-reference from *fish* to three of them: *Pisces* (the constellation), *piscatory* or *piscatorial,* and *porpoise.* In the latter it is the second syllable that is related; this comes through the French from a Late Latin compound word meaning 'pig-fish':[7]

Pisces 5: American Heritage, Klein, Oxford (?), Partridge,
Shipley.
piscatory, -ial 5: American Heritage, Klein, Oxford (?), Partridge,
Shipley.
porpoise 3: American Heritage, Klein, Shipley.

In these cases I require that the cross-reference be explicit to the English word as a cognate, rather than merely being a matter of translation, such as saying that Latin *piscēs* means 'fish (pl.)', or of synonymy, such as listing together as synonyms *full* and *complete.* This cross-referencing can be done by entering both words under the same word family in works such as American Heritage, Partridge, and Shipley. In several other works it is done by indicating the other dictionary entry heading in small capital letters. There can also be a chain of cross-references via other words, such as is illustrated by Laird for *adroit* in *The Word* (p. 113).

Similarly we can indicate the number and identification of dictionaries that give a cross-reference in the opposite direction, from the borrowed to the native word:

Pisces 9: American Heritage, Klein, Oxford, Partridge, Shipley,
Skeat, Universal, Webster's New World, Webster's Third.

piscatory, -ial 8: American Heritage, Klein, Oxford, Partridge,
   Shipley, Universal, Webster's New World, Webster's Second.
porpoise 9: American Heritage, Klein, Oxford, Skeat, Shipley,
   Universal, Webster's New World, Webster's Second, Webster's
   Third.

One sees a strong tendency toward unidirectionality in this respect; thus six more refer from *porpoise* to *fish* than from *fish* to *porpoise*.

We may more briefly consider the entries concerning the word *fire,* from Old English *fȳr.* Indo-European reconstructions are given by seven dictionaries, of which the last four appear on my listing for the first time:

American Heritage: pūr-. Fire.
Webster's New World: IE. base *pewōr-.
Shipley: peuor: fire; color of flames.
Klein: I.-E. base *pewōr-, *puwer-, 'fire'.
Partridge: The IE r. is prob. pu- to flame, with predominant extn
   pur-, a fire. The word is perh. Medit: cf. Eg. pa, flame, fire,
   and perh. gara, fire, furnace.
Universal: Aryan base *pŭ, 'bright, shining; clear, pure'; the
   meaning has, on the one hand, been specialized to 'fire'; on the
   other hand, to 'clean, pure'.
Skeat: √ PŪ.

These reconstructions show a somewhat surprising variety of shapes, with some uncertainty as to whether the root had one or two syllables. Partridge indulges here, as often, in unfortunate comparisons to Egyptian.

This is a widely attested root in the family, so that there can be no doubt of its Proto-Indo-European pedigree. Although not reflected in Latin, it does turn up in Italic Umbrian.[8] Thus the dictionaries give cognate words from as many as seven branches, including the twentieth-century discoveries Tocharian and Hittite. They all show at least the Greek word, which is the one borrowed into English:

Klein 8/7: Toch. A por, B pwār, 'fire', Arm. hur, 'fire, torch', Gk.
   πῦρ, Umbr. pir, 'fire', Czech pyř, 'hot ashes'. Compare, with -*n*
   for -*r,* OPruss. panno, 'fire'. Cp. also, with -*r* in the nom. and
   -*n* in the gen., Hitt. pahhur, gen. pahhuenash, 'fire'.
Partridge 7/7: Arm hur, Gr pur, Umbrian pir, Cz pyr, live coal,
   Hit pahhur, pahhuwar, Tokh A puwar, por, Skt pu-, flame.

Oxford 6/6: Gr. pûr, Umbrian pir, Czech pýř, Arm. hūr, Toch. por, pwār; cf. Skt. pāvakás fire.

OED 4/4: Gr. πύ-ιρ, πῦρ, Umbrian pir, Arm. hūr, of same meaning; cf. Skr. pū, pāvaka fire.

Webster's Third 3/3: Umbrian pir, Gk. pyr, Arm. hur fire, torch.

Webster's Second 2/2: Gr. pyr, Armen. hur.

Webster's New World 2/2: Gr. pyra PYRE, Czech pýř glowing.

Skeat 2/2: Gk. πῦρ; Cf. Skt. pāvaka- (from pū), purifying, also fire.

American Heritage 1/1: Gk. pur, fire.

Universal 1/1: Gk. pûr, 'fire'.

Random House 1/1: Gk. pŷr.

Shipley 1/1: Gk. pur; purros: fiery red.

Weekley 1/1: G. πῦρ.

This word shows an interesting archaism whereby, as Klein points out, the final *r* would have alternated with *n* in certain inflected forms.[9] This creates a problem that is ignored by the Proto-Germanic reconstructions, which end in *r,* although the *n* shows up in Gothic and Old Norse:

American Heritage: Germanic *fūri-.
Oxford: WGerm. *fūir.
Skeat: Teut. type *fū-ir.
OED: OTeut. *fûir- (cons. stem).

At least Oxford labels its reconstructions as specifically West Germanic, and OED indicates that the Icelandic words ending in *r* may be borrowings from West Germanic. Otherwise the listings of Germanic forms mostly omit those in -*n,* as though not cognate:

Klein 10/3: OS., OFris. fiur, ON. fūrr, fȳrr, MDu., Du. vuur, OHG. fiur, MHG. viur, viuwer, G. Feuer 'fire'. Compare, with -*n* for -*r,* Goth fōn, gen. funins, ON. funi.

Partridge 10/3: OFris. fiōr, fiūr, OS fiur, OHG fiur, fuir, MHG viur, viuwer, G Feuer, MD vuy(e)r, fuer, vuer, MD-D vuur, ON fūrr, fȳrr. Cf. also the fu- of Go funins, gen of fōn, fire, syn ON funi.

OED 10/2: Com. WGer.: OFris. fiur, fior, OS. fiur (Du. vuur, Flem. vier), OHG. fiur, fûir (MHG. viur, fiwer, Ger. feuer); the Icel. fúr-r str. masc., fýre str. neut., fire, and Sw., Da. fyr, lighthouse, beacon, may be of German or Eng. origin.

Skeat 7/2: Du. vuur, Icel. fȳri, Dan. and Swed. fyr, G. feuer,
   M.H.G. viur, O.H.G. fūir.
Oxford 6/2: OFris., OS. fiur, Du. vuur, OHG. fiur, fūir, G. feuer,
   ON. had poet. furr, fyrr, m.
Webster's Second 5/2: D. vuur, OS. & OHG. fiur, G. feuer, ON.
   fȳrr, fūrr.
Webster's Third 3/3: OHG fiur fire, ON fȳrr, fūrr, funi, Goth. fon.
Universal 2/2: O.H.G. fūir, fiur; O.N. (poet.) furr, 'fire'.
Random House 2/2: Icel. fūrr, G. Feuer.
Weekley 2/1: Du. vuur, Ger. feuer.
Webster's New World 1/1: G. feuer.

Another word of this type, incidentally, is the word *water*, where the
North and East Germanic words similarly end in *n*. It is also worth
mentioning that the Romance language words for 'fire', such as
French *feu* and Spanish *fuego*, do not belong to this cognate set, but
rather come from Latin *focus* meaning 'hearth' (to which we return
below).

I next indicate the number of cross-references to the doublets *pyre*
and *pyro-* (as in *pyromaniac* and *pyrotechnics*), both ultimately from
Greek:

pyre 7: American Heritage, Klein, Partridge, Shipley, Universal,
   Webster's New World, Webster's Second.
pyro- 4: American Heritage, Partridge, Shipley, Random House.

And the number of cross-references from these words to *fire:*

pyre 10: American Heritage, Klein, Oxford, Partridge, Shipley,
   Skeat, Universal, Webster's New World, Webster's Second,
   Webster's Third.
pyro- 9: American Heritage, Klein, Oxford, Partridge, Shipley,
   Universal, Webster's New World, Webster's Second, Webster's
   Third.

As with *fish*, we see a strong propensity toward referring back to the
native word rather than away from it, by a ratio of 10 : 7 for *pyre* and
9 : 4 for *pyro-*.

Let us finally consider, more selectively, the entries for the word
foot, which comes from Old English *fōt*. Although I do not show reconstructions or actual cognate forms here, one thing that struck me
is that while the usual dictionaries give the Proto-Germanic recon-

struction for *foot*, none show it for the plural *feet* (Old English *fēt*, from Proto-Germanic **fōtiz*), thus leading to the possibility, as with *fen*, of mistaking the actual umlaut for ablaut, especially since the latter is prominent in this set, as between the Latin-derived words with *e* and the Greek-derived ones with *o*.

This root is even more widely spread, thus leading to citation of cognates from as many as eight Indo-European branches:

Klein 10/8: OI., Avestic, Toch. A, B, Arm., Gk., L., Lith., OSlav., Russ.
Webster's Second 6/6: L., Gr., Skr., Armen., Lith., Tocharian A.
Partridge 6/5: L, Gr, Skt, Tokh A, Tokh B, Lith.
American Heritage 5/5: Latin, Greek, Russian, Sanskrit, Middle Persian.
Oxford 5/5: Skr., Lith., L., Gr., Arm.
Universal 5/5: Scrt., Russ., Lith., Gk., Lat.
OED 4/4: Skr., Lith., Gr., Lat.
Webster's New World 3/3: Sans., Gr., L.
Webster's Third 3/3: L., Gk., Skt.
Skeat 3/3: L., Gk., Skt.
Weekley 3/3: L., G., Sanskrit.
Shipley 2/2: Gk., L.
Random House 2/2: L., Gk.

Here we can see most clearly a principle of selectivity that has applied in some of these works, whereby four of them display just Latin, Greek, and Sanskrit, and two just Latin and Greek. Under its policy of representation in English, American Heritage cites Russian with respect to *podzol*, Sanskrit for the coins *pie* and *naya paisa*, and Middle Persian as yielding *pajamas* and *teapoy*.

Cognates also run throughout the Germanic languages, so that we find a range of language citations comparable to that for *fish:*

OED 10/3: OFris., OS., Du., OHG., MHG., mod. Ger., ON., Sw., Da., Goth.
Klein 9/3: OS., ON., Swed., Dan., Du., OHG., MHG., G., Goth.
Partridge 8/3: OFris, OS, OHG, MHG, MD, D, Go, ON.
Oxford 7/3: OFris., OS., Du., OHG., G., ON., Goth.
Webster's Second 7/3: D., OHG., G., ON., Sw., Dan., Goth.
Skeat 6/3: Du., Icel., Dan., Swed., Goth., G.
Universal 4/3: O.H.G., Mod. Germ., Goth., O.N.

Weekley 4/3: Du., Ger., ON., Goth.
Webster's Third 3/3: OHG, ON, Goth.
American Heritage 1/1: OHG.
Webster's New World 1/1: G.
Random House 1/1: G.

Again only Shipley cites none, and Webster's New World cites only German, in this case joined by Random House. American Heritage cites only Old High German *vizzelach* 'fetlock', as being akin to the Germanic source of English *fetlock*.

Just as *foot* has many cognates, it also has many doublets within English. The following listing indicates the number of cross-references that are found in each dictionary from *foot* to any among a set of twelve doublets. These words are, within Germanic, *fetter* and *fetlock,* and from Latin *ped-* (nominative *pēs*) or Greek *pod-* (nominative *poús*) or their hybrids, the initial parts of *pedal, pes, podium,* and *pew,* and the final parts of *octopus, tripod, tripos, trivet, polyp,* and *trapeze:*

11: Shipley.
10: American Heritage, Klein.
 9: Webster's Second.
 8: Partridge.
 3: Oxford.
 2: OED, Skeat.
 1: Universal.
 0: Random House, Webster's New World, Webster's Third,
    Weekley.

Similarly we can indicate the number of cross-references back from any of these doublets to *foot:*

12: American Heritage, Klein, Partridge, Webster's New World.
11: Webster's Second.
10: Oxford, Shipley, Universal, Webster's Third.
 7: Skeat.
 2: Random House, OED, Weekley.

Comparing the two listings, we can see that high scores are obtained in both directions by American Heritage, Klein, Shipley, and Webster's Second, and low scores by OED, Random House, and Weekley, while a sharp asymmetry in the direction already noted is displayed by Universal, Webster's New World, Webster's Third, and to a lesser degree by Oxford, Partridge, and Skeat.

To further investigate the adequacy of cross-referencing of doublets, we may take up several samples containing a dozen pairs of words, sorted out according to different historical relationships and patterns of word formation.

Our first group consists of doublets related via Proto-Indo-European. Eight of them show again the *f-* : *p-* sound correspondence, where the borrowed word comes either from Latin (or French), listing the native word first: *farrow—pork, feather—pen, fee—pecuniary, fish—Pisces, foot—pedal, full—plenty;* or Greek: *fire—pyre;* or Sanskrit: *five—punch* (the drink). Other sound correspondences obtain in borrowings from Latin: *quick—vivid;* French: *head—chief, hound—kennel;* and Greek: *sow—hyena.* The following are the numbers of references from the native word to the borrowed doublet given by our dictionaries:

12: American Heritage, Klein, Partridge, Shipley.
10: Webster's Second.
7: Oxford, Universal.
3: Webster's New World.
2: Skeat.
1: OED, Weekley.
0: Random House, Webster's Third.

And the number of reverse references from the borrowed doublet to the native word in this set:

12: American Heritage, Klein, Partridge, Shipley, Webster's New World, Webster's Third.
11: Oxford, Webster's Second.
10: Universal.
7: Skeat.
3: Random House.
0: OED, Weekley.

This is a very similar pattern to what we have seen for doublets of *foot* above, although Oxford, Partridge, and Universal do a little better here.

When the related part of a borrowed doublet is noninitial because of compounding or prefixation, there is some tendency to overlook it in cross-referencing. Let us consider a group of such words, again related via Proto-Indo-European. Once more, eight of the native words begin with *f-*, with doublets borrowed from the Latin-French continuum:

feather—compete, fish—porpoise, foot—trivet, full—complete; or from Greek: *feather—symptom, foot—octopus, foot—polyp, foot—tripod.* The other initial consonant correspondences also involve Latin-French: *head—precipice, head—kerchief;* and Greek: *quick—microbe, work—liturgy.* We then find the following numbers of cross-references from these native words to their doublets involving noninitial parts:

12: Shipley.
11: American Heritage.
10: Klein.
 8: Webster's Second.
 5: Partridge.
 2: Oxford.
 1: Universal, Weekley.
 0: OED, Random House, Skeat, Webster's New World, Webster's Third.

And references back to the native words:

12: American Heritage, Klein.
11: Shipley.
10: Oxford, Universal, Webster's New World, Webster's Second, Webster's Third.
 9: Partridge.
 4: Skeat.
 2: Random House.
 0: OED, Weekley.

One notes a general decline in the number of cross-references, most striking in the cases of Oxford, Partridge, and Universal, with respect to cross-references starting from the native word.

We turn to sets of doublets that are more closely related, either within Germanic or even within English itself. Our next dozen include the following doublets that have developed within English, out of the weakening of formerly productive derivational patterns, no borrowing being involved: *comb—unkempt, drink—drench, fall—fell, foot—fetter, full—fill, freeze—frore, ten—tithe.* The remainder arose out of borrowing from other West Germanic languages: *comb—cam, eat—etch, ship—equip, ship—skiff, stone—stein.* The following are the numbers of references from the primary native word (listed first in each pair):

11: American Heritage.
10: Klein.
9: Webster's Second.
8: Partridge.
6: Oxford, Shipley, Skeat.
3: Weekley.
1: OED, Random House, Universal.
0: Webster's New World, Webster's Third.

And references back to the primary native word:

12: American Heritage, Webster's New World, Webster's Second, Webster's Third.
11: Klein, Oxford, Universal.
10: Partridge, Skeat.
9: OED, Random House.
8: Weekley.
7: Shipley.

The asymmetry is again striking, in that the low numbers move up when it comes to referring from the doublet to the primary native word.

We may next consider a group of doublets where one word is historically a compound word related in its first part. The following have developed within English, with the relationship having become obscured by phonetic change: *burn—brimstone, loaf—lord, many—manifold, stair—stirrup, sty—steward, toad—tadpole, wife—woman.* The remaining members of this batch involve borrowing within Germanic: *earth—aardvark, foot—fetlock, house—husband, stone—steenbok, whale—walrus.* The references are as follows from the primary native word to the compound:

10: Klein.
9: Partridge.
8: Webster's Second.
7: American Heritage, Oxford, Shipley.
5: Skeat.
4: Weekley.
2: Universal.
1: OED, Webster's New World.
0: Random House, Webster's Third.

And from the compound back to the primary native word related to its first part:

12: American Heritage, Klein, Webster's Third.
11: Oxford, Universal, Webster's New World, Webster's Second.
10: Partridge, Weekley.
9: OED, Shipley, Skeat.
8: Random House.

A similar pattern of asymmetry presents itself.

Finally, we may consider a group of doublets where again one word is historically a compound, but where the relationship is to its second part. The following pairs do not involve borrowing: *dairy—lady, hundred—thousand, poll—tadpole, rope—stirrup, ward—lord, wife—hussy*. Another half dozen consist of borrowed compounds taken from other Germanic languages: *eye—window, farrow—aardvark, horse—walrus, stone—tungsten, whale—narwhal (narwal), work—bulwark*. The following numbers of references are made to the compound word:

11: Klein.
8: American Heritage, Webster's Second.
7: Shipley.
6: Partridge.
2: Oxford, Skeat, Weekley.
1: Random House.
0: OED, Universal, Webster's New World, Webster's Third.

And from the compound back to the primary native word related to its second part:

12: American Heritage, Klein.
11: Oxford, Webster's New World, Webster's Third.
10: Partridge, Shipley, Weekley.
9: Skeat, Universal, Webster's Second.
8: Random House.
7: OED.

The asymmetry of direction of cross-reference still obtains, in addition to which it seems that Oxford, Skeat, and Partridge do less well when it comes to referring to these noninitial parts.

The sets of doublets we have looked at so far all contain at least one native English word. But doublets may also arise among exclusively borrowed words, that is, when two or more related words are borrowed from other languages. One type of relationship may be illustrated (to continue with words in *f-*) by *focus,* a borrowing of the Latin word (of uncertain origin) meaning 'hearth', as related to its descendant forms borrowed from French, *fuel, foyer,* and the last part of *curfew* (a compound meaning 'cover-fire').[10] In cases like this, the Latin borrowing tends to be treated practically like a native word with respect to the asymmetry of cross-referencing. Thus we find the following numbers of cross-references from *focus* to the French borrowings:

fuel 4: American Heritage, Klein, Partridge, Webster's Second.
foyer 4: Klein, OED, Partridge, Webster's Second.
curfew 3: Klein, Partridge, Webster's Second.

This contrasts with a much higher number of cross-references from these French borrowings to *focus:*

fuel 12: American Heritage, Klein, OED, Oxford, Partridge,
 Random House, Skeat, Universal, Webster's New World,
 Webster's Second, Webster's Third, Weekley (?).
foyer 10: American Heritage, Klein, OED, Oxford, Partridge,
 Universal, Webster's New World, Webster's Second,
 Webster's Third, Weekley (?).
curfew 11: American Heritage, Klein, Oxford, Partridge, Random
 House, Skeat, Universal, Webster's New World, Webster's
 Second, Webster's Third, Weekley.

In such borrowed words the *f-* is naturally not a member of the sound correspondence arising from Proto-Indo-European $*p$ that we have observed in native English words. Rather, Latin initial *f* comes from Proto-Indo-European $*bh$, $*dh$, or, less commonly, $*g^wh$. The respective native English initial consonants in cognate words would be *b, d,* and *w* or *g.* Some doublets illustrating these correspondences are: *fraternal—brother, forum—door,* and *furnace—warm.* If a word is borrowed from Greek, an initial *f*-sound, spelled *ph,* would come from Proto-Indo-European $*bh$ and hence correspond to Latin *f* and English *b,* as illustrated by *phlox—flame—blaze.*

Doublets can arise through borrowing, not only by taking in a word and its descendants, as with *focus,* but also by borrowing of cognates from related languages. This relationship obtains between words borrowed from different Romance languages, such as *farm* from French and the musical term *fermata* from Italian, and it is even more predominant between words borrowed from separate branches of Indo-European, such as words relating to *foot* that we have met above, like *pedal* from Latin beside *podium* from Greek (via Latin).

To investigate the adequacy of cross-referencing of doublets of this type, when there is no native English word to serve as an anchor, we can use words related to *firm*, which comes to us through French from Latin *firmus*, and is another doublet of *farm* and *fermata*. The Latin *f-* here is from Proto-Indo-European **dh-*, which means that Greek cognates will contain *th-* and Sanskrit ones, *dh-*; English doublets of *firm* borrowed from these languages are *throne* and *dharma*. We find the following numbers of references from *firm* to these words:

> *throne* 6: American Heritage, Klein, Partridge, Shipley, Universal, Webster's Second.
> *dharma* 4: American Heritage, Klein, Shipley, Webster's Second (?).

And from these to *firm:*

> *throne* 8: American Heritage, Klein, Partridge, Shipley, Universal, Webster's New World, Webster's Second, Webster's Third.
> *dharma* 5: American Heritage, Klein, Shipley, Webster's Second, Webster's Third.

Here we do not find very high numbers in either direction (but in the case of *dharma* this correlates with its absence as an entry from six of these dictionaries).

To test whether the presence of a native cognate increases the number of such cross-references, we can look at a final set of doublets whose ancestor also began with **dh:* the Latin group of borrowings *forum, forensic, foreign,* and *forest,* all based ultimately on Latin *forēs* 'door', beside native English *door* and Greek-derived *thyroid* (originally meaning 'shield-like', the Greek rectangular shield resembling a door). Letting *foreign* stand for this group of Latin-derived words, we find relatively few references to it from the other words:

> *door* 6: American Heritage, Klein, Oxford, Partridge, Shipley, Webster's Second.
> *thyroid* 4: American Heritage, Klein, Oxford, Shipley.

And similarly few references to *thyroid:*

> *door* 4: American Heritage, Klein, Shipley, Universal.
> *foreign* 4: American Heritage, Klein, Shipley, Universal.

The references to the native *door* are moderately higher:

> *foreign* 9: American Heritage, Klein, Oxford, Partridge, Skeat, Universal, Webster's New World, Webster's Second, Webster's Third.
> *thyroid* 8: American Heritage, Klein, Oxford, Random House, Shipley, Universal, Webster's New World, Webster's Third.

Since we find twice as many references from *throne* to *firm* (8) as from *thyroid* to *foreign* (4), I draw the conclusion that the presence of a native doublet does not necessarily increase the likelihood of cross-references among borrowed doublets, even though it is available as a link in a chain of cross-references. Admittedly, *thyroid* is a more learned word than the rest (and is absent as an entry from Skeat).

The treatment of loanwords in themselves raises issues that we can merely adumbrate. It is clear that our dictionaries give in principle as complete a treatment to words borrowed from other Indo-European branches, such as *focus, firm,* and *foreign,* as to native words. This entails, of course, the same differences of emphasis that we have already brought out. But when the branch of Indo-European is a more exotic one than Latin or Greek, the treatment is apt to be less adequate. The trajectory of transmission via other languages may not be specified, and the word is not necessarily analyzed or compared to cognates in other languages. For just one example (sticking to *f-*), we can consider *firman* 'a decree issued by an Oriental sovereign' (Klein). This comes from a Persian word, transmitted to English via Turkish. Seven variables in its treatment may be observed, which are mostly not mutually exclusive: (1) there is no entry for the word; (2) the Persian form *fermān/farmān* is cited, without analysis or comparison to cognates; (3) the transmission via Turkish is indicated; (4) the Old Persian form *framānā* 'command' is also cited; (5) comparison is made to closely related Sanskrit *pramāṇa-* 'measure, authority'; (6) the word is analyzed into prefix *pra-* and stem *mā-* (or earlier versions **pro-* and **mē-*), either explicitly or by comparing Sanskrit *mimāti* 'he measures'; and (7) reference is made to English Latin-derived doublets *measure* or *meditate.* Our dictionaries fit into these categories as follows:

no entry 3: American Heritage, Partridge, Shipley.

merely cite Persian *fermān* 3: Random House, Universal, Webster's New World.

mention Turkish transmission 4: Klein, Random House, Webster's Second, Webster's Third.

give Old Persian *framānā* 6: Klein, OED, Oxford, Skeat, Webster's Second, Webster's Third.

compare Sanskrit *pramāna-* 6: Klein, OED, Oxford, Skeat, Webster's Second, Weekley.

analyze into *pra-* (*pro-*) + *mā-* (*mē-*) 4: Klein, Oxford, Skeat, Webster's Second.

refer to *measure* or *meditate* 3: Klein, Oxford, Webster's Second.

It will be seen that the most adequate treatments are given by Klein and Webster's Second, followed by Oxford and Skeat.

Loanwords coming from families other than Indo-European, such as Semitic, Finno-Ugric, Altaic, and Algonquian, are characteristically treated more cursorily, being less likely to be analyzed, and usually not being compared to cognates in their family.[11] For a final example (beginning, of course, with *f-*), we can notice the Arabic borrowing *fellah* 'a peasant or agricultural laborer in Arab countries' (American Heritage). We may group the treatments into five categories: (1) no entry for the word; (2) the source is identified as Arabic and the meaning of the Arabic word is indicated, but the Arabic form is not shown; (3) the Arabic source-form *fallāḥ* is shown; (4) the Arabic word is shown, in most cases in its dialectal variant *fellāḥ*, and is related to its root, cited in the perfect category formation *falaḥa* 'cultivate, till' (rather than as the actual triconsonantal root *flḥ*);[12] and (5) the preceding information is given, plus the information that the root in this sense is borrowed from Aramaic, and cognates (beginning with *p-*) in Hebrew and Aramaic-Syriac are shown. Our dictionaries sort out as follows:

no entry 2: Partridge, Shipley.

Arabic + meaning 2: Random House, Universal.

Arabic *fallāḥ* 2: Webster's Second, Webster's Third.

Arabic *fellāḥ* + root *falaḥa* 6: American Heritage, OED, Oxford, Skeat, Webster's New World, Weekley.

preceding + other Semitic 1: Klein.

Klein thus stands apart in his treatment of comparative Semitic, and he is generally superior in his handling of Oriental material.[13]

Thus we see that the same information is not provided by all these works, and different parts of the whole story of a word's etymology tend to be left out by different ones. This suggests, of course, the desirability of utilizing several of them, when feasible.

The reader wanting to get an idea of the word family coming from one root is best advised to consult American Heritage, with Partridge as a second choice. The recent Shipley work is probably to be avoided as being too inexplicit as to the nature of the relationships, as well as incomplete and unreliable in various respects. The reader wanting good information about the etymology of a given word might go to these same works, as well as to Klein, Oxford, or Webster's Second. Since slow but steady progress in etymological research has taken place, the older works should be more cautiously utilized, especially Skeat and Weekley, and to a lesser extent Universal, OED, and Webster's Second. Desired words are more often found to be missing from Skeat and Shipley, and to a lesser extent Weekley and Partridge, than from the others. We have seen that Klein is strong in Oriental material. Dates of first occurrences of words are given by OED, Oxford, and the recent specialized listing by Finkenstaedt.

Pokorny's comparative Indo-European dictionary, organized by roots, and Ernout-Meillet's exemplary etymological dictionary of Latin, organized by word families, but indicating the survival of the Latin words, not only in Romance languages, but as borrowings into Germanic, as well as Celtic and Slavic, are useful supplements to these English-oriented dictionaries, as is Feist's etymological dictionary of Gothic.[14]

The heavy hand of commercialism is regretfully to be noted in the fact that Webster's Third systematically excised the references to English doublets found in Webster's Second, just as in the fact that more recent editions of American Heritage omit the etymological appendix. The latter, however, has recently been issued separately in a revised and expanded version as Indo-European Roots.[15]

We can now return to an initial question and see that the concept of a root can be utilized in two rather different ways. On the one hand, it is the core part of a word or a set of related words already in Proto-Indo-European and continuing on down.[16] On the other, it can be a data-organizing device to bring together cognates or doublets. These functions are quite independent and both are dispensable. Thus neither kind of root is used by Random House or Weekley. The root as a reconstruction for its own sake is found in Klein and Webster's New World. Shipley uses it rather as a data-organizing device. American Heritage shows both functions, but with some tension between them. Thus some apparent roots are introduced for the purpose of heading an entry connecting two or more English words when it is clear that the root did not occur in Proto-Indo-European, such as those standing behind the English words *wine* (related to *vine* and *oenology,* among others), *hemp* (related to *cannabis* and *canvas*), *merchant,* and *phylaxis.* Even the Semitic root *slm* is introduced for the same reason (connecting *salaam, Islam, Muslim; shalom, Solomon;* and *Salome*).[17] Yet other Semitic roots standing behind borrowings from Arabic are not used, for example, the *šrb* that would connect *sherbet, sorbet, syrup,* and *shrub* (the beverage). This in spite of the fact that numerous Indo-European roots are entered with unitary reflexes in English, whether native Germanic like *pen-* (standing behind *fen*) and *kelb-,* or borrowings from Latin (*nsi-, ō-*), Greek (*obhel-, terp-*), Sanskrit (*gweyə-*), or Slavic (*wer-*[9]). Shipley also has roots for *merchant* and *phylaxis,* and an equally dubious one connecting *sponge* and *fungus,* but as he is not unduly concerned with assigning a word to its actual root, he cheerfully enters *hempe* under *kel, wine* under *em,* and *salaam* under *dekm!*[18]

Occasionally relationships between words have become apparent only when their Proto-Indo-European reconstructions were compared. A classic case is the derivation of *hundred* from *ten,* which is recognized by eight dictionaries in our sample, even when, as with Webster's Third, they do not show the reconstructions.

These differences in the employment of roots, and more generally in the organization and selection of aspects of the data to be presented, should not blind us to the large common core of knowledge that these dictionaries offer. They represent the results of generations of scholarly labor: the working out of the history of the Indo-European languages, as well as of the general principles underlying language history, is one of the triumphs of modern (largely nineteenth-century) science. The sound correspondences linking cognates and doublets have been known in their essentials for over 150 years. But one must regretfully agree with Laird (*The Word,* p. 111) in lamenting the lack of diffusion of this knowledge and its sporadic treatment in our educational system. The average person doubtless still thinks of etymology in terms of the "romantic stories of word origins" approach.[19] Although, as Laird points out, the study of etymology in schools has largely emphasized the consideration of Latin and Greek elements of the English vocabulary, even this has declined along with the study of the classical languages. Thus the typical consulter of dictionaries for etymologies has not developed the appropriate mental framework, starting out with the layers of the family tree, for interpreting the information provided. The study of Indo-European roots and their proliferation in English along the lines indicated by Laird is thus to be advocated, perhaps not so much as he implies as a matter of vocabulary building (cf. *The Word,* pp. 112–15), but rather as an introduction to a challenging field of study whose existence is widely unsuspected.[20]

Notes

1. Cf. now Charles F. Hockett, "Distinguished Lecture: F," *American Anthropologist* 87 (1985): 263–81. This article presents the interesting, although doubtless controversial, hypothesis that the sound *f* (and its voiced counterpart *v*) are relatively recent innovations in human language, having been incited by a change of dentition brought about by the introduction of agriculture. Hockett summarizes (pp. 271–73) the principal historical sources of these sounds, the most common for *f* indeed being *p* (or aspirated *ph*), as also in Arabic and Hungarian (and for *v* being *w*).

2. I retain the alternative abbreviations and language names used by these dictionaries, as symptomatic of the other differences. The following abbreviations for languages occur in these extracts (normalizing with respect to the occurrence of periods): Arm., Armen., Armenian; Br., Breton; CGerm., Common Germanic; CIE, Common Indo-European; Com. WGer., Common West Germanic; Cor., Corn., Cornish; Cz., Czech; D., Dutch; Da., Dan., Danish; Du., Dutch; Eng., English; Flem., Flemish; G., German or Greek; Ga., Gael., Gaelic; Gaul., Gaulish; Ger., German; Gk., Greek; Go., Goth., Gothic; Gr., Greek; Hit., Hitt., Hittite; Icel., Icelandic; IE., Indo-European; Ir., Irish; L., Lat., Latin; Lith., Lithuanian; MD., MDu., Middle Dutch; MIr., Middle Irish; MLG., Middle Low German; mod. Ger., Mod. Germ., Modern German; Mx., Manx; OC., Old Celtic; OE., Old English; OFris., Old Frisian; OHG., Old High German; OI., Old Indic; OIr., Old Irish; ON., Old Norse; OPruss., OPrussian, Old Prussian; OS., Old Saxon; OSlav., Old Slavic; OTeut., Old Teutonic; pre-Teut., pre-Teutonic; Russ., Russian; Sans., Scrt., Skr., Skt., Sanskrit; Sw., Swed., Swedish; Teut., Teutonic; Toch., Tokh., Tocharian; Umbr., Umbrian; W., Welsh; WGer., WGerm., West Germanic.

3. Pokorny (p. 807) also cites cognates from these three branches, and additionally thinks of the Illyrian name *Pannonia.*

4. Citing only *pen-* would be an instance of the first flaw in current ety-

mological practice discussed by Heller: "The failure to bring the etymology consistently back to the form which actually underlies the word rather than to some canonical reference form." Louis G. Heller, "Lexicographic Etymology: Practice versus Theory," *American Speech* 40 (1965): 113–15.

5. A competing word for 'fish' is Greek *ikhthús,* which has cognates in Baltic and Armenian; yet other words occur in other branches. Weekley (column 568) points out the parallel distribution to congeners of *mere* and Latin *mare* 'sea'. Another similarly distributed word family, touched on below, is that of English *farrow* and *pork.* For more, see Antoine Meillet, *The Indo-European Dialects,* trans. Samuel N. Rosenberg (University, Ala.: University of Alabama Press, 1967), pp. 33–39, 161–63.

6. Universal does go on to say: "Further connexions are doubtful, but two suggestions have been put forward; (i.) relationship w. Latin *pinna,* 'fin'; O.E. *finn,* see **fin;** (ii.) w. Scrt. *picchā,* 'slime', *picchalaš,* 'slimy'."

7. The uncertainty regarding Oxford reflects the fact that reference is made overtly only to *piscina,* but this entry is in the same paragraph, headed by *piscary,* as *piscatorial, piscatory,* and *Pisces.*

8. The Latin word for 'fire' is *ignis,* the source of English *igneous* and *ignite, ignition.* This has cognates in Baltic, Slavic, and Indic. Thus it seems there were two words for 'fire' in Proto-Indo-European, the etymon of *fire* being of neuter gender, that of *ignis* being masculine and personified (cf. the Sanskrit god *Agni*). Descendant languages mostly kept just one of them.

9. On the archaism of the *r/n* alternation, see Robert Lord, *Comparative Linguistics* (London: English Universities Press, 1966), pp. 172–73.

10. Three dictionaries, Partridge, Webster's New World, and Pokorny, think of a root **bhok-* 'to flame, burn' relating *focus* to words in Armenian. This is dubious because of the scanty attestation, and also because this shape violates a well-known constraint on the consonants that may co-occur in a root. See Winfred P. Lehmann, *Proto-Indo-European Phonology* (Austin: University of Texas Press and Linguistic Society of America, 1952), p. 17.

11. Note the explicit instructions for Webster's Third in Gove for a differential treatment of Indo-European and non-Indo-European etyma with respect to the citation of cognates. Philip B. Gove, "Etymology in *Webster's Third New International Dictionary,*" *Word* 22 (1966): 60.

12. Citing such a root in this traditional form, and as a consequence failing to account for the vocalism of the actual Arabic word in question, would be an instance of the second flaw discussed by Heller: "The failure to etymologize all the morphemes of every word" (Heller, "Lexicographic Etymology," pp. 115–16, with discussion of *hegira*).

13. This strength of Klein is also noted by Laird in *The Word: A Look at the Vocabulary of English* (New York: Simon and Schuster, 1981), pp. 114, 323.

14. Etymologies receive little attention in recent discussions of dictionaries. Thus Kenneth G. Wilson et al., *Harbrace Guide to Dictionaries* (New

York and Burlingame: Harcourt, Brace and World, 1963), pp. 45–90, recognizes seven kinds of dictionaries but fails to allow for etymological ones. Sidney I. Landau's recent book *Dictionaries: The Art and Craft of Lexicography* (New York: Charles Scribner's Sons, 1984) devotes only 6 out of 310 pages of text (pp. 98–104) to etymology. There is even less in Ladislav Zgusta, *Manual of Lexicography* (The Hague/Paris: Mouton, 1971) and in R. R. K. Hartmann, ed., *Lexicography: Principles and Practice* (London: Academic Press, 1983). A good short discussion of etymologies in general-purpose dictionaries is found in Patrick Drysdale's article "Dictionary Etymologies: What? Why? and for Whom?" in *Papers of the Dictionary Society of North America 1979*, ed. Gillian Michell (London, Ont.: School of Library and Information Science, Univ. of Western Ontario, 1981), pp. 39–50. Drysdale considers the treatment of the doublets *door* (native English), *thyroid* (from Greek), and *foreign, forest, forum* (from Latin or French), as well as the treatment of loanwords as illustrated by *canoe, chipmunk,* and *lariat,* and he outlines ten degrees of information that can be given in an etymology. William Morris, in his article "The Making of a Dictionary—1969," *College Composition and Communication* 20 (1969): 198–203, happens also to have thought of *door* and its doublets, substituting *forensic* for *forum,* as an example of unsuspected relationships (p. 203). Alan S. C. Ross gives extracts of etymologies from twenty-three dictionaries of different languages in his book *Etymology: With Especial Reference to English* (London: André Deutsch, 1958), pp. 43–68, and he also presents selected English etymologies (pp. 141–64). M. M. Mathews leads the reader through a few dictionary etymologies for *anecdote* in *Words: How to Know Them* (New York: Henry Holt, 1956), pp. 56–64. A good brief exposition of technical limitations of dictionary etymologies is given by Heller in "Lexicographic Etymology," where he recognizes five "major flaws." (One of them, "the failure to mark relevant prosodic features," has encouraged me to include in my dictionary annotations an indication of the treatment of suprasegmentals, using Latin length and Greek accents as touchstones.) Gove's "Etymology in *Webster's Third*" is an enlightening publication of the actual guidelines for the etymologists of Webster's Third; see especially sections A57 *OE Etys.* (pp. 60–62) and A72 *System of Cross-References* (pp. 73–76) for the policies that have concerned us. More personal accounts of dictionary planning are given by Eric Partridge in *The Gentle Art of Lexicography as Pursued and Experienced by an Addict* (New York: Macmillan, 1963), pp. 85–101, and by Morris in "The Making of a Dictionary—1969," p. 203 (for American Heritage). V. Kiparsky, in "Über etymologische Wörterbücher," *Neuphilologische Mitteilungen* 60: 216–21, presents a comparison with respect to five characteristics of sixteen etymological dictionaries of individual languages, none of them English. Yakov Malkiel, in *Etymological Dictionaries: A Tentative Typology* (Chicago and London: Univ. of Chicago Press, 1976), gives a fuller discussion of many scholarly etymological dictionaries in accordance with eight "distinctive features"; he has something to say about Holthausen, Klein, Oxford, Partridge, Skeat, and Weekley. Laird, in *The Word* (p. 114, fn. 8), comments on Partridge, Webster's New World, American Heritage, Oxford, and Klein. Clarence L. Barnhart, in "American Lexicography, 1945–1973," *American Speech* 53 (1978); 93–94, 112–13, 117, 119, and 120, characterizes the handling of etymologies in Klein, Oxford, Webster's Third, Webster's New World, and American Heritage.

15. Mathews in *Words,* p. 60, praises Webster's Second for its references to related words, listing some of them for *stand* (cf. also pp. 59–60, 66–67). The Webster's Third policy is officially stated in Gove, "Etymology in *Webster's Third,*" pp. 73–74. Laird, in *The Word,* p. 327, also notes the continuing usefulness of Webster's Second. The change in American Heritage is noted by Landau in *Dictionaries,* pp. 101–2. The separation of Indo-European Roots from American Heritage has the disadvantage, of course, of segregating the historical and prehistoric parts of etymologies in different works. Although Watkins in Indo-European Roots, p. ix, states that "many new roots have been added," others have been removed or combined, so that the total is increased by only six, from 1,396 to 1,402. Revisions to the extracts shown from American Heritage include, for Indo-European, labeling of zero ablaut-grade (*pisk-) and presentation of uncontracted forms (standing behind *pūr-), and for Germanic, citation of complete words (*fanjam) and indication of internal morpheme boundaries (*fisk-a-, *fūr-i-).

16. Cf. the explanation by Calvert Watkins in American Heritage, p. 1497, and Indo-European Roots, p. xvi, and Lord, *Comparative Linguistics,* pp. 166–70. One no longer accepts the evolutionary sequence, exemplified by Greenough and Kittredge, according to which roots originally occurred in isolation, so that language went through a root-period, followed by a stem-period, and culminated in an inflectional period. James B. Greenough and George L. Kittredge, *Words and Their Ways in English Speech* (New York: Macmillan, 1901), pp. 168–84.

17. This root has been removed from Indo-European Roots. American Heritage and Indo-European Roots indicate such data-subsuming roots by enclosing them in brackets: *[slm], [vīnum]* for *wine* (etymologically better would be *[woino-]*), *[phulax]* for *phylaxis* (which might have been projected backwards as *[bhulak-]*), *[merc-],* changed to *[merk-²],* for *merchant,* but unenclosed *kannabis* for *hemp.* There are 98 roots that are so flagged in American Heritage. Indo-European Roots omits 13 and adds 3 to give 88. They correspond to a diversity of sources, but preponderantly Germanic, Greek, and Latin.

18. Shipley uses preposed ? to indicate doubt about a root's historical validity: *?(s)pong* for *sponge,* *?phulax* for *phylaxis,* *?merc* for *merchant.*

19. Cf. the comments of Landau, *Dictionaries,* pp. 98, 101–2, regarding dictionary users' interest in etymology.

20. A highly recommended fuller guide to English doublets is Mario Pei, *The Families of Words* (New York: Harper and Bros., 1962), which presents family trees for about two hundred roots, grouped according to increasing numbers of Indo-European branches that have provided words to English. Similar but much less comprehensive is Peter Davies, *Roots: Family Histories of Familiar Words* (New York: McGraw-Hill, 1981), giving family trees for one hundred roots, arranged in alphabetical order.

Appendix A

American Heritage: *The American Heritage Dictionary of the English Language*. Edited by William Morris. Boston: American Heritage Publishing and Houghton Mifflin, 1969. 1 + 1550 pp.
[General-purpose dictionary, alphabetically arranged, with appendix of Indo-European roots, to and from which reference is made; reconstructions for Proto-Indo-European roots and for derived Proto-Indo-European and Proto-Germanic forms; Indo-European and Germanic cognates cited only if they have led to English borrowings (suprasegmentals shown); extensive cross-references to doublets via Proto-Indo-European, good but incomplete cross-references to doublets within Germanic or English.]

Indo-European Roots: *The American Heritage Dictionary of Indo-European Roots*. Revised and edited by Calvert Watkins. Boston: Houghton Mifflin, 1985. xxvii + 113 pp.
[Separate publication of a revised and expanded version of the appendix of Indo-European roots in American Heritage. An index of English derivatives has been provided.]

Klein: *A Comprehensive Etymological Dictionary of the English Language: Dealing with the Origin of Words and Their Sense Development Thus Illustrating the History of Civilization and Culture*. By Dr. Ernest Klein. Amsterdam, London, New York: Elsevier Publishing, 1966, 1967. 2 volumes. xxvi + 1776 pp. Reprinted 1969; reprinted in one volume 1971.
[Etymological dictionary, alphabetically arranged; often Proto-Indo-European but no Proto-Germanic reconstructions; thorough citing of Indo-European and Germanic cognates (suprasegmentals shown, Greek alphabet); extensive cross-references to doublets.]

OED: *The Oxford English Dictionary: Being a Corrected Re-issue with an Introduction, Supplement, and Bibliography of A New English Dictionary on Historical Principles*. Oxford: At the Clarendon Press, 1933. 13 volumes.
[Unique historical dictionary, alphabetically arranged; Proto-Germanic reconstructions, occasionally Proto-Indo-European roots; limited citing of Indo-European cognates, but thorough citing of Germanic cognates

(suprasegmentals shown, Greek alphabet); few cross-references to
doublets.]
Oxford: *The Oxford Dictionary of English Etymology*. Edited by C. T.
Onions, with the assistance of G. W. S. Friedrichsen and R. W. Burchfield. Oxford: At the Clarendon Press, 1966. xvi + 1025 pp.
[Etymological dictionary, alphabetically arranged; Proto-Germanic reconstructions, and frequently Proto-Indo-European roots; good citing
of Indo-European and Germanic cognates (suprasegmentals shown);
moderately good cross-references to doublets (weak on noninitial
parts).]
Partridge: *Origins: A Short Etymological Dictionary of Modern English*. By
Eric Partridge. 4th edition. New York: Macmillan, 1966. xix + 972 pp.
Reprinted 1983: New York: Greenwich House.
[Etymological dictionary, alphabetically arranged entries grouping together numerous related words under one head word (although not
always all that come from one Proto-Indo-European root), with cross-
references; occasional Proto-Indo-European and Proto-Germanic reconstructions; good citing of Indo-European and Germanic cognates (suprasegmentals inconsistently shown); extensive cross-references to doublets
(weaker on noninitial parts).]
Random House: *The Random House Dictionary of the English Language*.
Jess Stein, Editor-in-Chief; Laurence Urdang, Managing Editor. New
York: Random House, 1966. xxxii + 2059 pp.
[General-purpose dictionary, alphabetically arranged; no reconstructions;
limited citing of Indo-European and Germanic cognates (suprasegmen-
tals shown); few cross-references to doublets.]
Shipley: *The Origins of English Words: A Discursive Dictionary of Indo-
European Roots*. By Joseph T. Shipley. Baltimore and London: Johns
Hopkins University Press, 1984. xxxiii + 637 pp.
[Etymological dictionary, alphabetically arranged under simplified Indo-
European roots, with index of English words (many words entered else-
where than under their actual root); no other reconstructions; Indo-
European cognates cited only if they have led to English borrowings,
Germanic cognates not cited (no suprasegmentals); extensive citing of
doublets via Proto-Indo-European, more limited citing of doublets
within Germanic or English.]
Skeat: *A Concise Etymological Dictionary of the English Language*. By the
Rev. Walter W. Skeat. New and corrected impression. Oxford: At the
Clarendon Press, 1911. xvi + 664 pp. Reprinted 1963: New York: Capri-
corn Books.
[Etymological dictionary, alphabetically arranged; frequent Proto-
Germanic reconstructions and occasional Proto-Indo-European roots;
limited citing of Indo-European cognates, less limited for Germanic cog-

nates (suprasegmentals shown, Greek alphabet); few cross-references to doublets via Proto-Indo-European, some to doublets within Germanic.]

Universal: *The Universal Dictionary of the English Language.* Edited by Henry Cecil Wyld. New York: E. P. Dutton, 1932. xx + 1431 pp. Reprinted 1961: London: Routledge and Kegan Paul.
[General-purpose dictionary, alphabetically arranged; occasional Proto-Indo-European and Proto-Germanic reconstructions; moderate citing of Indo-European and Germanic cognates (suprasegmentals shown); occasional cross-references to, but extensive cross-references from, doublets.]

Webster's New World: *Webster's New World Dictionary of the American Language.* David B. Guralnik, Editor-in-Chief. Second College Edition. New York and Cleveland: World Publishing, 1970. xxxvi + 1692 pp. Later printings: Simon and Schuster.
[General-purpose dictionary, alphabetically arranged; Proto-Indo-European roots but no Proto-Germanic reconstructions; limited citing of Indo-European cognates and very limited citing of Germanic cognates (no suprasegmentals); few cross-references to, but extensive cross-references from, doublets.]

Webster's Second: *Webster's New International Dictionary of the English Language.* 2nd edition, unabridged. William Allan Neilson, Editor-in-Chief; Thomas A. Knott, General Editor; Paul W. Carhart, Managing Editor. Springfield, Mass.: G. and C. Merriam, 1934. cxxxvi + 3194 pp.
[General-purpose dictionary, alphabetically arranged; no reconstructions; limited citing of Indo-European cognates, less limited for Germanic cognates (no suprasegmentals); extensive cross-references to doublets.]

Webster's Third: *Webster's Third New International Dictionary of the English Language.* Unabridged. Philip Babcock Gove, Editor-in-Chief. Springfield, Mass.: G. and C. Merriam, 1961. 72a + 2662 pp.
[General-purpose dictionary, alphabetically arranged; no reconstructions; limited citing of Indo-European and Germanic cognates (no suprasegmentals); no cross-references to, but extensive cross-references from, doublets.]

Weekley: *An Etymological Dictionary of Modern English.* By Ernest Weekley. London: John Murray, 1921. Reprinted 1967: New York: Dover Publications. 2 volumes. xx + 1660 pp.
[Etymological dictionary, alphabetically arranged; no reconstructions; limited citing of Indo-European and Germanic cognates (seldom Latin length, Greek alphabet); few cross-references to doublets via Proto-Indo-European, some to doublets within Germanic.]

Appendix B

Ernout-Meillet: *Dictionnaire étymologique de la langue latine: Histoire des mots*.
By Alfred Ernout and Antoine Meillet. 4th edition. Paris: C. Klinck-
sieck, 1959–60. 2 volumes. xviii + 829 pp. Reprinted 1979.
[Etymological dictionary of Latin, in French.]
Feist: *Vergleichendes Wörterbuch der gotischen Sprache mit Einschluß des
Krimgotischen und sonstiger zerstreuter Überreste des Gotischen*. By Sig-
mund Feist. Leiden: E. J. Brill, 1939. xxviii + 710 pp.
[Etymological dictionary of Gothic, in German; index of English (mostly
Old English) words, pp. 646–58.]
Finkenstaedt: *A Chronological English Dictionary, Listing 80000 Words in
Order of Their Earliest Known Occurrence*. By Thomas Finkenstaedt,
Ernst Leisi, and Dieter Wolff. Heidelberg: C. Winter, 1970. xvi + 1395 pp.
Funk and Wagnalls: *Funk and Wagnalls New Standard Dictionary of the Eng-
lish Language*. Isaac K. Funk, Editor-in-Chief. New York: Funk and
Wagnalls, 1963. lxx + 2816 pp.
[General-purpose dictionary, alphabetically arranged; no reconstructions;
no citing of Indo-European cognates, very little citing of Germanic cog-
nates (no suprasegmentals); very few cross-references to doublets.]
Holthausen: *Etymologisches Wörterbuch der Englischen Sprache*. By Ferdinand
Holthausen. 3. neubearbeitete und vermehrte Auflage. Göttingen: Van-
denhoeck und Ruprecht, 1949. vii + 226 pp.
[Etymological dictionary of the core vocabulary, in German, alphabetically arranged; few reconstructions; limited citing of Indo-European
cognates and very limited citing of Germanic cognates (suprasegmentals
shown); some cross-references to doublets.]
New Century: *The New Century Dictionary of the English Language*. Edited
by H. G. Emery and K. G. Brewster. Charles H. Fitch, Revision Editor.
New York, London: D. Appleton-Century, 1948. 2 volumes. viii + 2798 pp.
[General-purpose dictionary, alphabetically arranged; no reconstructions;
limited citing of Indo-European and Germanic cognates (no Latin length,
Greek alphabet); very few cross-references to doublets.]
Pokorny: *Indogermanisches Etymologisches Wörterbuch*. By Julius Pokorny.
Bern, Munich: Francke Verlag, 1959–69. 2 volumes. 1183, 495 pp.
[Comprehensive etymological dictionary of Indo-European, in German,
alphabetically arranged under Indo-European roots; reconstructions for
Proto-Indo-European roots and for derived Proto-Indo-European and
Proto-Germanic forms; thorough citing of Indo-European, including
Germanic, cognates (suprasegmentals shown); few indications of later
borrowings; second volume has indexes of English (mostly Old English)
words, pp. 317–45.]

Shorter OED: *The Shorter Oxford English Dictionary on Historical Principles.* Prepared by William Little, H. W. Fowler, J. Coulson. Revised and edited by C. T. Onions. 3rd edition, revised with addenda. Oxford: At the Clarendon Press, 1944. 2 volumes. xxii + 2494 pp.
[Abridged historical dictionary, alphabetically arranged; Proto-Germanic reconstructions, occasionally Proto-Indo-European roots; limited citing of Indo-European cognates and very limited citing of Germanic cognates (suprasegmentals shown); few cross-references to doublets.]

Webster's New Twentieth Century: *Webster's New Twentieth Century Dictionary.* 2nd edition. Cleveland: William Collins Publishers, 1979. xiv + 2129 + 160 pp. Reprinted 1983 as *Webster's New Universal Unabridged Dictionary.* Deluxe 2nd edition. Dorset and Baber.
[General purpose dictionary, alphabetically arranged; no reconstructions; very little citing of Indo-European or Germanic cognates (no suprasegmentals); no cross-references to doublets.]

The Lexicographer as
Social Chronicler

David B. Guralnik

IN the little biographical note that Charlton Laird supplied for
the jacket of his last published book, *The Word,* he referred to
himself as a "generalist." That was a characteristically modest
assessment and true as far as it went, for Larry was, indeed, a
generalist in the best sense of that word—Lewis Mumford called Aristotle the supreme generalist—but, in his ranging widely across the
field of English linguistics, he often introduced original and important theses that he offered to the specialists for further investigation.
In his review of *Language in America,* Robert Chapman refers to
Larry's tentative theory that there must be a felt human need for the
quality of language, as there is a felt need for language itself; that is,
the efficiency of a language as an intellectual mode of communication
"is paralleled or perhaps overweighed by its function as a symbolic
vehicle of the speaker's peculiar percepts and attitudes and of a whole
culture's apprehension of reality. As these change, language will
change in vocabulary and even in structure to embody them." And
that, in effect, is the theme of my talk.

But let me return to Larry for a moment. I made his acquaintance
shortly after World War II, when I returned to work on the dictionary that the now defunct World Publishing Company was preparing.
I had met Helene Gent, later Larry's wife, even earlier, when I first
came to World in 1941. In the early 1950s, I was asked to read and
evaluate a manuscript of Laird's. I read it and enthusiastically recommended its publication. It came out in 1953 as *The Miracle of Language,* and over a span of years, in both hard and soft covers, close to
a million copies appeared in print throughout the world. Perhaps I
can demonstrate the impact that this instructive, yet entertaining

DAVID B. GURALNIK is editor emeritus of *Webster's New World Dictionary* and retired vice president and dictionary editor-in-chief of Simon and
Schuster. A distinguished lexicographer, he has written and lectured widely
on the lore of words.

book on language has had by reading two little excerpts from letters I received in recent months. The first was written in April, less than a month before Larry died, and the writer says, "I noted in Laird's *Language in America* that he was paying an acknowledgment to you. This interested me, because he has always been one of my favorite authors. I have, over the years, purchased perhaps two dozen copies of his *Miracle of Language,* and have given them away. Now, I have been looking for two more copies, and have been completely unable to locate any." This, mind you, more than thirty years after its publication. The other was sent in July by a Japanese admirer in Tokyo. He writes, "I am sorry to hear that Dr. Laird passed away in May. I learned about the history of American English from his book more than from any other book on the subject. I should have expressed my gratitude to him when I was teaching at my graduate school." It was my privilege to have some slight, incidental connections with others of Larry's books published by my various employers, *The Tree of Language,* written with Helene for young folks, *Language in America, The Word,* and, of course, his *New World Thesaurus,* based upon his earlier *Promptory.* He was one of the first outside scholars whom I invited to take part in the planning conference, in 1963, for the Second College Edition of our dictionary, and his uncommon common sense has stood us in good stead all these years. And I prevailed upon him to write the introductory article, "Language and the Dictionary," for that edition, an article that, as I have learned, is required reading in English courses at many colleges. I last saw Larry when I visited him here in Reno in 1980, not too long after Helene's death, and first learned of his early novels, a copy of one of which he was kind enough to give me. I miss his chatty and perceptive letters, but I take some small solace from this conference dedicated to the memory of a first-rate scholar, a most honorable man, and a good friend. So, let me begin.

Dr. Johnson—one of the canonized members of the lexicographical fraternity—defined *lexicographer* as "a harmless drudge" and *patron* as "a wretch who supports with insolence and is paid with flattery." The American patron saint of dictionaries, Noah Webster, defined *Jacobin* as "one who opposes government from an unreasonable spirit of discontent," a definition that neatly balances Johnson's etymology for *Tory:* "a cant term derived, I suppose, from an Irish word signifying a savage." In their definitions, these gentlemen were indulging in a privilege not accorded the modern dictionary-maker.

The last feeble attempt at personal lexicography in English, with all the richness of invective that bias or a fleeting sense of fun could impart, was made by Henry Cecil Wyld, whose *Universal Dictionary of the English Language* appeared in 1932, and who in that work illustrated the expletive *damn* with "Damn this dictionary!"

Modern lexicographers are not allowed the luxury of venting their spleen upon those persons, institutions, and ideas that find little favor with them, at least not in their dictionaries. Nor do they take it upon themselves to pass personal judgment upon the validity of a term, as Johnson did at the entry *emergency,* for the meaning that is today the predominant one, which he declared a sense "not proper," or at the entry *clever,* where he adds: "This is a low word, scarcely ever used but in burlesque or conversation"—this forthright judgment despite the fact that Johnson accompanies it with citations of the use of *clever* by no less personages than Addison and Pope. Today's dictionary-makers may or may not share the distaste felt by some at the free use of the terminal combining form *-wise* in such compounds as "*weatherwise* there is a 20% chance of rain" or "*budgetwise* we won't make it this year," but their lexical entry for that suffix is likely to be something as unemotional as this from our own dictionary: "with regard to; in connection with: in this sense a revival of an earlier usage." For one thing, the modern dictionary is no longer the product of a single pair of gifted hands, sorting out the uses to which a word is put, constructing, mostly by conjecture, an interesting etymology, and carefully molding the phonemic contours of the term to fashion the pronunciation that the lexicographer would like to hear universally used. Today's dictionary is, *pace* the late Eric Partridge, the product of a group of specialists, each analyzing the word from his or her own area of expertise and reporting the findings in as objective a manner as the human mind can manage. Absolute objectivity is probably as unattainable as that other goal of the lexicographer, an error-free dictionary, and for the same reason. Dictionaries are, after all, compiled by human beings, who are both fallible and prone to hold opinions. Nevertheless, in this form of participatory democracy that is twentieth-century lexicography, each vocabulary listing is likely to be scrutinized by at least half a dozen pairs of eyes, so that any one person's inadvertent bias will almost certainly be called—triumphantly—to his or her attention for correction.

For another thing, the modern lexicographer is the beneficiary, if not the slave, of the science of linguistics. We know, for example, that the primary use of the dictionary we are preparing is for our time, and not for all times. We know that etymology is the historical retracing by means of available evidence of the forms through which a word has found its way from some ancient parent tongue to its present usage and that all the pretty fictions, such as that *posh* is an acronym of the phrase "port outward starboard home," are meaningless without the hard evidence to substantiate them. We know that the pronunciation or pronunciations of a word are those which a careful monitoring of cultivated native speakers of the language tells us are the ones most frequently heard, and that, much as some of us would have liked to preserve *rash uh NAY lee* as the etymologically informative pronunciation of this direct borrowing from Latin, we must report *rash uh NAL*, as though the word had entered our language via French, to be the overwhelmingly prevailing pronunciation of educated speakers. We know that the definitions of a term must be constructed on the evidence of actual citations in context. And, above all, we know that our position as recorder of the state of the language is a self-appointment and that no governmental or scholarly body—no Language Academy—has delegated us the arbiters of elegance or style or even logic in usage.

But these differences between dictionary editors today and their predecessors have to do with the conscious, the deliberate, taking on of prerogatives. There is, however, an area in which the lexicographer of Georgian England and his counterparts in America today serve a common, albeit inadvertent, role. Let us look at the dictionary as a kind of Sears catalog, that is, a broad listing of an inventory of currently available items, with a description (sometimes an illustration) of each item, some indication of the best uses to which it could be put, and its current value, in terms of either price or status. In 1984, the principal function of such a catalog, mercantile or linguistic, is to make known the available inventory.

In 1984, however, the 1904 catalog may serve another purpose not specifically intended by its compilers, and in 2084, it may be presumed, the 1984 catalog will also serve such a purpose. And that is as a record of social history, of mass attitudes, beliefs, fads, and taboos prevailing at the time the dictionary was constructed. The 1904 Sears-Roebuck catalog is generally recognized as an accurate source book of U.S. living conditions, tastes, and buying habits in that period. A careful and sensitive reading of a dictionary—any good dictionary—will be equally productive. Immediately apparent is the rhetorical style of the definitions—for example, the balanced, cadenced, but relatively terse prose of the eighteenth-century Johnson dictionary in keeping with the classical, balanced elegance of the music and painting and architecture of that period. Or the simpler, more direct, but often more discursive style of Noah Webster, reflecting the more forthright, even austere, quality of Colonial Puritanism. Take Johnson's often quoted definition of *network:* "any thing reticulated or decussated, at equal distances, with interstices between the intersections." And Webster's treatment: "a complication of threads, twine or cords united at certain distances, forming meshes or open spaces between the knots or intersections." An interesting footnote: having improved measurably upon Johnson's baroque poem, Webster still feels the need to pay homage to the great man and so he adds: "reticulated or decussated work." Incidentally, in his *Language in America,* Laird describes Webster as "the preeminent cracker-barrel lexicographer . . . more a hack of all intellectual trades than a scholar." Conceding Webster's intelligence and practicality, Laird adds: "But he had neither the wit nor profundity, and he probably never felt the lack of either quality." A dictionary of our own times is likely to have a definition more or less like the following example of twentieth-century prose: "any arrangement or fabric of parallel wires, threads, etc. crossed at regular intervals by others fastened to them so as to leave open spaces."

But it is in even more subtle lexical areas that the temper of the times may be read. The 1970s may well be remembered in history mainly as the period in which women for the first time in any concerted way, and with a sizable consensus, took positive action to expose the sexist aspects of our culture and to attempt to do something about them. The very word *sexism,* so familiar to our ears now, did not begin to appear with any frequency in the public prints until about a dozen years ago. That ours has been a male-dominated society in which women have been variously exploited is a charge that cannot be successfully refuted. Language, as a mirror of culture, can reflect such a situation, and English reveals traditional sexism in such respects as the absence of a neutral pronoun, for which *he* and *his* have been conventionally used ("everyone should bring his own lunch"), or in the absence, until quite recently, of a title for women which, like *Mr.,* would not reveal marital status. This latter defect has been remedied by the introduction of *Ms.,* which in just a few years caught on to an astonishing degree and is recorded in every up-to-date dictionary, as are the words *sexism* and *liberation,* in its newest meaning: "the securing of equal social and economic rights, as, the women's *liberation* movement." Artificial attempts have been made to construct genderless pronouns, but so far none of those proposed has been widely accepted. I recall one publication, the *Daily Beacon,* student newspaper at the University of Tennessee, that was determined to use such a set of pronouns consistently. That paper for several years, beginning in June of 1973, used the pronoun *tey* for *he* or *she, tem* for *him* or *her,* and *ter* for *his* or *her.* But for the most part, the exotic sound and look of such coinages have turned users off by opening their serious intent to ridicule. Probably the ultimate solution will be a practice already in common use for over 200 years, although still frowned on by purists, and that is the employment of the plural *they* or *their* when the antecedent is indefinite ("everyone should bring *their* own lunch"). There are actually times when its use is almost mandatory. Sample dialogue: "What's Jim doing?" "I don't know. I don't think *he* knows what he's doing." "I don't think anybody around here knows what he's doing" would be an ambiguous retort (is the antecedent of *he* Jim or anybody?), but not if you substitute *they* for *he.* Our own dictionary has for some time taken cognizance of that practice with notes at *they* and *their* ("also used with a singular antecedent, as *everybody, somebody, everyone*—everyone helped and it was good that they did").

The growing awareness of sexist attitudes reflected in our speech and writing has resulted in a conscious effort to become aware of them and to take steps to eliminate them. These measures may take the form of a voluntary effort by writers and publications to avoid pejorative or condescending terms for women, such as *suffragette* for *suffragist* (the *-ette* suffix clearly diminishes the importance of the activity; a *drum majorette* is cute and fluffy and lacks the solid, martial magnificence of a *drum major*) or the use of *my girl* for *my secretary* or *my assistant* indulged in by many executive types. Or it may take the extreme form of the fiat handed down a couple of years back by one book publisher in the form of a handbook strictly forbidding editors or even authors to use such terms as *mankind* ("use humanity instead") that are felt to have sexist connotations. In any case, all this ferment, these linguistic feints and parries, are bound to have an effect on the language, and the dictionaries are beginning to reflect that change. Already the efforts to eliminate the terminal combining form *-man* from many long-established terms is recognized in dictionaries by the inclusion a few years back of the combining form *-person* ("*a comb. form meaning* a person of either sex in a specified activity: used in coinages, as *chairperson,* to avoid the masculine implications of *-man*"). It is interesting to note that a number of the compounds with *-man* name activities in which women have been participating for some time, so linguistically sensitive dictionaries have for many years recognized that *statesman,* for example, which Noah Webster defines as "a man versed in the arts of government," should be defined as "a *person* who shows wisdom, skill, and vision in conducting state affairs . . . or one engaged in the business of government." Margaret Thatcher, Indira Gandhi, and Golda Meir are or were, after all, statesmen among statesmen, with all the perquisites attached to that appellation, including, as we have been reminded to our horror, vulnerability to assassination. The nineteenth-century view of women in politics is reflected in Noah Webster's entry *stateswoman,* which he defines as "a woman who meddles in public affairs," or in his entry for *ambassadress,* defined simply as "the wife of an *ambassador.*" Incidentally, the U.S. Department of Labor, in its fourth edition of *The Dictionary of Occupational Titles* prepared a few years ago, did a major overhauling of that list to, as they put it, eliminate "sex and age referent titles considered to be potentially discriminatory." There are no longer *foremen* (they are now *supervisors*) or *linesmen* (they are *line repairers*), and so on. Although it will be some time before all of society adopts these linguistic practices, lexicographers must monitor the language regularly and record the changes as they occur.

One area in which dictionaries can be very revealing about the culture in which they are compiled is the illustrative examples or cited quotations used to exemplify a usage. A good barometer for the change in sexist attitudes that is taking place today might be such illustrations. As an experiment, I chose a word of generally neutral connotation with many meanings, the word *set,* which occupies nearly a full page of our Second College Edition. Dr. Johnson uses actual citations from printed literature to illustrate the meanings, whereas we use briefer, manufactured illustrative examples. Among Johnson's citations I counted all nouns and pronouns that clearly had gender. The score reads: males, 216—females, 28, and many of the latter were in pejorative contexts. Most of the verbal illustrations in our dictionary tend on the whole to be genderless, but in our First College Edition, published in 1953, there were nine examples with gender within the entry *set,* seven of them masculine, two feminine. The current Second College Edition has only one example with gender, and that one is feminine. This change is not the result of a ukase handed down to editors but rather a general awareness on their part of the danger of falling into stereotypes or making women the nearly invisible half of humanity.

But let me move on to another point. The use of euphemism would seem to be ingrained in the human psyche. We tend to avoid the unpleasant, to delude others or ourselves, or to bypass that which is taboo by a kind of sleight-of-tongue, a magical use of softer or more oblique terms that gloss over a painful fact—terms that tell it like it isn't. It seems to be a universal characteristic, and, as such, it is a feature of all languages. In English, until quite recently, death was a phenomenon to be euphemized by "passings on," "departures," and "lateness." Illness, too, has been a subject for euphemizing. Until relatively recently, *cancer* was taboo in normal discourse, and even such a word as *disease* was once a euphemism. Dis-ease—a mere inconvenience. This demonstrates another facet of language. Through continued usage, a euphemism loses its softening quality and must in turn be euphemized. At least one of the common vulgate sexual terms, until quite recently taboo at most social levels, probably began life as a euphemism for an earlier, now forgotten term. A study of any dictionary reveals those aspects of our culture which seemed to require that kind of delicate substitution in its particular period. A current dictionary tells us something about the hunger for status in our culture as revealed in the changes of occupational designation. The old-fashioned *family doctor* became a *general practitioner,* who today is a *specialist in internal medicine,* although I note the beginning of a return to *family medicine.* And taking the next occupation in logical sequence, the old-fashioned *undertaker* became a *mortician,* whose heir to the family business today is a *funeral director* operating out of a *funeral home.* The *hairdresser* became a *beauty parlor operator,* who then went to school and became a *cosmetologist,* whose place of business changed from a *parlor* to a *salon,* which is fast becoming a *villa, bazaar, boutique,* or *house of hair fashion.* And *barbers,* I'm afraid, are rapidly metamorphosing into *hair stylists.* The *elderly* (itself a euphemism) were invested with the diadem of *golden agers,* then *senior citizens,* until they themselves, in the wisdom of their years, rejected the brass crown and began calling themselves *older* (or *senior) adults. Janitors* were elevated to *custodians* and have since rocketed to the heady stratosphere of *superintendency*. Just think what a difference one small *s* can make, at least in salary. Compare the *superintendent of the school* with the *superintendent of the schools*. All these meteoric ascents are of course a matter of record in the dictionary. But it is not only persons who are so elevated. I recently saw an ad for *energy systems*, which turned out to be wood-burning stoves. And the Yellow Pages tell us that florists and greenhouses now often sell *foliage systems*. The *complete shaving system* in another ad turned out to be a razor with a reasonably compatible blade. Are we becoming more systematized?

The areas of government and politics have always been fertile fields for the culture of linguistic obfuscation and flimflam, but it is in the twentieth century, if dictionaries are any record of the fact—and they are—that the real proliferation is taking place. Professor William Lutz, who is the editor of the splendid *Quarterly Review of Doublespeak,* could tell you much more about these linguistic shenanigans than I can, but let me just say that it is in this century that Orwell gave us *Newspeak* and it is in this century that official lies became first a *credibility gap* and then *inoperative statements,* that *no-knock laws* were instituted which might more descriptively have been called *bust-in laws,* since that's what actually happens to the suspect's door. This is the century in which those suffering the degradation of poverty, those whom Dickens had in the *poor* house, are called the *underprivileged,* though, one may note in passing, there is no parallel *overprivileged* in the dictionary for those who may have more than they need or morally deserve. And in which those who seek to leave the abyss of poverty are *striving for upward mobility.* This is the century in which terrorists are called *liberationists,* totalitarian governments are called *democracies, doing one's own thing* in the sixties meant doing exactly as others in one's peer group were doing—a century in which nuclear bombs whose radioactive fallout has a half-life of only five thousand years are *clean bombs,* and in which the devastation of a peasant village is a form of *pacification.* It is to be hoped that the researcher of today's dictionary in the year 2084 will look upon these terms as curious and incomprehensible relics of an earlier and darker age.

Earlier I mentioned taboo as one of the causes of euphemism. Humanity has had its taboos in all periods, apparently must have such taboos, especially in language, for unless you have a stock of generally forbidden words, what release valve is there, other than the Saturday night special, in moments of great stress or frustration? At one time, such taboos were largely religious in origin and based on the ineffability of the name of God or of Jesus, or on the profanity in the use of such terms as *damn* and *hell,* and so the dictionaries have been variously filled over the years with such evasions as *zounds* and *odd's bodkins,* and *gadzooks,* and *gee whiz,* and *Jiminy crickets* and *cripes* and *gosh* and *golly* and *darn* and *heck.* For a very long time, and still to some extent today, the principal taboo has operated against the use of a number of old vernacular terms dealing with sex and excretion, the so-called dirty words.

Until quite recently—and some of us tend to forget how very recently, indeed, it has been—these half dozen or so unmentionable words, which had long been mentioned, these unwhisperable words, which were much whispered, were also unprintable words which did remain unprinted. Even Captain Grose's innovative work, *A Classical Dictionary of the Vulgar Tongue,* published in London in 1785, the first work of its kind to deal extensively with slang, cant, and underworld jargon, could do no more than print the initial letter of each of these words followed by the proper number of asterisks to complete it, a practice still advocated in the Associated Press and United Press International stylebooks, and the ultimate word does not appear even in this laundered form in Grose's work. Johnson and Bailey and Noah Webster simply ignore these terms altogether, as does the great 13-volume OED, which professes to enter all terms for which the editors had adequate citation. I must add, however, that the first three volumes of a supplement to that work now in process, which have appeared in the last few years, do enter several of the formerly taboo terms, with citations going back to the thirteenth century. This in a supplement which, the preface states, is restricted to "accessions to the English language . . . from 1928 to the present day" along with most of the entries in the 1933 supplement, which also ignored the taboo terms. In fact, immediately following the *Lady Chatterley's Lover* obscenity trial in 1959, which was won by the defense, the publishers of the OED took the trouble to announce publicly that the words which had been the gravamen of that trial would not appear in the Oxford dictionaries. Sometimes dictionaries will tell you as much about the culture they report in their omissions as in their inclusions. It is clearly not the organs and acts described by these terms that have been verboten. If the words for them are fashioned out of the syllables of the International Scientific Vocabulary, even cunnilingus and fellatio might safely be recorded. It was only the Old English terms of common use that were forbidden. Robert Graves tells the story of the soldier who was shot in the buttocks and, asked by a member of royalty visiting the hospital where he had been wounded, replied, "I'm so sorry, Ma'am, I don't know. I never learned Latin." The taboo was so strong that, for example, Greenough and Kittredge, devoting a chapter to euphemism in their classic *Words and Their Ways,* never allude, even by indirection, to that class of "dirty words."

The epoch-making decision of Judge Woolsey in 1933, permitting the publication and distribution of Joyce's *Ulysses* in the United States, theoretically lowered the bars, but publishers remained cautious and for the most part these taboo words were kept out of print, except in materials sold under the counter, until the 1960s. Even today, most newspapers, including the "all the news that's fit to print" *New York Times,* rarely allow these terms on their pages, although the *Times* temporarily lifted its ban when it printed transcripts of taped conversations in the Oval Office during the Watergate hearings, as revelatory of the atmosphere in the White House at that time (or should I say at that point in time?). Not too many years ago, the acerbic comic Lenny Bruce was arrested and temporarily jailed for uttering only one of these words in a nightclub act. You have noticed, I'm sure, that I, uncertain of the sensibilities of my audience, have studiously avoided enunciating these earth-shaking syllables.

Let me tell you of a personal incident. During the planning conference for our Second College Edition, which was held in January of 1963 and was attended by staff and by academic consultants including, as I mentioned earlier, Larry, I put on the agenda the question of including these taboo terms for the first time in any general, commercial dictionary. At that time, our citation file was already beginning to show a number of uses for some of these terms. Nearly all of these early citations were from dialogue in novels, virtually none from periodicals or newspapers, except for a few from the *Village Voice* and some other subterranean publications. There was much discussion of the question, but the decision, virtually unanimous, was that it would be unwise at that juncture to invite the banning of the dictionary in many areas. We knew, for example, that the state of Texas would peremptorily forbid the use of the dictionary by students throughout the state. And judging by what has been going on in many other areas in the past few years, we would likely have had trouble elsewhere getting the book into the hands of the students for whom it was being specifically prepared. Bear in mind that this was 1963. Possibly our conference would have come to quite another conclusion in 1973, although I note that the Supreme Court has just now agreed to hear a couple of cases dealing with the state of Washington's obscenity law, which could lead to a redefinition of "community standards."[1]

At any rate, with the publication of the book early in 1970, I made the inevitable promotional tour, appearing on television and radio shows in various cities. On one talk show in Washington, D.C., the conversation led inexorably to these rediscovered jewels, the "dirty dozen," and the moderator of the show asked for an explanation of their omission from our dictionary, even though she had read the foreword to the book, where our reasoning is given clearly and, I believe, candidly. I repeated that explanation and added my thesis of this afternoon—that dictionaries are a barometer of social climate. And that if our culture is still in large measure puritanical and prudish—"Prudish! How can you say 'prudish?'" the moderator interjected. "Why these words are heard and seen everywhere these days." "Well," I replied, "why all this circumlocution, then? We might as well talk about the words themselves. I'll begin with fu—." "Stop!" she screamed, on the verge of apoplexy. My point, I think, had been made.

During the planning conference at which the decision on the taboo words was reached, we also tackled the question of how to deal with the vernacular terms used contemptuously for members of various racial and ethnic groups. For racism, no less than sexism, has long characterized our culture. It is, of course, clear that a desk dictionary the size of our college editions, currently at about 160,000 vocabulary entries, represents a selection of only a fraction of the more than a million lexical units that could conceivably be incorporated in a dictionary, but that no dictionary has ever attempted to encompass, not even the multivolume OED. The process of lexical selection is not an easy one. While it is based essentially on frequency of usage, it is not a simple statistical exercise of counting citations. *Where* the citations are found and over *what span of time* are factors that must be considered along with the mere number.

At any rate, the planning conference decided—this time with less than unanimity but nevertheless a substantial majority—that we would be well within our lexicographical responsibilities to omit these vulgate terms of opprobrium. For one thing, a strange development seemed to be taking place. During the very period that our files were being inundated with the newly liberated taboo terms, citations for all but a few of the derogatory names were dwindling to a trickle. And even in oral usage, a change seems to be taking place. Where thirty or forty years ago such epithets were likely to be heard equally and unselfconsciously from the Archie Bunkers *and* their sons-in-law, as well as from gentlemen of cultivation sipping brandy in their clubs, today it is chiefly the Bunkers who hold on to the traditions, and even they are beginning to show a curious reticence. Is it possible that people, who, as I've suggested, seem to have a built-in need for taboos, in the process of freeing the terms of eroticism and scatology are simultaneously creating a new category of taboos?

Recently a correspondent wrote concerning the use of *white meat* and *dark meat* to refer to parts of a chicken, a usage that he declared originated in Victorian disapproval of the words *breast, leg,* and *thigh*. Actually, the American ban on those terms antedated Victoria's accession to the throne—see Captain Marryat's *Diary in America*. Incidentally, there is a story, perhaps apocryphal, about Winston Churchill, who as a guest at dinner was asked which joint of chicken he preferred. When he asked for the breast, he was informed by his hostess that, yes, he could have a piece of "white meat." The next day he sent a bread-and-butter letter, accompanied by a corsage, which he suggested she wear on her white meat. Well, the letter goes on to say: "I had lunch at a counter yesterday and, looking at the menu, asked what came with the 'chicken dinner.' 'You has your choice,' I was told by the waitress, 'of breast and wing or leg and thigh.'" He then adds: "'White and dark meat' have acquired racial connotations, whereas 'breast and thigh' are no longer offensive. A nice turnabout?" It would be an interesting development if for once in our language the truly obscene became unspeakable. The next decade or two will show whether such concomitant developments are, in fact, taking place—and if they are, all dictionaries will reflect that turn of events.

Some of you may recall that a few years back the publishers of the OED were involved in a court case on the very issue of the pejorative terms. A class libel suit had been filed against them back in 1969 charging that the OED's entry for the word *Jew* defamed all Jews and asking that a correction be made in the forthcoming supplement. The entry in question has a noun that reads: "a person of Hebrew race . . . : applied to a grasping or extortionate money-lender or usurer, or a trader who drives hard bargains or deals craftily." And there is a verb reading: "to cheat or overreach in a way attributed to Jewish traders or usurers." There is no indication that these terms are in any way pejorative or that their use might be taken as offensive.

In a speech that the editor of the OED delivered to a philological society shortly before the case came to trial, he defended the OED's practices in this regard and stoutly proclaimed that they had no intention of altering their methods. Now, the OED's entries for *Jew* and for *dago* and for *nigger* may not give us much factual information about these peoples, but as part of a social chronicle they do tell us much about the British attitude toward such minority groups. Equally revealing was the trial judge's gratuitous remarks, after he had dismissed the suit as failing to show damage to the plaintiffs: "I am happy to say this in open court, that there are many fine persons who are Jewish by birth or creed, persons of utmost integrity, honesty, reputation, skill and ability." And then he added, "If there be Jews, and no doubt there are, who do not in fact measure up to that standard, there are many people not Jews who are just as bad or worse, and there are many non-Jews to whom these derogatory words could very properly be applied." These derogatory words, I presume, being the noun *Jew* and the verb *Jew*, as defined in the OED.

These fatuities aside, the real question is: to what extent have dictionaries perpetuated and even given sanction to these expressions of hatred and contempt? A correspondent a while back uncovered for me an interesting letter to the editor printed in the *Chicago Tribune* on March 13, 1872. That was a letter from the G. and C. Merriam Company, the dictionary publishers in Springfield, Massachusetts, in reply to a complaint about the entry of the opprobrious verb *jew*. The editors conceded that the complaint was justified, that a search of earlier British dictionaries reveals no record of such a usage and that "they do not recall seeing it employed in literary composition." One of the OED's defenses was that the term was of very long standing in the language and in literature, although they originally offered no citations earlier than the middle of the nineteenth century. I note that the OED supplement now has a citation from a diary compiled in 1825 but that did not appear in print until 1929. In any event, the Merriam editors in their reply added that "we fear it must have been drawn from Worcester, where we first find it" and that they intended to drop it from future editions. Joseph Worcester was the editor of a dictionary competing with the Merriams in the nineteenth century.

Not too long ago, I uncovered the information that Worcester, in response to a similar complaint, conceded that he had no real evidence for a generic use and dropped the term from a later edition. Somehow the term found its way back into the dictionaries, possibly as a result of its entry in the OED in the 1890s. To what extent dictionaries have influenced this usage, as distinct from merely recording it, would be hard to say.

Time has allowed us to do only a little strip mining on the rich beds of ore buried in the archival dictionary. The perceptive researchers of the year 2084 will learn much from the 1984 dictionary about the post–World War II *counterculture* (that term itself is very revealing), about the disillusion of youth with the *Establishment* (that, too, is a relatively recent extension of the term), about its *anomie*, or rootlessness, as revealed through a flourishing drug culture, with *its* extensive lexicon, or through the search for truths in the mysticism of *Zen Buddhism, Hare Krishna, mantras,* and the *lotus position.* Or, from more recent editions of our lexicons, they will learn about the growing counter-counterculture, as exemplified by *upscale Yuppies* and *Yumpies, gentrification* and *time-share condominia,* and the search for truths through being *born again, Pro-Life,* and one of the *Moral Majority.* They will detect a growing concern over possible *ecocide* and for *zero population growth,* and they will learn about our sprawling *megalopolises* and the need for *urbanologists.* They will note the preponderance of newer terms from the hard sciences and technologies, from physics and chemistry and medicine, over terms from the humanities, from philosophy or literature or the arts. They will also note the rapidly proliferating lexis of computer science from *EBCDIC* through *electronic mail* through *user-friendly software.* And they will observe that in the second half of the twentieth century, the language was enriched—some might say impoverished—by the addition of many hundreds of acronyms, from *laser* through *AWACS* through *AIDS.* They will also learn something about the moral climate of our times from such recorded lexical items as *genocide, Watergate, yellow rain,* the *Holocaust,* the *neutron bomb,* and *star wars.* But despite all that, I remain optimist enough to believe that there will be researchers in 2084 studying the dictionaries of 1984.

Note

1. On June 19, 1985, the Court ruled on two cases (*Brockett* v. *Spokane Arcade* and *Eikenberry* v. *State Statute*) to decide the constitutionality of a Washington State obscenity law that permitted authorities to take legal action against any material that incited "lasciviousness or lust." The Court ruled (6 to 2) that the statute is constitutional. The 9th U.S. Circuit Court of Appeals had struck down the law because of the ban against "lust," which it said is "a healthy, wholesome human reaction common to millions of well-adjusted persons." The Supreme Court, while agreeing that "material that provoked only normal, healthy sexual desires should not be suppressed as obscene," added that the appellate court should have limited itself to invalidating the part containing the word *lust,* but should not have struck down the entire law.

Social Dialects
Educational Implications of the Study of Black English

Robert H. Bentley

IT should surprise no reader of this collection of essays that the study of language often has political, social, and educational implications. Language exists in a social context. To study language is to study people and at least one aspect of the way they behave.

Certainly one of the serious linguistic—and ultimately educational—issues of the past two decades has been the dispute over the status of socially nonstandard dialects in society generally and in the school particularly. This paper examines the educational implications of the results of the past twenty years of research in these nonstandard dialects, with special attention to the work in Black English.

The social turbulence of the late 1960s rather directly gave new importance to the study of linguistics generally, and social dialects particularly. While students marching in demonstrations against the conflict in Vietnam were charging colleges and universities with social irresponsibility and irrelevance, major cities became battle zones. Ethnic minority groups, especially blacks, demanded both respect and equal opportunities.

Society looked to its educational institutions to solve the problems. The demands for "relevance" and respect gave rise to the programs in Black Studies and Hispanic Studies which proliferated in the early seventies. The demands for equal opportunity presupposed adequate educational preparation, and it was clear to just about everyone that inner-city education was anything but adequate.

Formal studies validated what black parents had been saying for years: the schools were not teaching children to read and write.

R O B E R T H. B E N T L E Y is a professor in the Communication Department of Lansing Community College, Lansing, Michigan. He has written on social dialects, especially Black English, and has worked on textbooks on composition.

Without this basic literacy, all other educational doors remained closed. As Charlton Laird noted in 1970:

These [black] youngsters need to learn to use the standard language of the world outside their ghetto communities if they are to acquire a good education and hold good jobs. Standard English is a subject of instruction in the schools, but it is also the medium of instruction, so that the troubles of ghetto children are at least doubled.[1]

William Labov put the case even more strongly in the same year: "One of most extraordinary failures in the history of American education is the failure of the public school system to teach black children in the urban ghettos to read."[2]

The attacks on the quality—or lack of it—in inner-city schools put professional educationists on the defensive. To explain the "extraordinary failures," educationists—aided and abetted by some psychologists and linguists—formulated a number of deprivation theories. Urban students, and especially black students, were failing to read, they said, not because the schools were poor but because students were somehow "deprived" and unable to learn. One extreme deprivation model claimed the problem was actually cognitive deprivation—a fancy way of saying that whites are smarter than blacks. Another suggested that the problem was cultural deprivation. By far the most pervasive of the theories, and the one that haunts us still, charged that the problem in urban education was linguistic deprivation. These deprivation theories seem, in retrospect, to have one thing in common: they all blame the victim for the crime.

While the charges of cognitive and cultural deprivation provoked debate and inspired research, it was the charge of linguistic deprivation that most immediately involved linguists and—often—departments of English and which occupies me here.

A new "hyphenated discipline," called *socio-linguistics,* had been maturing during the early 1960s. Linguists such as Decamp and Labov and many others were building upon the solid foundations of dialect studies. Adding insights and methods from sociology to the findings about the nature of language and language change from both diachronic and synchronic linguistics, the early work in American sociolinguistics (with or without the hyphen) began to lay a solid foundation for a counterargument to then-current deprivation theories. Fueled by public and academic interest, and supported by freely flowing grant monies, research into social dialects, and especially Black English, proliferated.

Many fascinating debates erupted as data were collected and hypotheses constructed. The favorite debate topic? "Is there *really* such a thing as 'Black English'?" Another such is the debate over the origins of the dialect which some have now come to call Black English Vernacular.[3] One camp in this debate, typified by Dillard's book *Black English,* argues for African origins for BEV. Another view, held by Raven McDavid and others, is that BEV is merely southern speech transported north by blacks and "discovered" by northern linguists.

While these debates are both useful and interesting, they do not address the primary problem of the failure by the schools to impart literacy. From out of the smoke, roughly three positions have emerged which *do* attempt to explain this failure.

While the three positions overlap at times, I have nevertheless found it useful to lump some theories in categories I refer to as *linguistic deprivation, dialect interference,* and *attitude interference.* The first two have formed the basis for pedagogy, but—in my opinion—the third should be the cornerstone of pedagogy. The Black English controversy has stirred emotions and generated much name calling (and, in the case of the Ann Arbor "King" decision, a lawsuit).[4] My purpose here is to look at these positions with an eye toward discovering what linguistic science has to offer educators interested in basic literacy in the 1980s.

The first group, the *linguistic deprivationists,* are usually thought to have been inspired by the work of Bernstein, but many carried his views of elaborated and restricted codes far beyond what he could live with. In its most extreme form, the deprivationist view holds, quite simply, that speakers of BEV are linguistically crippled, not possessed of a full and complete human language.

The names most often associated with this view are Carl Bereiter and Siegfried Englemann. Finding the black children in their studies so linguistically retarded that it would be best to treat them "as if they had no language at all," Bereiter and Englemann set out to teach preschoolers to speak English, using behavioral methods.[5]

Their work has been thoroughly dissected, of course, in Labov's famous polemic "The Logic of Nonstandard English,"[6] and need not be elaborated upon. My point here is that deprivationist theories were able to take root and flourish in education departments, psychology departments, and in many English departments where literary studies had all but crowded out the study of language.[7]

I have heard astro-physicist Carl Sagan lament the public fascination with (and widespread belief in) astrology. In his view, even otherwise educated and rational people are capable of ignoring several hundred years of solid scientific evidence in favor of a kitchen necromancer's seriously flawed astral charts.

It should be no great surprise, then, that otherwise educated and reasonable people could ignore the findings of several hundred years of language study stretching all the way back to Panini to embrace the myth that blacks are "nonverbal."

One consistent finding of language study has been precisely the linguistic *competence* of human beings. Nowhere, to my knowledge, has a culture been found whose inhabitants are not able to communicate their thoughts and needs through a fully developed human language.

Nor can it be argued that no attempts to communicate these findings to audiences outside of linguistics have been made. Attempts to popularize the findings of modern linguistics stretch back to Hall's *Leave Your Language Alone* (1950) and Laird's *The Miracle of Language* (1953).[8]

The success of the deprivationists in convincing educators that blacks were "nonverbal"—and in convincing them to purchase a massive basal reading system incorporating the premise—is sobering. As Professor Kenneth Johnson (who is black) once quipped at an NCTE panel on Black English, "Educators who think blacks are nonverbal ought to roll their windows down the next time they drive through the ghetto."

A second group consists of those who have embraced the position I am calling *dialect interference*—the assumption that the way one speaks affects how one reads and/or writes. This position evidently assumes that prevailing middle-class dialects are virtually identical with standard written English. Nonstandard dialects therefore allegedly impede acquisition of print codes because they are markedly different from written English.

Let me say from the outset that it is obvious that speaking *any* dialect which is socially nonstandard interferes with one's "upward social mobility" in a society that judges people by the way they talk.

In *You and Your Language,* Laird puts the case this way:

> A linguist would . . . say that all dialects are equal, that Black speech is as good as any other. If it is not as fashionable as Back Bay Bostonese, it preserves what the fashionable dialects never had and would have been lost except for so-called dialect speakers. Yet it is not standard speech, and being "underprivileged" results more from not commanding standard speech than from any other one thing.[9]

Those who hold the "Pygmalion" view of the problem argue that probably the simplest solution is to teach speakers of nonstandard dialects to speak standard English. For the most part, those who advocate the "bidialectal" position acknowledge the adequacy and legitimacy of all varieties of language, but believe that, nevertheless, nonstandard speakers must learn the prevailing tongue.

In a piece that has become something of a classic in the heated politics of the debate over BEV, "Doublespeak: Dialectology in the Service of Big Brother,"[10] James Sledd describes the extent of the bidialectal movement and mounts a furious attack against it. His most serious accusation can probably be repeated today with undiminished force: expensive programs to impart standard English to speakers of nonstandard dialects have failed to produce bidialectalists. As Thomas Kochman has noted, it is hard to persuade a child to give up the language of his or her own culture. As many of us remember, putting on linguistic airs can be dangerous to one's health on the playground at recess. Conversely, those who find it desirable to master the standard tongue seem to do so without the aid of linguists.

Another aspect of "dialect interference" is still being actively researched (if not litigated). Roughly, this position says that the "massive failure" of reading and writing instruction in the schools is caused by dialect interference. Put another way, nonstandard dialects (and especially BEV) are so different from standard written English that they might as well be foreign languages. Students fail to read and write, therefore, because they are unable to grasp the oral/written connection.[11]

Anyone who has worked with the writing of "hard core" BEV speakers will find this hypothesis tempting. While teaching writing in a federally funded job training program some years ago, I was able to gather examples of BEV grammar and pronunciation from student papers at will: "My biggest grife is our race and discrimashun. Why doesn't all races have a together nest?" And: "I be always coming to class late!"

And if dialect interferes with writing, surely it interferes with reading—obviously a prior skill. Again, examples are easy to come by. I have, for example, recorded a young BEV speaker reading the sentence "I asked her if she went" as "I axed her, do she go?"

Looking at this sort of evidence led many to the position that the spoken dialect must be blocking the efforts of children to read and write. This further strengthened their conviction, discussed above, that the BEV speakers would have to learn to speak standard English if they were to succeed in literate society.

But it also led to the hypothesis that materials written in BEV might be easier to read, initially, and students could gradually be weaned off the materials written in Black English and onto standard materials. A number of linguists argued convincingly for such materials and even helped to design those reading materials.[12]

Of course, the use of dialect materials in a public school setting is highly controversial. Some parents object to the use of materials they consider to be written in "bad English." Not all students in inner-city schools are black. Not all blacks speak BEV. Finally, as Sledd and others note, we don't even have a full and accurate description of what constitutes so-called standard English as a point of departure.

In addition, three recent articles argue that dialect interference—in reading or writing—is a myth (Hartwell, Rubin, and Schwartz).[13] In his article, Hartwell notes that psycholinguistic research by Goodman, Smith, and others has shown convincingly what most of us ought to know intuitively: the student who reads "I axed her, do she go?" has *not* made a mistake in reading. In point of fact, the student read the specimen sentence ("I asked her if she went"), understood it, and translated it into good, "standard," BEV.

Ken and Yetta Goodman, tapping psycholinguistic research in the reading approach widely known as "miscue analysis,"[14] have offered methods to distinguish among genuine errors, "miscues," and mere surface dialect features. Much of the alleged interference simply turns out to be the ignorance of the teacher who can't tell a dialect feature from a reading error.

The excitement over "linguistically appropriate reading materials" seems to have abated in recent years: In part, this is no doubt due to the volatility of the materials themselves, but it is certainly due to their general failure to live up to expectations. Learning to crack the print code is no small intellectual task, and the dialect reading materials simply introduced another learning activity: first the students have to learn how to read the dialect materials, and then they have to go on and learn to read conventional materials. I have seen no convincing evidence that the approach works, but I have seen some evidence that it does not.

Dialect interference in writing is a bit trickier. As I mentioned earlier, most writing teachers who have worked with BEV speakers have seen evidence of spoken influence in their students' writing. Hartwell puts it this way:

> The most widely accepted argument for dialect interference in writing would seem to be common sense, judging from the lack of formal discussion and from informal talks with teachers. Students say "bofe" [for *both*] and they write *bofe;* they say "he tall" and they write *he tall.* It's simply common sense that the one causes the other.
>
> There's a primitive attractiveness to this argument; it has the surface simplicity that *post hoc ergo propter hoc* arguments always have. It should be clear, however, that common sense alone, without more analytic support, is inadequate to support such a crucial position. (One might imagine a doctor, on a similar common sense basis, mistaking the symptom for the disease— perhaps by treating measles by painting the spots.) [15]

After reviewing the empirical evidence for dialect interference in writing, and demonstrating that it is shaky indeed (for example, research shows that white students who do *not* speak BEV make essentially the same errors as black students, although not as frequently), Hartwell advances his thesis that errors in the writing of "basic writers" are reading—not dialect—related.

> All apparent dialect interference in writing is reading-related. More precisely, apparent dialect interference in writing reveals partial or imperfect mastery of a neural coding system that underlies both reading and writing. That is to say, writers turn to the surface features of the phonology and grammar of their spoken dialect when they do not have available mental equivalents of the print forms. [16]

Before turning to my discussion of attitude interference, let me quickly reiterate what I hope I have demonstrated so far: we obviously have a major literacy problem in the United States, and most observers agree that our greatest failure has been in educating students whose dialects are nonstandard. It seems to me, however, that linguistic science has demonstrated what the problem is *not:* nonstandard dialects are not *sub*standard dialects. BEV, for example, is as legitimate a dialect, as expressive, as any other. Moreover, the interference theories are unconvincing, after one has admitted the truism that speakers of nonstandard dialects are disadvantaged because they are discriminated against because they speak nonstandard dialects.

This brings me, then, to my third position, which I'm calling *attitude interference.* By this I mean simply that the attitudes of society generally, but particularly those often found in the school system, may be the root of the problem. Sam Crawford and I put it this way in 1973:

> Some linguists and educators (the authors among them) now think that the massive failure to teach reading and writing skills to "inner-city" children is not a failure in method at all, but a failure to restructure the linguistic attitudes of teachers.[17]

If changing the linguistic behavior of BEV speakers is wrongheaded and impossible to do anyway, about all that is left is to try to solve the problem by changing the attitudes of the people involved, while we get on with the real business of imparting literacy. I believe, with Hartwell, that no dialect "interferes" with learning to read and write.[18]

William Labov has most forcefully asserted this attitude interference hypothesis in the aforementioned "Logic of Nonstandard English." He asserts that the biggest block to reading success for ghetto-dwelling BEV speakers may well be the attitudes of teachers toward the language of students. In the early 1970s, I was the linguistics consultant to a project that attempted to test Labov's hypothesis. We spent a year working with teachers in an inner-city elementary school in Flint, Michigan, attempting to improve the teaching of reading by offering instruction in linguistics, and especially social dialects, in addition to instruction in reading theory and reading methods and information on problems affecting black families as they confronted the educational system.

In order to carry out the project, we found it necessary to devise some method to test or measure the attitudes people held toward nonstandard speech. We devised an instrument which consisted of a tape with a large number of sentences spoken by blacks and whites. Some sentences were BEV, said by whites, and some by blacks. We also had BEV speakers read "standard" sentences, along with whites reading "standard" sentences. For good measure, we threw in a few specimens of white working-class dialect. Test-takers were asked to "rate" each sentence according to a number of criteria such as "harsh"-to-"soft" and "pleasant"-to-"unpleasant."

We also employed a multiple choice test which attempted to measure the test-taker's knowledge about language and linguistics. What we were trying to find out, of course, was whether a basic working knowledge of linguistics affected the way a person perceived social dialects. We used these tests, not only in the inner-city school reading project, but also as pre- and post-tests for in-service and pre-service teachers in a Right-to-Read project. I have since given the tests to many more students and had linguistics students give them to members of the general public.

What I have seen as a result of all this testing can be easily generalized. Basically, many people find nonstandard dialects offensive, and many middle-class educators, including blacks, are often very hostile toward dialects which differ from the prevailing "standard." Here, of course, empirical study confirms just what many of us thought or suspected anyway. The important finding, from my point of view, is that hostility toward nonstandard dialects generally decreases after instruction in linguistics!

How permanent this change in attitude may be, I cannot say. It does, however, make sense to me that if one replaces ignorance with knowledge, attitudes will change and prejudices may be lessened. I can't prove it, but I strongly suspect that most believers in astrology have never had a college-level course in astronomy—and know little about the scientific method in general.

Eliminating attitude interference or erasing the widespread prejudice against nonstandard dialects may seem at first blush to be an overly idealistic and impossible goal. But I would argue that replacing linguistic myths with the findings of linguistic science is both feasible and vital.

We might consider major paradigm shifts that have occurred repeatedly and routinely in human history: Copernicus and his followers provide an excellent example. It has been a while since attacks on the Ptolemaic model of the solar system were considered heresy. First the minds of scientists were changed, and gradually the public was educated.

And it is clear that public attitudes can be changed through the educational process. We have, for example, seen a gradual but steady change in public attitude toward smoking as the findings of medical science continue to pile up. People *can* be educated, thank God!

Now, changing attitudes is not a cure-all. In the inner-city reading project I described, we discovered that many black kids still came to school hungry, no matter how liberal we were, from homes without books, and still felt alienated by "the system." However, changing teacher attitudes at least removed one barrier to learning.

I am, of course, arguing that we need to continue attempts to communicate the findings of research to wider audiences. I realize that I may well be preaching to the choir here, but the controversy of the 4C's resolution on students' rights to their own language and the Ann Arbor King decision of 1979 make it clear that we still have a long way to go.[19]

While students of language are not charged with ending discrimination and poverty in our society, it does seem to me that we *can* do much to eradicate linguistic prejudice based upon ignorance. It seems to me, for example, that no university should graduate an elementary teacher who has not been exposed to the major findings of linguistics regarding the linguistic adequacy of all dialects in some systematic way. Certainly no English department should graduate a student who has no formal training in the English language and the rudiments of linguistics.

"Freshmen English"—a course that touches virtually every student in the two- and four-year colleges of America—could include at least some instruction in the nature of the medium itself, to make students more open to the language of their culture.

Finally, public schools might revitalize their language arts curricula by including units on the richness and variety of the English language. Excellent dialect records and linguistic atlases are already available. Such study might even bolster the sagging study of geography and make it more interesting.

Those of us who were students of Charlton Laird learned from his infectious enthusiasm for language that such studies need not be dull. In these essays we hope to honor Laird. He believed deeply in scholarship, and was himself a scholar. But he also believed that we must communicate our views of language to wider audiences. The facts about human language are too important to keep to ourselves.

Notes

1. Charlton Laird, *Language in America* (Englewood Cliffs, N.J.: Prentice-Hall, 1972), p. 389.

2. William Labov, "Language Characteristics: Blacks," in *Black Language Reader*, ed. Robert H. Bentley and Samuel Crawford (Glenview, Ill.: Scott, Foresman, 1973), p. 96.

3. "Black English Vernacular" is the dialect spoken widely in lower-class black communities. It is often abbreviated BEV—a convention I employ here.

4. In the King school case, parents of black students charged that their children were being denied equal educational opportunities because of their unfamiliarity with the dialect usually called "Standard English":

> U.S. District Judge Charles W. Joiner July 12, 1979, ordered the Ann Arbor, Michigan, school system to draft a plan within 30 days to teach standard English to children who spoke only "black English." He ruled that the black dialect was not inherently a language barrier, but became a learning obstacle when teachers did not take it into account in their instructions for reading and writing standard English. The Ann Arbor school board July 21 voted, 5–4, not to appeal the order.
>
> (*Facts on File,* B-1, August 10, 1979, p. 597).

5. Carl Bereiter and S. Englemann, *Teaching Disadvantaged Children in the Preschool* (Englewood Cliffs, N.J.: Prentice-Hall, 1966). Readers interested in the theories of Basil Bernstein might see, for example, his "Elaborated and Restricted Codes: Their Social Origins and Some Consequences," in *Communication and Culture,* ed. A. G. Smith (New York: Holt, Rinehart and Winston, 1966).

6. William Labov, "The Logic of Nonstandard English," in *Report of the Twentieth Annual Roundtable Meeting on Linguistics and Language Studies,* ed. James E. Alatis (Washington, D.C.: Georgetown University Press, 1970), pp. 1–43 (widely reprinted).

7. The deprivationist theory is still alive: see Thomas J. Farrell, "IQ and Standard English," *College Composition and Communication* 34 (1983): 470–84. Farrell argues that nonstandard dialects contribute to cognitive deficiencies.

8. Robert A. Hall, Jr., *Leave Your Language Alone!* (Ithaca, N.Y.: Linguistica, 1950). In a subsequent edition, Hall toned down the title a bit: *Lin-*

guistics and Your Language; Charlton Laird, *Miracle of Language* (Cleveland and New York: World, 1953).

9. Charlton Laird, *You and Your Language* (Englewood Cliffs, N.J.: Prentice-Hall, 1973), p. 134.

10. In *College English* 33 (January 1972): 439–56.

11. This is most thoroughly articulated in Walter A. Wolfram and Ralph W. Fasold, "Toward Reading Materials for Speakers of Black English: Three Linguistically Appropriate Passages," in *Teaching Black Children to Read,* ed. Joan Baratz and Roger W. Shuy (Washington, D.C.: Center for Applied Linguistics, 1969), pp. 138–55.

12. Ibid., for example.

13. The articles are: Patrick Hartwell, "Dialect Interference in Writing: A Critical View," *Research in the Teaching of English* 14 (1980): 101–18; Donald L. Rubin, "The Myth of Dialect Interference in Written Composition," *Arizona English Bulletin* 22:3 (1980): 55–67; Judith I. Schwartz, "Dialect Interference in the Attainment of Literacy," *Journal of Reading* 25 (1982): 440–46.

14. Many citations are possible here. Here are two: Kenneth S. Goodman and C. Buck, "Dialect Barriers to Reading Comprehension Revisited," *Reading Teacher* 27 (1973): 6–12; Kenneth Goodman and Yetta Goodman, "Learning about Psycholinguistic Processes by Analyzing Oral Reading," *Harvard Educational Review* 47 (1977): 317–33.

15. Hartwell, "Dialect Interference," p. 103.

16. Ibid., p. 108.

17. *Black Language Reader,* p. 10.

18. When working on a grant proposal, Hartwell and I once "brainstormed" a list of successful readers/writers who spoke "nonstandard" social or geographical dialects. It included William Shakespeare, John Keats, John F. Kennedy, and Jesse Jackson.

19. The interested reader should see *Black English and the Education of Black Children and Youth: Proceedings of the National Invitational Symposium on the King Decision,* ed. Geneva Smitherman (Detroit: Wayne State University, 1981).

Something About Language and Social Class

James Sledd

Praise in Parting

IT would be impertinent for me to say anything in praise of Charlton Laird. I knew him, admired him, used *Language in America* in my course in American English; but to me Mr. Laird was mainly a respected elder. That much I *have* to say, for otherwise my remarks tonight would be grievously misunderstood. I think it is not just my own age and dyspeptic disposition which make me believe that the academic humanist of the 1980s is a very different person from the academic humanist of the 1930s and 1940s, when I was introduced to English studies by men whom I still revere—men like J. M. Steadman, C. L. Wrenn, Rudolph Willard, D. T. Starnes. I think of Mr. Laird as more nearly their contemporary than mine, a department chairman when I was still a graduate student; and my own generation and the younger people around me now seem to me to suffer painfully by comparison with such predecessors. The typical American state university is in my view no longer a university but instead an appendage of the multinational corporations which run the United States, and the typical academic is no longer a dedicated member of a community of learners and teachers but a corporate employee, afflicted with the self-seeking, the itch for upward mobility, and the consequent subservience which the new way of the university world imparts and demands. Tonight I intend to speak my mind concerning that new world and its ways; but I am condemning

JAMES SLEDD, a grammarian and linguist at the University of Texas at Austin, has written on a wide variety of subjects. His books and articles include "Bidialectalism: The Linguistics of White Supremacy," *A Short Introduction to English Grammar, Dictionaries and THAT Dictionary,* and *English Linguistics.*

myself, my contemporaries, and my juniors, not the teachers (Mr. Laird among them) to whom I owe an inestimable debt.

A Concrete Abstract

Let me attract your attention and your disbelief at once by at least trying to commit the academic's unforgivable sin—namely, to tell the truth in public.

State-supported education supports the state. When the state is unjust, state-supported education maintains injustice. That is the situation in the United States today, and academics can be counted on to do just nothing at all about it. The dream of today's academics is to become the brains of the great interlocking bureaucracies of government, business, industry, and the military—like the little spaniels in Shakespeare, to gobble up the goodies that fall from Power's table. Academic humanists in particular are now a pompously futile bunch. We scorn the cultivation of literacy among the masses of ordinary undergraduates, the one undertaking which might really win us Power's favor. We whine about the damaging effects of television on our students' writing, but never state the obvious truth that television is simply the reflection of our own universities' richly supported departments of advertising, marketing, and management. We complain that our students are incapable of the critical thinking which we claim to teach, yet we ourselves do not think critically enough to see and say that our society punishes critical thinking while it rewards the image-makers who turn predation into patriotism.

When we talk about the language whose purity we say we defend, we display our ignorance of the nature, history, and social functions of standard languages in general while we applaud the demands by the College Board and Educational Testing Service that all college *entrants* should control our own particular standard language in both its written and its spoken form. If that same mastery were demanded of college *faculties,* the job-lists of the professional societies would be the size of their annual bibliographies; and if governments made provision for the *cultivation* of that mastery in all our schoolrooms, there would be no money left for star wars, protracted nuclear massacres, or the eventual balancing of the budget which this year was to have been balanced. But academic humanists prefer not to think the thoughts which Power finds offensive. Instead, we quote Shakespeare and flatter Lady the brach, providing cultural titillation for the petulant wives of the Big Rich; and meanwhile the relationships of language to social class are ignored as the gurus of education fret and sweat vainly over SAT scores. When I close this initial statement of my thesis by saying that at this very moment many of our university presidents are aiding and abetting the executives of the monstrous corporations in a final takeover of U.S. education, you will settle into disbelieving anger. Visiting humanists are supposed to be mildly amusing about nothing much. Truth is only to be told in private, among consenting adults.

Banalities Descriptive and Historical

Having said, now, what I came to say, I will relapse for a while into the mildly scholarly descriptive and historical banalities which support my contention.

In present fact, the standard languages of western Europe and North America are "clique languages," the dialects of the dominant; and in saying so I have often wrapped myself in respectability by quoting the late Charles Fries, the grand old man of English linguistics at the University of Michigan, and Einar Haugen, Harvard emeritus. It was Haugen, in his Voice of America paper on "National and International Languages," who assured his listeners that the standard languages "are everywhere the result of a concentration of political power, which establishes dominion over an area in which it is convenient for that power to have a single language for communicating with its subjects." Haugen went on to say that "the standard languages have usually come into being in a small community, often an élite which was recruited from various parts of the country or the empire."[1] It was Fries, as long ago as 1940, who taught the NCTE that the standard English of the United States, the language of "the *socially acceptable*" among us, is standard not because of its intrinsic merit but because it is "the particular type of English" used by our decision-makers.[2]

Tonight, however, instead of borrowing respectability from Fries and Haugen, I will amuse myself by finding authority among perhaps less well-known scholars, writers so very different that to cite them is to demonstrate that my remarks are indeed banalities and therefore richly American in the year of a presidential election. I will begin with Margaret Shaklee of UCLA, whose essay "The Rise of Standard English" would please my students because it denigrates their teacher. Shaklee maintains that the characteristics of English in the southern states "have become features of the lower-class dialect of American English because the southern laborer has settled in all American cities, particularly those of the Northeast and Midwest, where much of the economic power of the United States resides." "In contrast," Shaklee says, "the characteristics of middle- and upper-class dialect of those areas have become the hallmarks of 'standard' American English." You hear where that puts me. I console myself, however, for the downward mobility of the speech of the privileged in old Atlanta by observing that I am now domiciled in Lyndon Johnson's Pedernales Valley, the heart of that Texas whose residents include fifty-two of *Forbes* magazine's four hundred richest Americans; and I bolster my argument by observing also that even a misguided Californian like Margaret Shaklee nonetheless agrees that a standard language is often "the sociolect of the economically powerful."[3]

My next exhibit is not an American at all, but an emeritus professor of linguistics at the University of Manchester, who cunningly conceals his given name of William by signing himself simply W. Haas. W. Haas points out that "the desirability of a standard . . . is not tied to the prestige of a dominant social class."[4] That is true. A standard language is a technology, usable for good as well as evil; and because standard English has been the linguistic vehicle of all the activities which our rulers have chosen to regulate, it has become the form of English which any intelligent child would wish to be born to if the neonate had that choice. But the abstract possibility that a technology may serve good purposes does not determine what purposes it serves in the real world. W. Haas has therefore to acknowledge the further truth that "when a form is selected as 'standard' and others are rejected as 'sub-standard' there are frequently neither linguistic nor any more general social reasons to justify the preference."[5] The only reason for preferring *isn't* to *ain't* is "the social prestige" of those who say *isn't*. Standard English in reality has always been the language of the dominant. It was another Englishman, Professor Norman Blake, who coolly remarked, in his book on the literary use of *non*standard English, that "it might be difficult to persuade an English audience that a man who spoke with an East End accent was intellectually serious . . . rather than merely comic."[6] After fourteen centuries, the Gospel is still bad news in England.

The last descriptive banality which time allows me is from a little book entitled *Language and Control,* by two academics in Australia and two in England, including Roger Fowler of the University of East Anglia. They write from the academic Left. "Variation in types of discourse," they insist on their very first page, "is inseparable from social and economic factors." Linguistic variation expresses and consolidates "the structured social differences" which are its causes, reaffirming "specialized systems of ideas relevant to events such as political demonstrations, to processes such as employment and bargaining, to objects such as material possessions and physical environment." Thus "a major function of sociolinguistic mechanisms," my Commonwealth foursome says, "is to play a part in the control of members of subordinate groups by members of dominant groups," to conceal truth and to maintain social inequality.[7]

So much for my *descriptive* banalities concerning standard English as the dialect of the dominant in the English-speaking countries. Fries, Haugen, Shaklee, Haas, Blake, Fowler—I gathered their testimonies just from the books on my own shelves; and my promised *historical* banalities were just as easy to collect from just as various authorities. At least since M. L. Samuels's essay on "Some Applications of Middle English Dialectology," in *English Studies* for 1963, it has been fashionable to refer to "the basis of modern written English" as "Chancery Standard," which Samuels found in "that flood of government documents that starts in the years following 1430," roughly the time "when London English was adopted . . . instead of French and Latin for the purposes of official business."[8] Samuels's lead has been followed in essays by John Fisher and others,[9] and Fisher has now collaborated in producing *An Anthology of Chancery English.*[10] The advertisement for the anthology, which costs a disgusting $49.50, says that it "contains all of the letters written by the Signet clerks of Henry V, who established the first forms and style of the official written language"; and Fisher's collaborator Malcolm Richardson argues that Henry's "motive for using the vernacular was undoubtedly to win support for the war" and that his example was "a major factor . . . in the increase in the importance of English in the Chancery and elsewhere."[11]

It is Fisher's fondness for bureaucratic power, I take it, which prompts him to call Chancery English "an administrative language, independent of the spoken dialect of any region or class, and, in the long run, imposing its own structure and idiom upon those who conduct the affairs of the nation."[12] I would deny that independence, just as I reject the personification of language as if it were an active human agent; but I happily accept Fisher's generalization that "official languages have always been the prerogatives of ruling hierarchies."[13] Indeed they have, and rulers use them to promote their own arrogant ambitions.

Much the same story has been told about the development and recognition of a *spoken* standard English in the *sixteenth* century. E. J. Dobson, the bad-mannered Australian professor at Oxford, characterizes it as the speech of scholars, administrators, and unaffected aristocrats in the south of England. "The standard language was," he says, "the creation . . . of the educated professional and administrative class of London."[14] But a less repetitious and maybe more persuasive example of the relationship between standard English and centralized national power can be found, not in English itself, but in English attacks on the Celtic languages and in the collapse of standard Scots, the descendant of Northumbrian Old English which from the late fourteenth to the early seventeenth century was the language of both literature and administration in Scotland. From early in the 1500s, when both written and spoken standards for English were developed and recognized, various attacks have been made on "the indigenous cultures and mother tongues of the Celtic periphery."[15] Thus Henry VIII's Act of Union between England and Wales, complaining in 1536 that the use of Welsh had led to "great Discord, Variance, Debate, Division, Murmur and Sedition," provided that in Wales the courts and all official business should be conducted in English and excluded monoglot Welshmen from public office.[16]

In the next year, 1537, Irish was denigrated in an "Act for the English Order, Habit and Language," which made remarkably ambitious provisions for the spread of English in Ireland's homes and schools; and early in the following century Scots Gaelic came under attack as "one of the cheif and principall causis of the continewance of barbaritie and incivilitie amongis the inhabitantis of the Ilis and Heylandis."[17] James VI and I hoped to assimilate the Gaelic-speaking Highlands to the Lowlands; but even the standard Scots of the Lowlands, whose poets actually called their language English, did not survive such blows as the Union of the Crowns (1603) and the later Act of Union (1707).[18] When there was no longer a center of independent national power in Scotland, an independent standard language could not be maintained.

Revenges of the Whirligig of Time

I see no reason to believe that standard English, since the seventeenth century, has changed its essential nature, so I turn now from historical banalities to some familiar consequences of that history in present-day relations between language and social class.

It is a commonplace of sociolinguistics that linguistic variation distinguishes one social stratum from another. I learned that before I was twelve years old. I learned (without being taught) that the boys around the corner from our big house were not as good as I was because they called a faucet a *spicket* and because they made *foul* into a dissyllable at the baseball game when they sneakingly called a fair ball a "fow-el." *My* mother would have called *their* mother common and ordinary, maybe even as common as pigtracks. Academics, however, do not believe what they know from direct experience. Since we don't need a government grant to have direct experience, we say instead that "more research is needed"; and accordingly the sociolinguists have spent lots of time and money in proving what we all knew to begin with. I cite some of their familiar results as an antidote to such poisonous notions as that of E. D. Hirsch, who pretends that standard English is a classless and unchanging grapholect which universal schooling has made available to all.

Here again Charles Fries provides my first ammunition. The American people, Fries says, "have been devoted to education because education has furnished the most important tool of social advancement." Consequently the schools have set out (though with dubious success) to train "every boy and girl, no matter what his original background and native speech," to use the "class dialect" of "the *socially acceptable*."[19] To determine how the socially acceptable wrote, Fries studied the language of some thousands of letters by writers whom he classified by education, occupation, and income;[20] and he devoted most of his *American English Grammar* to displaying the differences that he found. He found, to just nobody's surprise, that rich and poor write differently and that his middle and lower classes fractured standard English more than his upper class. The reader doesn't need to be told that it was not a status-holder who wrote, "The mule that throwed him and cracked his skull has Engered his mind that he is not real bright at times."[21]

But mules are as unfamiliar as virgins to contemporary undergraduates. Since it might be argued that universal schooling has accomplished its glorious work since 1940, I take my next quotation from Mina Shaughnessy's famous *Errors and Expectations,* which made a great splash in 1977 because it promised to teach the oppressed the language of their oppressors without endangering the structure of oppression. In her "Preface," Shaughnessy recounts her dismay when she read her first set of papers by "poverty-area youth" (as she describes them in the standard English of the welfare bureaucrat). "The writing," she says, "was so stunningly unskilled that I could not begin to define the task nor even sort out the difficulties. I could only sit there, reading and re-reading the alien papers, wondering what had gone wrong. . . ."[22] Though I have always admired Ms. Shaughnessy's courage and devotion, I have always wondered what on earth she had expected. People will never talk alike and write alike unless they *live* together and *live* alike, a situation which would never be tolerated in the indivisible nation under God where all people have been created equal, with equal rights to the pursuit of happiness.

That not just writing but speech as well is socially graded has been among the vaunted discoveries of sociolinguists like William Labov in the United States and Peter Trudgill in Britain. Everybody remembers Labov's ingenious experiment in New York, where he showed, by asking questions of salespeople in three department stores, that the frequency of the prestigious dog's letter, postvocalic /r/, declined from Saks Fifth Avenue to Macy's to S. Klein in Union Square.[23] Trudgill's work, in Norwich, for example,[24] is not quite so generally familiar in the United States as Labov's, and I suppose I am pushing the limits of banality when I also cite R. K. S. Macaulay's Glasgow study, *Language, Social Class, and Education.*[25]

To determine social class and social status, Trudgill used his subjects' occupations and incomes, their housing and the neighborhood of their housing, and their *fathers'* incomes. Eventually he divided his subjects into five classes, descending from a "middle middle-class" of "professional people" to "a lower working-class . . . consisting mainly of labourers and other unskilled workers."[26] These divisions correlated quite well with the subjects' use of such linguistic variables as the so-called dropping of the *-g* from present participles (*singin'* for *singing*) and the *s*-less third person singular in the present tense (*she sing* for *she sings*). The frequency of use of these sinful forms increased systematically from each higher class to the next lower, and—within each class—frequency increased from formal speech to casual speech.[27] In Trudgill's Norwich, then, anybody who said *she sing* instead of *she sings* could at once be judged as lower middle class or lower still. I will say nothing about Trudgill's conclusions concerning sex differentiation in Norwich speech, since in all likelihood they would offend any feminist hearers, and I expect to have enough trouble on my hands without that confrontation.

New York and Norwich are very different one from the other, and different still from Glasgow, which has been described as the height "of sheer obscenity in modern urban life";[28] but social stratification in Glasgow, too, is marked by the varying use of English. Beginning with a set of four classes based on occupation and excluding both the very highest and the very lowest Glaswegians, Macaulay later reduced the set of four to three by lumping skilled and unskilled manual laborers together;[29] and he discovered both that differences in pronunciation distinguished among his classes and made the proper class-assignments for individuals and that his informants correspondingly "categorise[d] their fellow citizens by their speech."[30] More disturbingly, he showed that middle-class ten-year-olds are in some respects closer than middle-class adults to the speech of "their peers in the other social class groups" and that "quality of speech is often an important factor in success in higher education and employment."[31] In my own words, children have to be *taught* to use language as a way of making damaging social distinctions as the adults around them do, but at last they learn very well to fire that loaded gun.[32]

There, then, is one bad consequence of the nature and history of standard English as the dialect of the dominant: we use the use of English to assign people to different social classes, and the higher classes use the language of the lower classes—the one language which the whole society makes available to them—to keep those low-down working people properly subservient to the inheritors of privilege and to risen rednecks like the Texas billionaire H. Ross Perot. A striking example is the abuse of SAT scores, which so largely determine young people's chances for decent higher education. Everybody has heard the great yowling about the way those scores declined from the early 1960s until just the last two or three years, and everybody has read at least one report proclaiming, because of that decline, that the intellectual sky is falling, that the Japanese are destroying us in economic war, and that Russian technology can kill all living creatures deader than our own technology can kill them. Never before have schools and schoolteachers taken such savage criticism, and never have so many of the uneducated set out to put education right.

What people have usually *not* heard, however, is that although the test-makers used the furor to promote the sale of their tests, they themselves admitted that the search for the *causes* (and hence the significance) of the declining SAT scores "is essentially an exercise in conjecture."[33] Those are the words of the report by the College Board's "blue-ribbon panel" appointed "to investigate and interpret" the decline, and the report concludes with a warning that "the statistical averages on a set of standardized examinations" are a quite inadequate measure "of either educational or broader human purpose."[34] Instead of advertising its conjectures, the panel would have done better to stress the really crucial facts that SAT scores systematically parallel parental income and that the gap between the average scores of blacks and whites is much greater than the decline which set the blue-ribbon panelists to guessing.[35] What SAT scores really show is the extent of social injustice in the U.S.A. The gatekeepers of education demand, for example, that aspiring youth should recognize *intensify* as the antonym of *mitigate*;[36] but the society systematically restricts the opportunity of minorities and the poor to learn such things.

I am not saying, of course, that English-speaking children do not need to learn the foreign-learned vocabulary. They do; and they *would* if they had the chance and were not encouraged to care more about football and a fast buck than about language and quick thinking. But not *all* the distinctive features of standard English have communicative value, especially not all the shibboleths which are invented or maintained by such word-catchers as E. B. White, Dwight Macdonald, Edwin Newman, and John Simon.

These prescriptivists, though they do little for communication, do have a socioeconomic function. In a partially open society where everyone dreams of upward mobility and some few achieve it, the difficulty of changing one's speech after adolescence guarantees that risen rednecks will often still be marked with the speech-stigmata of the powerless. Their children, however, will learn *their* English among their peers in privilege; and both the risen rednecks and their offspring will wish their speech to *advertise* their privilege. Like all the upwardly mobile, they may then turn to the prescriptivists for guidance—the prescriptivists who manage to claim for English teachers equality with well-trained maids or butlers in households newly rich. Because no one can claim lordly status by shunning the speech of mere peasants, the prescriptivists accordingly prescribe a *super*-standard, recommending niggling distinctions which have nothing to do with communication but which (because they *are* arbitrary and hard to learn) provide badges of dubious honor for those who have nothing more serious to do than to learn them.

Prescriptivists enjoy their greatest triumph when they assume a higher status than those new members of the dominant economic class who remain strangers to traditional linguistic and literary cultivation. So English teachers rejoice when Professor Douglas Bush, in Phi Beta Kappa's magazine, rebukes John Connally, one of several millionaire ex-governors of Texas, for confusing *virulent* with *virile*.[37] E. B. White and the *New York Times* proudly denounce the well-formed and useful verb *to finalize*, though when John F. Kennedy used it in 1961 the *Times* of London had already used it six years before.[38] In all such fulminations, the thunderers must systematically conceal what is really going on and must avoid all efforts to define a *rational* standard. In particular they must never admit that a *single* rational standard is forever impossible, just because universal agreement in definitions of goodness, truth, and beauty is impossible. The much be-granted researchers who think they can achieve "uniform assessment" of freshman themes and freshman courses are quite, quite mad. On my list of time's revenges, the last I wish to cite is that the nature and history of standard English make so many discussions of it so very silly.

Toward a Just Policy for Teaching Standard English Now

Exactly no one, so far as I know, opposes the teaching of standard English in right ways and for right reasons. I wish myself that some of our well-known sociolinguists were better acquainted with it. Of course, some people do oppose the sort of mindless drill which structural linguists imposed on a whole unhappy generation; some people oppose the notion that the primary aim of education is to facilitate "upward mobility in the mainstream culture"; and some oppose the linguists' belief that all languages and all dialects are equal in both complexity and value—a belief that reduces the teaching of standard English to unmotivated tyranny.

Unless estimates of the relative value of languages and dialects have validity, the assertion that all are equally valuable is meaningless; and if some such estimates indeed are valid, then standard English may plausibly be considered the most useful all-purpose dialect we have. Quite certainly, every language and every dialect serves some purposes which no other serves so well. Otherwise, nonstandard dialects, like minority languages, would not survive so tenaciously as they do. But the value of a dialect depends on its usefulness, on the purposes it does serve; and I believe that standard English serves a wider range of purposes than dialects which have not been so expanded and codified. An argument that it should not be taught would in my opinion be quite impossible to make out.

I would argue instead that a just educational policy demands that the standard dialect be made genuinely accessible to all who wish to learn it and that the wish to learn it should be encouraged. But a just policy also demands the recognition that for a long time to come, many good and able people either won't be able to learn the standard (because the circumstances of their lives prevent that learning) or will *choose* not to learn it (either because the promised rewards are too improbable or because the abandonment or partial abandonment of the native dialect seems to be a betrayal and a threat to cherished personal identity). Since the standard dialect thus seems likely to remain, for the foreseeable future, the dialect of a privileged minority, it should not be required where other dialects can function just as well, as indeed they can in many situations. To say that the users of nonstandard English will be forever denied economic opportunity and social acceptance is to say that the dominant will forever grind their heels in the faces of the dominated.

The Actual Policy of the Crisis-Criers

Standardized tests of verbal aptitude, like the College Board's Test of Standard Written English or the verbal part of the SAT, obviously test the knowledge of the standard dialect in which they are phrased. It is odd, then, that persons who are alarmed by declining test scores should strengthen their demands for standard English without demanding just as strongly that the standard be made accessible to all. That oddity, however (to call it by too kind a name), is precisely what we now observe. Looking as usual at just the batch of anxious reports on education which happen to be lying around my office, I repeatedly encounter the strong demand for standard English. I have yet to read a single explanation how the majority of young Americans can meet that demand.

Characteristically, the College Board uses its Educational EQuality Project in ways which promote inequality. The Board's pamphlet, *Academic Preparation for College,* defines what the Board calls "the Basic Academic Competencies" (with capital letters)—"the broad intellectual skills essential to effective work in all fields of college study. . . . Without such competencies," the pontificators go on, "knowledge of history, science, language, and all other subjects is unattainable."[39] Two of the "competencies" are the ability to speak and write standard English. More specifically, the Board tells us that college entrants should have the ability to write Standard English sentences with correct:

—sentence structure;
—verb forms;
—punctuation, capitalization, possessives, plural forms, and
   other matters of mechanics;
—word choice and spelling.

College entrants should also have

the ability to conceive and develop ideas about a topic for the purpose of speaking to a group; to choose and organize related ideas; to present them clearly in Standard English; and to evaluate similar presentations by others.[40]

Those demands for written and spoken standard English are only two on a longer list under the headings "Writing" and "Speaking and Listening." College entrants who really had the specified abilities would immediately be eligible for appointment to the composition faculties of their colleges, but the Board isn't content to demand only such superbly qualified freshmen. After cosponsoring "dialogues" among "business people and educators," the Board announced a "consensus" that "the Basic Academic Competencies are as necessary for work as for college,"[41] where (you will recall) nothing can supposedly be learned without them. "In the world of work, competency in writing is required"—competency in writing "accurately" and "succinctly," in a good hand and "with correct spelling"; and employees also "must develop the technique of speaking on their feet—using standard English to organize their thoughts as they proceed."[42]

As the Great Communicator demonstrated in his recently televised debates,[43] many wealthy executives lack the skills which the College Board would require of all the employees of those same executives.

Like you, I would be delighted, though a little frightened, to have freshmen students fit to be colleagues (or, on the Board's terms, colleagues fit to be freshmen); and I know from experience that employers get a bang out of bossing employees who are more intelligent than they themselves are. Accordingly, I look eagerly for the means by which the College Board would work its miracles—but I find only empty exhortations, with no workable concrete suggestions. "Arbitrary standards must not be imposed," the Board intones, "without concern for enabling students to meet them."[44] Quite so; but the Board itself is utterly arbitrary and in fact dead wrong in its assertion that without "the basic competencies," knowledge is unattainable, and the Board would never suggest (for just one example) the immediate halt to the unimaginably expensive arms race which would be necessary to the provision of adequate funding for American education. Such a suggestion would offend "the military-industrial complex" (to use the Eisenhower phrase), which promises to defend us by impoverishing not us alone but our posterity as well.

Similarly, the College Board would never anger administrators and tweedy faculty by pushing for the costly tutorial programs which would be necessary if colleges were genuinely to accept the responsibility of raising all their "incoming students" to the level of "the basic competencies." At the University of Texas at Austin (my corporate employer), the majority of the juniors and seniors in my classes lack those abilities; but President Peter Flawn has proudly insisted that UT Austin does not and will not offer "remedial work," and the greater part of our lower-division teaching is left to an army of underpaid but overworked lecturers and graduate students, of whom the lowest are assigned to work with the weakest freshmen.

It would be wrong, however, to suggest that the College Board's campaign has had no practical effects. It has. Some "business people" have joined the cry for "the basic competencies"; and many have enthusiastically volunteered for the campaign to "bridge the gap between the academic and business worlds"—a bridge which would allow the invading corporate army to complete and perpetuate its control of education in the land of the free. "'Business *is* the primary user of the schools' products,' said Bill Funderburk, Manager of Business Services for the Birmingham Area Chamber of Commerce."[45]

The Funderburkian diction should prompt anxious thought at a conference on language. "Business *is* the primary user of the schools' products"—as if business were some privileged individual, students were pig-iron or sides of beef, and the schools were steel mills or slaughterhouses. That's what the schools *will* be if the corporate executives have their way.

For the purposes of the great corporations, as they move in on education, are altogether clear. What was the agency of the Education Commission of the States which gave us the report entitled *Action for Excellence?*[46] It was the Task Force on Education for Economic Growth, and the imperial Task Force echoes and re-echoes the phrase *economic growth* as it insists that "the business community" must "lead the improvement of education" so that the "work force" will have "the changing work skills that are necessary *for economic growth* [emphasis added]."[47] Naturally, as "the business community gets more involved in both the design and the delivery of education," the executives whose language so betrays them maintain that "everyone stands to benefit";[48] but their claim is more than dubious.

The future which the self-deified executives intend for the "work force" is barbarous. Assuming that they themselves must control technology and its application for the sake of "economic growth" and corporate profit, the executives plan to wipe out old jobs and (maybe) create new ones by constant technological innovation to meet the demands of what they call "the new economic realities." Workers must therefore be prepared to live as rootless and unstable nomads, moving repeatedly from job to job and place to place as the executives strive to regain and consolidate their threatened dominance of the world's markets. "We don't believe," says the Task Force on Education for Economic Growth, that "a high school graduate in 1985 will retire 35 years later from the same job for which he was hired—during that period he will need to be trained and retrained many times."[49] The basis for that alleged need is simply the executives' determination to hold on to their own privilege as America's unfair share of the world's irreplaceable resources is reduced and as mobility downward, not upward, on the scale of wasteful consumption becomes the fate of most Americans.

For the worker, the future under corporate domination may be even less attractive than the nomadic life of a deracinated technician. It is highly questionable that high technology under the direction of the Du Ponts and IBM will multiply highly paid jobs for highly skilled workers.[50] The Education Commission of the States, in its seventeenth "issuegram," has itself admitted that "office computerization . . . will reduce the skills needed for many routine jobs";[51] and the Business–Higher Education Forum actually reports a more widely devastating prediction by the Bureau of Labor Statistics of the U.S. Department of Labor. According to that prediction, of the workers who will hold half the new jobs in the 1980s, the top ten groups are secretaries, nurses' aids and orderlies, janitors and sextons, sales clerks, cashiers, nurses, truck drivers, fast food service workers, general office clerks, and waiters and waitresses.[52]

By the standards of the brave new high tech world, those slaveys may be lucky. As the Forum goes on to say, during the next twenty-five years the eighteen to twenty million new workers will compete for jobs *both* "with millions of experienced employees" who "have been directly displaced by technology" or "who have lost their jobs as a result of industrial decline" *and* with the multiplying robots which still other robots will be making.[53] The director of Stanford's Institute for Research on Educational Finance and Governance, Henry M. Levin, says flatly that "high technology will simplify or reduce the skill requirements for performing a particular work task so that, excepting a small number of highly specialized positions, most jobs will not require higher skill levels."[54]

That is the dismal shape of things to come if control of the means of production remains in the hands of the Big Rich. The situation is already bad enough. According to *Forbes* magazine, in 1984 the four hundred richest Americans had net worth of 125 *billion* dollars, and 1.6 million people (less than 1 percent of the total population) held almost a third of the nation's personal wealth. In the same vein, a survey by the Federal Reserve Board determined that 2 percent of American families own "50 percent of all stocks in private hands, 71 percent of all tax-free bonds and 20 percent of all real estate."[55] What distinguished contributions to human welfare have justified that concentration of wealth? Of the *Forbes* four hundred, Gene Autry got rich from *Rudolph the Red-Nosed Reindeer,* Edwin Claiborne Robinson from flea collars and the Dalkon Shield, Atlanta's Woodruff from Coca-Cola, Chicago's Wrigley from chewing gum, Robert Lee Vesco by activities which have made him a fugitive; and under "primary sources" of the wealth of the four hundred, *Forbes* lists "inheritance" some two hundred times.

In the future, we must conclude, the gap between rich and poor will widen. The huge national deficits in our Orwellian world of willed perpetual war will remain a gold mine for the lenders of money at high interest rates, and the relatively small number of technically accomplished but socially docile upper servants of the bosses will be allowed to share the bosses' goodies; but the "new poor" will multiply as the lower reaches of the middle class become just lower, and at the very bottom the underclass of the helpless and hopeless will grow larger. The consequences for linguistic stratification are obvious. If standard spoken and written English continues to be demanded as a prerequisite for higher education and well-paid jobs, the majority of young Americans will be neither well educated nor well paid. Their language will proclaim and perpetuate their disadvantage.

But that prospect doesn't dismay the Business–Higher Education Forum, if it allows itself at all to contemplate such a future. The Forum, which reports to the president of the United States at the president's invitation, enthusiastically promotes the dominance of the multinational corporations. As it planned the nation's economy in its initial report to the president, *America's Competitive Challenge,* the Forum attacked "national economic planning, income redistribution," "health, safety, environmental and other regulatory requirements," and "tax, regulatory and patent policies" when they "hamper the ability of industry to commercialize innovations" and improve productivity; but it happily proposed tax reductions, tax incentives, and tax credits for the big corporations and urged that the corporate fox be put in charge of the people's henhouse by increased "interactions between regulators and affected private sector parties."[56] Higher education and indeed the entire population was to accept one "central objective" for the United States in the 1980s—namely, "to improve the ability of American industry and American workers to compete in markets at home and abroad."[57] As a later report transparently phrased the recommendation, "all business corporations and institutions of higher education" must "develop means to cooperate with and assist each other"; but "at the same time, higher education institutions must recognize that business corporations, unlike foundations, are not created for the purpose of making contributions to education. . . . They . . . must earn profits for their shareholders. . . ."[58]

I ask you to remember that "50 percent of all stocks in private hands" are owned by the 2 percent of American families "earning $100,000 or more a year."[59] I also ask you to remember that the Business–Higher Education Forum includes the chief executives of the

University of Alabama, Harvard, Princeton, Cedar Crest College, Carnegie-Mellon, Goucher College, the University of North Carolina, California Institute of Technology, the University of Chicago, Georgetown University, the University of Notre Dame, Radcliffe College, the University of Illinois, *et cetera, et cetera,* through some twenty-two more names.[60] Members of the Task Force and signers of its first report include the presidents of Harvard, Notre Dame, Carnegie-Mellon, Radcliffe, the American Council on Education, the State University of New York System, and the universities of California, Pittsburgh, and Florida.[61]

The Responsibility of Students of Language

I began with an acknowledgment and an abstract. I will end with a summary and a recommendation.

By its nature and history, standard English has always been, among other important things, the English of the dominant and an instrument of their domination. One bad consequence of that nature and history is that we use English to assign people to different social classes and that the higher classes use the language of the lower classes to keep the lower classes lower. One device which is currently much in favor is to demand control of standard spoken and written English as prerequisites for higher education and well-paid jobs but to make no adequate provision for the accessibility of standard English to all classes of the population. As the multinational corporations move to extend and consolidate their control of American education, we must expect ourselves and our fellow citizens to be more sharply divided into a minority of haves and a great majority of have-nots; and linguistic stratification will consequently grow sharper, both cause and effect of deepening social injustice. There is no present indication that students of language and languages, traditionally at the center of the humanities, will resist those ugly changes. In fact, the presidents of many colleges and universities have joined with corporate executives to actively promote them.

Without the slightest hope that my absurdly puny efforts can do anything to help avert the looming disasters, I still believe that a man who at least aspires to be honorable can best do honor to an honorable man by speaking the unpalatable truth. As teachers and students of standard English, we must do whatever we can (1) to make sure that demands for its use are not arbitrary but functionally justified, (2) to make sure that the standard dialect is accessible to all the people, not just the privileged minority, and (3) to make sure that those intelligent *young* people who through no fault of their own either cannot or will not learn the standard dialect are not denied economic opportunity and social acceptance. That means that we must do whatever we can to revive the old dreams of liberty and equality, sisterhood and brotherhood—dreams which are presently insulted by the self-styled defenders of traditional values. Finally, we must not let the certainty of failure breed self-pity or abort a sense of humor. When the devotees of Uncle Matthew die before Fort Folly, I intend to be in the tavern, singing "Back and side go bare!" I might even be inside the fort—but shunning the company of the *dux stultorum* who sets out to improve education by spending less money on the schools and more on bombs.[62]

Notes

1. Einar Haugen, "National and International Languages," in *The Ecology of Language: Essays by Einar Haugen,* ed. Anwar S. Dil (Stanford: Stanford University Press, 1972), pp. 258–59.

2. Charles Carpenter Fries, *American English Grammar* (New York: D. Appleton-Century, 1940), p. 13.

3. Margaret Shaklee, "The Rise of Standard English," in *Standards and Dialects in English,* ed. Timothy Shopen and Joseph M. Williams (Cambridge, Mass.: Winthrop Publishers, 1980), p. 37.

4. W. Haas, "On the Normative Character of Language," in *Standard Languages Spoken and Written,* ed. W. Haas (Manchester: Manchester University Press, 1982), p. 9.

5. Ibid., pp. 9–10.

6. N. F. Blake, *Non-standard Language in English Literature* (London: Andre Deutsch, 1981), p. 185.

7. Roger Fowler, Bob Hodge, Gunther Kress, and Tony Trew, *Language and Control* (London: Routledge and Kegan Paul, 1979), pp. 1–2.

8. "Some Applications," reprinted in *Approaches to English Historical Linguistics,* ed. Roger Lass (New York: Holt, Rinehart and Winston, 1969), p. 411; Samuels, *Linguistic Evolution* (Cambridge: Cambridge University Press, 1972), p. 168.

9. John H. Fisher, "Chancery and the Emergence of Standard Written English in the Fifteenth Century," *Speculum* 52 (1977): 870–99; Malcolm

Richardson, "Henry V, the English Chancery, and Chancery English," *Speculum* 55 (1980): 726–50.

10. John H. Fisher, Malcolm Richardson II, and Jane L. Fisher, *An Anthology of Chancery English* (Knoxville: University of Tennessee Press, 1984).

11. Richardson, "Henry V," pp. 739–40.

12. Fisher, "Chancery," p. 870.

13. Ibid.

14. E. J. Dobson, "Early Modern Standard English," reprinted from *Transactions of the Philological Society* (1955) in *Approaches,* ed. Lass; see pp. 419, 424.

15. Victor Edward Durkacz, *The Decline of the Celtic Languages* (Edinburgh: John Donald Publishers, 1983), p. 1.

16. Ibid., p. 3.

17. Ibid., pp. 4–5.

18. Ibid., p. 4; Glanville Price, *The Languages of Britain* (London: Edward Arnold, 1984), p. 187.

19. Fries, *American English Grammar,* pp. 13–14.

20. Chapter 3, "The Materials Here Examined and the Scope of the Investigation."

21. Fries, *American English Grammar,* p. 230.

22. Mina P. Shaughnessy, *Errors and Expectations* (New York: Oxford University Press, 1977), p. vii.

23. William Labov, *The Social Stratification of English in New York City* (Washington, D.C.: Center for Applied Linguistics, 1966), chapter 3.

24. Peter Trudgill, *The Social Differentiation of English in Norwich* (Cambridge: Cambridge University Press, 1974).

25. R. K. S. Macaulay, *Language, Social Class, and Education* (Edinburgh: Edinburgh University Press, 1977).

26. Trudgill, *Norwich,* pp. 36, 60–61.

27. Ibid., pp. 60–63, 84, 92–93.

28. *Guardian,* May 8, 1973, p. 18; quoted from Macaulay, *Language,* p. 3.

29. Macaulay, *Language,* pp. 18, 60, 63, 65.

30. Ibid., pp. 31–32, 46–47, 58–60, 63, 65, 76, 82.

31. Ibid., pp. 32–33, 46–47, 131.

32. I take the metaphor from Dwight Bolinger, *Language—The Loaded Weapon* (London: Longman, 1980)—a book of which I otherwise do not approve.

33. *On Further Examination: Report of the Advisory Panel on the Scholastic Aptitude Test Score Decline* (New York: College Entrance Examination Board, 1977), p. 25.

34. Ibid., p. 48.

35. Ibid., p. 15. For more detail, see Allan Nairn and Associates, *The Reign of ETS* (Washington, D.C.: Ralph Nader, 1980), pp. 199–207 and passim.

36. This question was used on twelve different tests, including four SATs, between 1948 and 1973 (Nairn, *Reign,* pp. 146–47).

37. Douglas Bush, "Polluting Our Language," *American Scholar* (Spring 1972): 240.

38. James Sledd, "Like Gag Me with a Spoon!" in Jerome B. Agel, *Test Your Word Power* (New York: Ballantine Books, 1984), p. 111.

39. *Academic Preparation for College* (New York: College Board, 1983), p. 7.

40. Ibid., pp. 8–9. The mad classification of features of Standard English highlights the linguistic ignorance of the Board's test-makers.

41. *Academic Preparation for the World of Work* (New York: College Board, 1984), pp. 3, 5.

42. Ibid., p. 3.

43. If anything could have put Walter Mondale into the White House, President Reagan's performance in their first debate would have done it. It is hard to speak on feet that one has in one's mouth, as "Princess David" might now remind us (November 1985).

44. *Academic Preparation for College,* p. 33.

45. *Academic Preparation for the World of Work,* p. 2.

46. Task Force on Education for Economic Growth, *Action for Excellence: A Comprehensive Plan to Improve Our Nation's Schools* (Washington, D.C., June 1983).

47. Task Force on Education for Economic Growth, *Actions for Business, Industry and Labor* (Denver: Education Commission of the States, n.d.), p. 3; "fact sheet" supplied by the office of Governor James B. Hunt, Jr., of North Carolina.

48. *Action for Excellence,* p. 20.

49. Ibid., p. 16.

50. The chair of the Task Force was Governor Hunt. It was co-chaired by Pierre S. Du Pont IV and Frank T. Carey of IBM.

51. *Information Society Challenges Education, ecs issuegram 17* (Denver: Education Commission of the States, 1983), p. 2.

52. Business–Higher Education Forum, *The New Manufacturing: America's Race to Automate* (Washington, D.C., June 1984), p. 26.

53. Ibid., pp. 27, 29.

54. The College Board's news-sheet *Academic Connections* (Winter 1984), p. 5. In replying to Levin, Allen Odden (the assistant executive director of the Education Commission of the States) suggested that presently low-skilled job categories like that of secretary may be high-skilled in the future. His argument was that in the high-tech world, secretaries, orderlies, janitors, sales clerks, truck drivers, waiters, and waitresses will have to be highly educated and highly skilled. Apparently Mr. Odden doesn't read the Commission's issuegrams (note 51, above).

55. Associated Press dispatch, *Austin American-Statesman,* October 14, 1984, p. H1.

56. Business–Higher Education Forum, *America's Competitive Challenge: The Report in Brief* (Washington, D.C., April 1983), pp. 3, 4, 9, 10.

57. Ibid., p. 1.

58. Business–Higher Education Forum, *Corporate and Campus Cooperation: An Action Agenda* (Washington, D.C., May 1984), p. 11.

59. *Austin American-Statesman,* October 14, 1984, p. H1.

60. *America's Competitive Challenge: The Report in Brief,* p. iv.

61. Ibid., p. iii.

62. A few minutes with the 1981 *Index* to the *New York Times* will fully substantiate the claim of the president as educator to be King of the Castle of Fools.

Language, Appearance, and Reality
Doublespeak in 1984

William D. Lutz

L A N G U A G E is a tool, one of many human tools. But language is arguably our most important tool, for with it we have developed society and built civilization. As Charlton Laird observes in *Language in America,* "language and the ability to use language apparently provided man with the tools he needed to become human; certainly they permitted him to develop and preserve civilization."[1] Moreover, as societies and civilizations have developed, language has grown in importance. Laird notes that "communication with language and the promotion of thought through language have become ever more crucial" so that "language will be even more important" to human development.[2]

Language, however, like any other tool, can be abused, used as a tool not to build but to destroy, used not to communicate but to confuse, used not to clarify but to obscure, used not to lead but to mislead. Moreover, language is a unique tool used not simply to communicate but to apprehend and even give shape to reality. Edward Sapir, in his essay "Language and Environment," writes:

> Human beings do not live in the objective world alone, nor alone in the world of social activity as ordinarily understood, but are very much at the mercy of the particular language which has become the medium of expression for their society. . . . We see and hear and otherwise experience very largely as we do be-

W I L L I A M D. L U T Z, chair of the Department of English at Rutgers University, is widely published in the fields of rhetoric and composition. He is chair of the National Council of Teachers of English (NCTE) Committee on Public Doublespeak and editor of the *Quarterly Review of Doublespeak.* He has recently revised *Webster's New World Thesaurus* to include many new words.

cause the language habits of our community predispose certain choices of interpretation.[3]

Benjamin Lee Whorf later extended Sapir's thesis to what became known as the Sapir-Whorf hypothesis. In 1940 Whorf also argued that each language conveys to its users a ready-made world view. "Every language . . . incorporates certain points of view and certain patterned resistances to widely divergent points of view."[4] Whorf adds:

> Language is not merely a reproducing instrument for voicing ideas but rather is itself the shaper of ideas, the program and guide for the individual's mental activity, for his analysis of impressions, for his synthesis of his mental stock in trade. . . . the world is presented in a kaleidoscope flux of impressions which has to be organized by our minds—and this means largely by the linguistic systems in our minds.[5]

Language thus reflects our perception of reality, which in turn influences and shapes our reactions to people, events, and ideas. Language is a kind of conceptual blueprint used to organize our thoughts. In this sense, language becomes the means by which we shape reality and the means by which we communicate our perceptions of reality to others. Language can easily distort perception and influence behavior and thus can be a tool, or weapon, for achieving the greatest good or the greatest evil. Socrates and Aristotle understood well this power of language.

Literature is language of the highest order used to express hopes and fears, joys and sorrows, language used to give expression to myths and religions, to explore the human soul and the universe. With language, we can encompass the infinite. Language thus used has enabled us to develop societies and build civilizations. But there is also a use of language which can distort reality, corrupt the mind.

In his essay "Politics and the English Language," George Orwell writes that the "great enemy of clear language is insincerity. When there is a gap between one's real and one's declared aims, one turns as it were instinctively to long words and exhausted idioms, like a cuttlefish squirting out ink." Orwell goes on to express his belief in "language as an instrument for expressing and not for concealing or preventing thought."[6] "In our time," Orwell observes, "political speech and writing are largely the defense of the indefensible. . . . political language has to consist largely of euphemism, question-begging and sheer cloudy vagueness."[7] "Political language . . . is designed to make lies sound truthful and murder respectable, and to give an appearance of solidity to pure wind."[8]

Orwell is, of course, reflecting here the Sapir-Whorf hypothesis on the relation of thought and language, but he is also raising the political implications of this hypothesis. If language can be used to control minds, then those who control language can control minds and ultimately control society. Language is power; those who control language control the world. Power may come out of the barrel of a gun, but without the control of language there can be no real control of society.

Orwell's belief in the power of language to achieve and maintain political control is most clearly expressed in his novel *Nineteen Eighty-Four*. The Party in Oceania understands the power of language, for it has based its control of society on the control of language. Order is preserved through the Thought Police, terror, and torture, but disorder, dissent, rebellion, and even independent thought are prevented by the use of Newspeak. The thoughts, the inspirations, the ideas that could lead to disorder are controlled, even eliminated, through the control of langauge.

> If language is abused, if words can have entirely contradictory meanings at the same time, if the language necessary to express political opposition is destroyed, if notions of objective truth and unchanging history are abandoned, then since thought is dependent on language, all unorthodox modes of thought can be made impossible, history can be altered to suit the needs of the moment, the individual can be reduced to an automaton incapable of thought or disloyalty.[9]

In such a world one must reject the evidence of one's eyes and ears, for the great sin, "the heresy of heresies was common sense."[10]

In *Nineteen Eighty-Four*, O'Brien, Winston Smith's torturer and guide to understanding the reality of life in Oceania, instructs Winston that

> reality is not external. Reality exists in the human mind, and nowhere else. Not in the individual mind, which can make mistakes, and in any case soon perishes; only in the mind of the Party, which is collective and immortal. Whatever the Party

holds to be truth is truth. It is impossible to see reality except by looking through the eyes of the Party.[11]

And the only way to see reality properly is through the language of the Party. Language thus becomes the means of control in the world of *Nineteen Eighty-Four*.

The official language of *Nineteen Eight-Four* is Newspeak, a language that "was designed not to extend but to *diminish* the range of thought."[12] The purpose of Newspeak was not only to provide a medium of expression for the Party and its members, "but to make all other modes of thought impossible."[13] Newspeak is the medium used to express the mental process in

> the labyrinthine world of doublethink. To know and not to know, to be conscious of complete truthfulness while telling carefully constructed lies, to hold simultaneously two opinions which canceled out, knowing them to be contradictory and believing in both of them, to use logic against logic, to repudiate morality while laying claim to it, to believe that democracy was impossible and that the Party was the guardian of democracy, to forget, whatever it was necessary to forget, whenever it was necessary to forget, then to draw it back into memory again at the moment when it was needed, and then promptly to forget it again, and above all, to apply the same process to the process itself. . . . Even to understand the word "doublethink" involved the use of doublethink.[14]

The word *doublespeak* combines the meanings of *Newspeak* and *doublethink*. Doublespeak is language which pretends to communicate but really does not. It is language which makes the bad seem good, something negative appear positive, something unpleasant appear attractive, or at least tolerable. It is language which avoids or shifts responsibility: language which is at variance with its real and its purported meaning. It is language which conceals or prevents thought. Doublespeak is language which does not extend thought but limits it.

Hugh Rank has written that identifying doublespeak requires an analysis of language "in context with the whole situation" in which the language occurs: "who is saying what to whom, under what conditions and circumstances, with what intent and with what results."[15] According to Edward P. J. Corbett, this method of identifying doublespeak "encapsulates the whole art of rhetoric and provides a set of criteria to help us discriminate those uses of language that we should proscribe and those that we should encourage."[16] Applying this method of analysis to language will identify doublespeak in uses of language which might otherwise be legitimate or which might not even appear at first glance to be doublespeak.

There are at least four kinds of doublespeak. The first kind is the euphemism, a word or phrase that is designed to avoid a harsh or distasteful reality. When a euphemism is used out of sensitivity for the feelings of someone or out of concern for a social or cultural taboo, it is not doublespeak. For example, we express grief that someone has *passed away* because we do not want to say to a grieving person, "I'm sorry your father is dead." The euphemism *passed away* functions here not just to protect the feelings of another person but also to communicate our concern over that person's feelings during a period of mourning.

However, when a euphemism is used to mislead or deceive, it becomes doublespeak. For example, the U.S. State Department decided in 1984 that in its annual reports on the status of human rights in countries around the world it would no longer use the word *killing*. Instead, it uses the phrase *unlawful or arbitrary deprivation of life*. Thus the State Department avoids discussing the embarrassing situation of the government-sanctioned killings in countries that are supported by the United States. This use of language constitutes doublespeak because it is designed to mislead, to cover up the unpleasant. Its real intent is at variance with its apparent intent. It is language designed to alter our perception of reality.

A second kind of doublespeak is jargon, the specialized language of a trade, profession, or similar group. It is the specialized language of doctors, lawyers, engineers, educators, or car mechanics. Jargon can serve an important and useful function. Within a group, jargon allows members of the group to communicate with each other clearly, efficiently, and quickly. Indeed, it is a mark of membership in the group to be able to use and understand the group's jargon. For example, lawyers speak of an *involuntary conversion* of property when discussing the loss or destruction of property through theft, accident, or condemnation. When used by lawyers in a legal situation, such jargon is a legitimate use of language, since all members of the group can be expected to understand the term.

However, when a member of the group uses jargon to communicate with a person outside the group, and uses it knowing that the nonmember does not understand such language, then there is doublespeak. For example, a number of years ago a commercial airliner crashed on takeoff, killing three passengers, injuring twenty-one others, and destroying the airplane, a 727. The insured value of the airplane was greater than its book value, so the airline made a profit of three million dollars on the destroyed airplane. But the airline had two problems: it did not want to talk about one of its airplanes crashing and it had to account for three million dollars when it issued its annual report to its stockholders. The airline solved these problems by inserting a footnote in its annual report explaining that this three million dollars was due to "the involuntary conversion of a 727." Note that airline officials could claim to have explained the crash of the airplane and the subsequent three million dollars in profit. However, since most stockholders in the company, and indeed most of the general public, are not familiar with legal jargon, the use of such jargon constitutes doublespeak.

A third kind of doublespeak is gobbledygook or bureaucratese. Basically, such doublespeak is simply a matter of piling on words, of overwhelming the audience with words, the bigger the better. For example, when Alan Greenspan was chairman of the President's Council of Economic Advisors, he made this statement when testifying before a Senate committee:

> It is a tricky problem to find the particular calibration in timing that would be appropriate to stem the acceleration in risk premiums created by falling incomes without prematurely aborting the decline in the inflation-generated risk premiums.

Did Alan Greenspan's audience really understand what he was saying? Did he believe his statement really explained anything? Perhaps there is some meaning beneath all those words, but it would take some time to search it out. This seems to be language that pretends to communicate but does not.

The fourth kind of doublespeak is inflated language. Inflated language is language designed to make the ordinary seem extraordinary, the common, uncommon; to make everyday things seem impressive; to give an air of importance to people, situations, or things that would not normally be considered important; to make the simple seem complex. With this kind of language, car mechanics become *automotive internists,* elevator operators become members of the *vertical transportation corps,* used cars become not just *pre-owned* but *experienced cars.* When the Pentagon uses the phrase *pre-emptive counterattack* to mean that American forces attacked first, or when it uses the phrase *engage the enemy on all sides* to describe an ambush of American troops, or when it uses the phrase *tactical redeployment* to describe a retreat by American troops, it is using doublespeak. The electronics company that sells the television set with *non-multicolor capability* is also using the doublespeak of inflated language.

Doublespeak is not a new use of language peculiar to the politics or economics of the twentieth century. Thucydides in *The Peloponnesian War* wrote that

> revolution thus ran its course from city to city. . . . Words had to change their ordinary meanings and to take those which were now given them. Reckless audacity came to be considered the courage of a loyal ally; prudent hesitation, specious cowardice; moderation was held to be a cloak for unmanliness; ability to see all sides of a question, inaptness to act on any. Frantic violence became the attribute of manliness; cautious plotting, a justifiable means of self-defense. The advocate of extreme measures was always trustworthy; his opponent, a man to be suspected.[17]

Caesar in his account of the Gallic Wars described his brutal conquest as "pacifying" Gaul. Doublespeak has a long history.

Military doublespeak seems always to have been with us. In 1947 the name of the War Department was changed to the more pleasing if misleading *Defense Department.* During the Vietnam War the American public learned that it was an *incursion,* not an invasion; a *protective reaction strike* or *a limited duration protective reaction strike* or *air support,* not bombing; and *incontinent ordinance,* not bombs and artillery shells, fell on civilians. This use of language continued with the invasion of Grenada, which was conducted not by the United States Army, Navy, or Air Force, but by the Caribbean Peace Keeping Forces. Indeed, according to the Pentagon, it was not an invasion of Grenada, but a *predawn, vertical insertion.* And it wasn't that the armed forces lacked intelligence data on Grenada before the invasion, it was just that "we were not micromanaging Grenada intelligence-wise until about that time frame." In today's armed forces, it's not a shovel but a *combat emplacement evacuator,* not a toothpick but a *wood interdental stimulator,* not a pencil but a *portable, hand-held communications inscriber,* not a bullet hole but a *ballistically induced aperture in the subcutaneous environment.*

Members of the military and politicians are not the only ones who use doublespeak. People in all parts of society use it. Take educators, for example. On some college campuses what was once the Department of Physical Education is now the *Department of Human Kinetics* or the *College of Applied Life Studies.* Home Economics is now the *School of Human Resources and Family Studies.* College campuses no longer have libraries but *learning resource centers.* Those are not desks in the classroom, they are *pupil stations.* Teachers—*classroom managers* who apply an *action plan* to a *knowledge base*—are concerned with the *basic fundamentals,* which are *inexorably linked* to the *education user's* (not student's) *time-on-task.* Students don't take tests; now it is *criterion referenced testing* which measures whether a student has achieved the *operational curricular objectives.* A school system in Pennsylvania uses the following grading system on report cards: "no effort, less than minimal effort, minimal effort, more than minimal effort, less than full effort, full effort, better than full effort, effort increasing, effort decreasing." Some college students in New York come from *economically nonaffluent* families, while the coach at a southern university wasn't fired, "he just won't be asked to continue in that job." An article in a scholarly journal suggests teaching students three approaches to writing to help them become better writers: "concretization of goals, procedural facilitation, and modeling planning." An article on family relationships entitled "Familial Love and Intertemporal Optimality" observes that "an altruistic utility function promotes intertemporal efficiency. However, altruism creates an externality that implies that satisfying the condition for efficiency does not insure intertemporal optimality." A research report issued by the U.S. Office of Education contains this sentence: "In other words, feediness is the shared information between toputness, where toputness is at a time just prior to the inputness." Education contributes more than its share to current doublespeak.

The world of business has produced large amounts of doublespeak. If an airplane crash is one of the worst things that can happen to an airline company, a recall of automobiles because of a safety defect is one of the worst things that can happen to an automobile company. So a few years ago, when one of the three largest car companies in America had to recall two of its models to correct mechanical defects, the company sent a letter to all those who had bought those models. In its letter, the company said that the rear axle bearings of the cars "can deteriorate" and that "continued driving with a failed bearing could result in disengagement of the axle shaft and adversely affect vehicle control." This is the language of nonresponsibility. What are "mechanical deficiencies"—poor design, bad workmanship? The rear axle bearings "can" deteriorate, but *will* they deteriorate? If they do, what causes the deterioration? Note that "continued driving" is the subject of the sentence and suggests that it is not the company's poor manufacturing which is at fault but the driver who persists in driving. Note, too, "failed bearing," which implies that the bearing failed, not the company. Finally, "adversely affect vehicle control" means nothing more than that the driver could lose control of the car and get killed.

If we apply Hugh Rank's criteria for examining such language, we quickly discover the doublespeak here. What the car company should be saying to its customers is that the car the company sold them has a serious defect which should be corrected immediately—otherwise the customer runs the risk of being killed. But the reader of the letter must find this message beneath the doublespeak the company has used to disguise the harshness of its message. We will probably never know how many of the customers never brought their cars in for the necessary repairs because they did not think the problem serious enough to warrant the inconvenience involved.

When it comes time to fire employees, business has produced more than enough doublespeak to deal with the unpleasant situation. Employees are, of course, never fired. They are *selected out, placed out, non-retained, released, dehired,* or *non-renewed.* A corporation will *eliminate the redundancies in the human resources area,* assign *candidates for derecruitment* to a *mobility pool, revitalize the department* by placing executives on *special assignment, enhance the efficiency of operations, streamline the field sales organization,* or *further rationalize marketing efforts.* The reality behind all this doublespeak is that companies are firing employees, but no one wants the stockholders, public, or competition to know that times are tough and people have to go.

Recently the oil industry has been hard hit by declining sales and a surplus of oil. Because of *reduced demand for product,* which results in *spare refining capacity* and problems in *down-stream operations,* oil companies have been forced to *re-evaluate and consolidate their opera-*

tions and take *appropriate cost reduction actions,* in order to *enhance the efficiency of operations,* which has meant the *elimination of marginal outlets, accelerating the divestment program,* and the *disposition of low throughput marketing units.* What this doublespeak really means is that oil companies have fired employees, cut back on expenses, and closed gas stations and oil refineries because there's a surplus of oil and people are not buying as much gas and oil as in the past.

One corporation faced with declining business sent a memorandum to its employees advising them that the company's "business plans are under revision and now reflect a more moderate approach toward our operating and capital programs." The result of this "more moderate approach" is a "surplus of professional/technical employees." To "assist in alleviating the surplus, selected professional and technical employees" have been "selected to participate" in a "Voluntary Program." Note that individuals were selected to "resign voluntarily." What this memorandum means, of course, is that expenses must be cut because of declining business, so employees will have to be fired.

It is rare to read that the stock market *fell.* Members of the financial community prefer to say that the stock market *retreated, eased, made a technical adjustment* or a *technical correction,* or perhaps that *prices were off due to profit taking,* or *off in light trading,* or *lost ground.* But the stock market never falls, not if stockbrokers have their say. As a side note, it is interesting to observe that the stock market never rises because of a *technical adjustment* or *correction,* nor does it ever *ease* upwards.

The business section of newspapers, business magazines, corporate reports, and executive speeches are filled with words and phrases such as *marginal rates of substitution, equilibrium price, getting off margin, distributional coalition, non-performing assets,* and *encompassing organizations.* Much of this is jargon or inflated language designed to make the simple seem complex, but there are other examples of business doublespeak that mislead, that are designed to avoid a harsh reality. What should we make of such expressions as *negative deficit* or *revenue excesses* for profit, *invest in* for buy, *price enhancement* or *price adjustment* for price increase, *shortfall* for a mistake in planning or *period of accelerated negative growth* or *negative economic growth* for recession?

Business doublespeak often attempts to give substance to wind, to make ordinary actions seem complex. Executives *operate* in *time-*

frames within the *context* of which a *task force* will serve as the proper *conduit* for all the necessary *input* to *program a scenario* that, within acceptable *parameters,* and with the proper *throughput,* will *generate* the *maximum output* for a *print out* of *zero defect terminal objectives* that will *enhance the bottom line*.

There are instances, however, where doublespeak becomes more than amusing, more than a cause for a weary shake of the head. When the anesthetist turned the wrong knob during a Caesarean delivery and killed the mother and unborn child, the hospital called it a *therapeutic misadventure*. The Pentagon calls the neutron bomb "an efficient nuclear weapon that eliminates an enemy with a minimum degree of damage to friendly territory." The Pentagon also calls expected civilian casualties in a nuclear war *collateral damage*. And it was the Central Intelligence Agency which during the Vietnam War created the phrase *eliminate with extreme prejudice* to replace the more direct verb *kill*.

Identifying doublespeak can at times be difficult. For example, on July 27, 1981, President Ronald Reagan said in a speech televised to the American public: "I will not stand by and see those of you who are dependent on Social Security deprived of the benefits you've worked so hard to earn. You will continue to receive your checks in the full amount due you." This speech had been billed as President Reagan's position on Social Security, a subject of much debate at the time. After the speech, public opinion polls revealed that the great majority of the public believed that President Reagan had affirmed his support for Social Security and that he would not support cuts in benefits. However, five days after the speech, on July 31, 1981, an article in the *Philadelphia Inquirer* quoted White House spokesman David Gergen as saying that President Reagan's words had been "carefully chosen." What President Reagan did mean, according to Gergen, was that he was reserving the right to decide who was "dependent" on those benefits, who had "earned" them, and who, therefore, was "due" them.[18]

The subsequent remarks of David Gergen reveal the real intent of President Reagan as opposed to his apparent intent. Thus Hugh Rank's criteria for analyzing language to determine whether it is doublespeak, when applied in light of David Gergen's remarks, reveal the doublespeak of President Reagan. Here indeed is the insincerity of which Orwell wrote. Here, too, is the gap between the speaker's real and declared aim.

In 1982 the Republican National Committee sponsored a television advertisement which pictured an elderly, folksy postman delivering Social Security checks "with the 7.4% cost-of-living raise that President Reagan promised." The postman then added that "he promised that raise and he kept his promise, in spite of those sticks-in-the-mud who tried to keep him from doing what we elected him to do." The commercial was, in fact, deliberately misleading. The cost-of-living increases had been provided automatically by law since 1975, and President Reagan tried three times to roll them back or delay them but was overruled by congressional opposition. When these discrepancies were pointed out to an official of the Republican National Committee, he called the commercial "inoffensive" and added, "Since when is a commercial supposed to be accurate? Do women really smile when they clean their ovens?"

Again, applying Hugh Rank's criteria to this advertisement reveals the doublespeak in it once we know the facts of past actions by President Reagan. Moreover, the official for the Republican National Committee assumes that all advertisements, whether for political candidates or commercial products, are lies, or in his doublespeak term *inaccurate*. Thus the real intent of the advertisement was to mislead while the apparent purpose was to inform the public of President Reagan's position on possible cuts in Social Security benefits. Again there is insincerity, and again there is a gap between the speaker's real and declared aims.

In 1981 Secretary of State Alexander Haig testified before congressional committees about the murder of three American nuns and a Catholic lay worker in El Salvador. The four women had been raped and shot at close range, and there was clear evidence that the crime had been committed by soldiers of the Salvadoran government. Before the House Foreign Affairs Committee, Secretary Haig said,

> I'd like to suggest to you that some of the investigations would lead one to believe that perhaps the vehicle the nuns were riding in may have tried to run a roadblock, or may accidentally have been perceived to have been doing so, and there'd been an exchange of fire and then perhaps those who inflicted the casualties sought to cover it up. And this could have been at a very low level of both competence and motivation in the context of

the issue itself. But the facts on this are not clear enough for anyone to draw a definitive conclusion.

The next day, before the Senate Foreign Relations Committee, Secretary Haig claimed that press reports on his previous testimony were inaccurate. When Senator Claiborne Pell asked whether Secretary Haig was suggesting the possibility that "the nuns may have run through a roadblock," Secretary Haig replied, "You mean that they tried to violate . . . ? Not at all, no, not at all. My heavens! The dear nuns who raised me in my parochial schooling would forever isolate me from their affections and respect." When Senator Pell asked Secretary Haig, "Did you mean that the nuns were firing at the people, or what did 'an exchange of fire' mean?" Secretary Haig replied, "I haven't met any pistol-packing nuns in my day, Senator. What I meant was that if one fellow starts shooting, then the next thing you know they all panic." Thus did the secretary of state of the United States explain official government policy on the murder of four American citizens in a foreign land.

Secretary Haig's testimony implies that the women were in some way responsible for their own fate. By using such vague wording as "would lead one to believe" and "may accidentally have been perceived to have been" he avoids any direct assertion. The use of "inflicted the casualties" not only avoids using the word *kill* but also implies that at the worst the killings were accidental or justifiable. The result of this testimony is that the secretary of state has become an apologist for murder. This is indeed language in defense of the indefensible; language designed to make lies sound truthful and murder respectable; language designed to give an appearance of solidity to pure wind.

These last three examples of doublespeak should make it clear that doublespeak is not the product of careless language or sloppy thinking. Indeed, most doublespeak is the product of clear thinking and is language carefully designed and constructed to appear to communicate when in fact it does not. It is language designed not to lead but to mislead. It is language designed to distort reality and corrupt the mind. It is not a tax increase but *revenue enhancement* or *tax base broadening,* so how can you complain about higher taxes? It is not acid rain, but *poorly buffered precipitation,* so don't worry about all those dead trees. That is not the Mafia in Atlantic City, New Jersey, those are *members of a career offender cartel*, so don't worry about the influence of organized crime in the city. The judge was not addicted to the pain-killing drug he was taking, it was just that the drug had "established an interrelationship with the body, such that if the drug is removed precipitously, there is a reaction," so don't worry that his decisions might have been influenced by his drug addiction. It's not a Titan II nuclear-armed, intercontinental ballistic missile with a warhead 630 times more powerful than the atomic bomb dropped on Hiroshima, it is just a *very large, potentially disruptive re-entry system*, so don't worry about the threat of nuclear destruction. It is not a neutron bomb but a *radiation enhancement device*, so don't worry about escalating the arms race. It is not an invasion but a *rescue mission*, or a *predawn vertical insertion*, so don't worry about any violations of United States or international law.

Doublespeak has become so common in our everyday lives that we fail to notice it. We do not protest when we are asked to check our packages at the desk "for our convenience" when it is not for our convenience at all but for someone else's convenience. We see advertisements for *genuine imitation leather, virgin vinyl,* or *real counterfeit diamonds* and do not question the language or the supposed quality of the product. We do not speak of slums or ghettos but of the *inner city* or *substandard housing* where the *disadvantaged* live and thus avoid talking about the poor who have to live in filthy, poorly heated, ramshackle apartments or houses. Patients do not die in the hospital; it is just *negative patient care outcome*.

Doublespeak which calls cab drivers *urban transportation specialists,* elevator operators *members of the vertical transporation corps,* and automobile mechanics *automotive internists* can be considered humorous and relatively harmless. However, doublespeak which calls a fire in a nuclear reactor building *rapid oxidation,* an explosion in a nuclear power plant an *energetic disassembly,* the illegal overthrow of a legitimate administration *destabilizing a government,* and lies *inoperative statements* is language which attempts to avoid responsibility, which attempts to make the bad seem good, the negative appear positive, something unpleasant appear attractive, and which seems to communicate but does not. It is language designed to alter our perception of reality and corrupt our minds. Such language does not provide us with the tools needed to develop and preserve civilization. Such language breeds suspicion, cynicism, distrust, and, ultimately, hostility.

Doublespeak is insidious because it can infect and ultimately destroy the function of language, which is communication between people and social groups. If this corrupting process does occur, it can have serious consequences in a country that depends upon an informed electorate to make decisions in selecting candidates for office and deciding issues of public policy. After a while we may really believe that politicians don't lie but only *misspeak,* that illegal acts are merely *inappropriate actions,* that fraud and criminal conspiracy are just *miscertification.* And if we really believe that we understand such language, then the world of *Nineteen Eighty-Four* with its control of reality through language is not far away.

The consistent use of doublespeak can have serious and far-reaching consequences beyond the obvious ones. The pervasive use of doublespeak can spread so that doublespeak becomes the coin of the political realm with speakers and listeners convinced that they really understand such language. President Jimmy Carter could call the aborted raid to free the hostages in Tehran in 1980 an "incomplete success" and really believe that he had made a statement that clearly communicated with the American public. So, too, President Ronald Reagan could say in 1985 that "ultimately our security and our hopes for success at the arms reduction talks hinge on the determination that we show here to continue our program to rebuild and refortify our defenses" and really believe that greatly increasing the amount of money spent building new weapons will lead to a reduction in the number of weapons in the world.

The task of English teachers is to teach not just the effective use of language but respect for language as well. Those who use language to conceal or prevent or corrupt thought must be called to account. Only by teaching respect for and love of language can teachers of English instill in students the sense of outrage they should experience when they encounter doublespeak. But before students can experience that outrage, they must first learn to use language effectively, to understand its beauty and power. Only then will we begin to make headway in the fight against doublespeak, for only by using language well will we come to appreciate the perversion inherent in doublespeak.

In his book *The Miracle of Language,* Charlton Laird notes that

> language is . . . the most important tool man ever devised. . . . language is [man's] basic tool. It is the tool more than any other with which he makes his living, makes his home, makes his life.

As man becomes more and more a social being, as the world becomes more and more a social community, communication grows ever more imperative. And language is the basis of communication. Language is also the instrument with which we think, and thinking is the rarest and most needed commodity in the world.[19]

In this opinion Laird echoes Orwell's comment that "if thought corrupts language, language can also corrupt thought."[20] Both men have given us a legacy of respect for language, a respect that should prompt us to cry "Enough!" when we encounter doublespeak. The greatest honor we can do Charlton Laird is to continue to have the greatest respect for language in all its manifestations, for, as Laird taught us, language is a miracle.

Notes

1. Charlton Laird, *Language in America* (Englewood Cliffs, N.J.: Prentice-Hall, 1970), p. 533.
2. Ibid.
3. Edward Sapir, *Selected Writings of Edward Sapir,* ed. D. G. Mandelbaum (Los Angeles: University of California Press, 1949), p. 162.
4. Benjamin Lee Whorf, "Science and Linguistics," in *Language, Thought and Reality: Selected Writings of Benjamin Lee Whorf,* ed. John B. Carroll (Cambridge: MIT Press, 1956), p. 212.
5. Ibid., pp. 212–13.
6. George Orwell, *The Collected Essays, Journalism and Letters of George Orwell,* ed. Sonia Orwell and Ian Angus, 4 vols. (Berkeley: University of California Press, 1976), 4:137.
7. Ibid., 4:136.
8. Ibid., 4:139.
9. Stephen J. Greenblatt, "Orwell as Satirist," in *George Orwell: A Collection of Critical Essays,* ed. Raymond Williams (Englewood Cliffs, N.J.: Prentice-Hall, 1974), p. 114.
10. George Orwell, *Nineteen Eighty-Four* (New York: New American Library, 1961), p. 69.
11. Ibid., p. 205.
12. Ibid., p. 247.
13. Ibid.
14. Ibid., pp. 32–33.
15. Hugh Rank, "The Teacher-Heal-Thyself Myth," in *Language and Pub-*

lic Policy, ed. Hugh Rank (Urbana, Ill.: National Council of Teachers of English, 1974), p. 219.

16. Edward P. J. Corbett, "Public Doublespeak: If I Speak with Forked Tongue," *English Journal* 65: 4 (April 1976): 16.

17. Thucydides, *The Peloponnesian War,* 3.82.

18. David Hess, "Reagan's Language on Benefits Confused, Angered Many," *Philadelphia Inquirer,* July 31, 1981, p. 6-A.

19. Charlton Laird, *The Miracle of Language* (New York: Fawcett, Premier Books, 1953), p. 224.

20. Orwell, *The Collected Essays,* 4:137.

What Makes
Good English Good?

John Algeo

HUMAN beings are a peculiar species. We have a rage for order: out of the great booming chaos of the world around us, we obsessively make pattern and regularity. Out of the wilderness, we make cities. Out of experience, we make histories. Out of speech, we make grammars. And in the process of turning chaos into order, we create values.

The human species has been called *homo sapiens,* the earthy one who knows or experiences. But we might as well be called *homo judex,* the judge, because an inescapable human impulse is to distinguish between good and bad. For us, the good is its own warrant. As Mammy Yokum was wont to instruct her physically sound and morally pure, if intellectually disadvantaged, offspring, Li'l Abner: "Good is better than evil because it's so much nicer." Or, as *Webster's New World Dictionary of the American Language,* with which Charlton Laird was associated, defines the word, *good* is "a general term of approval or commendation, meaning 'as it should be.'"

Should is a powerful and distinctly human concept. Wars have been fought over it. Among English speakers, the Grammar Wars began in the seventeenth century, when pedagogues fell out over why and how to teach Latin. One camp wanted to teach grammar as an end in itself, because knowing grammar is good. Another camp wanted to teach grammar only so that young English scholars could read the great works of Latin literature. The two camps were roughly the equivalents three hundred years ago of scientific linguists and literary humanists (if I may use the word *humanist* without calling down the wrath of the Reverend Jerry Falwell). The equivalence is only approximate, however, because the grammar-as-an-end-in-itself advocates of the 1600s had a strong bent toward logic and neatening up the lan-

---

JOHN ALGEO of the University of Georgia is the author of many works including *Problems in the Origins and Development of the English Language, On Defining the Proper Name,* and co-author of *English: An Introduction to Language* and *Origins and Development of the English Language.*

guage, whereas the grammar-as-a-tool-for-literature advocates argued that the ancients could hardly have been wrong in the way they used their own language and thus needed no help from grammarians intent on regularizing and improving Latin.

Joseph Webbe, a doughty combatant in the lists of the Grammar Wars, scored against the grammarians in his 1622 book, *An Appeale to Truth*, by writing that

> they haue not onely weakned and broken speech, by reducing it vnto the poore and penurious prescript of Grammar-rules; but haue also corrupted it with many errors, in that they haue spoken otherwise than they ought to doo: well, in respect of rules; but ill, in respect of custome, which is the *Lady and Mistress* of speaking.[1]

Our modern Grammar Wars (chronicled by Edward Finegan in his *Attitudes toward English Usage: The History of a War of Words*) have seen a curious realignment of forces. Today it is those whose principal concern is with studying language as an end in itself who are most in sympathy with Webbe's position "that we can neither in the Latine, nor in any other Tongue, be obedient vnto other rules or reasons, than Custome and our sense of hearing,"[2] whereas it is some contemporary men and women of letters who ignore custom and their sense of hearing in favor of "the poore and penurious prescript of Grammar-rules." And so we have spawned a new subspecies, variously called *pop-grammarians* or *usageasters* (the latter by Thomas L. Clark).[3]

The Grammar Wars go on. And, as they were more than three hundred years ago, they are still concerned with the question of what good English is. What makes good English good? A variety of answers have been given to that question, and since the question has been so long with us, it is useful occasionally to summarize the answers that have been given.

What I propose to do briefly in this essay is to look at ten of the grounds that have been proposed for deciding what good English is. I focus on grounds proposed by Theodore M. Bernstein, mentioning a few other writers on usage to show that Bernstein is not a linguistic sport. I single out Bernstein, not because he is particularly better or worse than others of the tribe, but because he wrote a good bit on the subject of usage, because he is typical of the modern man of letters, and because he was kind enough to provide a handy list of criteria for determining good usage.

Communicative Criterion

In *The Careful Writer* (1965), Bernstein equates good English with successful communication: "What good writing can do . . . is to assure that the writer is really in communication with the reader, that he is delivering his message unmistakably."[4] Porter Perrin has a similar criterion for good English: "So far as the writer's language furthers his intended effect, it is good; so far as it fails to further that effect, it is bad, no matter how 'correct' it may be."[5]

These are pious statements, which, like promises never to curtail Social Security benefits, are made to be broken. Bernstein does not even get out of the introduction to his book before he fractures the ideal of communication: "Let us insist that *disinterested* be differentiated from *uninterested*."[6] He urges this difference as essential to the existence of good English, with no concern for communicating with those readers for whom the two words are synonyms. If Bernstein had been really concerned about successful communication, he would not have advised his readers to avoid *disinterested* in the sense 'uninterested' but rather told them not to use it at all, because the word is ambiguous. Bernstein's point about the need for communication is obviously well made, but it is seldom taken seriously by those who make it.

Bernstein goes on to enumerate six other sources for determining good English. It is worth looking at them seriatim.

Literary Criterion

Bernstein adduces "the practices of reputable writers, past and present."[7] This criterion, like that of successful communication, is practically de rigueur in any discussion of usage. It is also a criterion of respectable antiquity. Webbe in 1622 had cited authors like Cicero as models of good Latin, in distinction to the grammarians among his contemporaries who invented rules that imposed more order on Latin than was to be found in classical authors. The authority of the literati was also invoked by Thomas Lounsbury, who used an elegant chiasmus in his *Standard of Usage in English:* "The best, and indeed the only proper, usage is the usage of the best."[8]

As appealing as it may be to English teachers, the literary criterion suffers from several weaknesses. One is the difficulty of deciding which authors are reputable or best and which are not; there is a danger of circularity—writers who do not use good English (as the decider conceives it) are clearly not reputable or best, however widely read they may be. Another difficulty is that of deciding how far past or present one will look for models of good English: Joyce Carol Oates? Virginia Woolf? Ralph Waldo Emerson? Fanny Burney? Shakespeare? Chaucer? the Beowulf poet? In fact, popular writers on usage cite reputable writers as exemplifiers of good English rather infrequently. They are rather more apt to quote the words of famous authors as examples of blunders by the mighty, Homer nodding, and all that. Since the days of Bishop Lowth, citing errors from the works of great writers (or of one's opponents) has been a game rivaled only by the current popularity of Trivial Pursuit.

Scholarly Criterion

Bernstein's next criterion for good English is from "the observations and discoveries of linguistic scholars."[9] He carefully qualifies this criterion in two ways, however. First, "the work of past scholars has, when necessary, been updated," and second, "the work of contemporary scholars has been weighed judiciously." That is, *homo judex* is free to change (update) or to ignore (weigh judiciously) whatever he does not like. Although clearly subordinate to reputable writers, linguistic scholars seem like an authoritative group to invoke, especially if you don't have to pay any attention to them. We like being told that the message we are getting is backed by authorities: 9 out of 10 doctors, 64 percent of economists, any and all linguistic scholars. However, the fact that something is said to be recommended by doctors or economists or linguistic scholars is of no importance. What is important is the evidence on which doctors, economists, and linguistic scholars speak. And therefore this criterion is no criterion at all. It is not evidence, but publicity hype.

Pedagogical Criterion

The following criterion is even phonier. It is "the predilections of teachers of English, wherever—right or wrong, like it or not—these predilections have become deeply ingrained in the language itself."[10] It is not at all clear that any predilections of any teachers of English have ever become deeply ingrained in our language. There may be one or two trivial matters for which the sweat of English teachers has dripped so incessantly on the stone of real language that it has finally worn a small indentation—the pronunciation of the *t* in *often* is probably one—but on the whole, not only are English teachers over-worked, underpaid, and poorly educated, they are also ineffective.

The archetype of the starched schoolmarm who has devoted her life, at the sacrifice of all personal comfort and happiness, to uphold-ing standards and educating into self-awareness the pliable young minds entrusted to her charge is as mythological as Parson Weems's George Washington. Bernstein seems to be remembering with am-bivalent nostalgia some Miss Thistlebottom from the eighth grade, who, in the haze of fifty intervening years, has taken on the epic pro-portions of Candida, Martin Joos's Muse of Grammar.[11] The reality is likely to have been thinner and more wizened. The predilections of teachers of English that have become deeply ingrained in our lan-guage are probably a null set.

Logical Criterion

Bernstein's next criterion is "what makes for clarity, precision, and logical presentation."[12] This is another mom-and-apple-pie criterion. However important clarity, precision, and logic are, our impression of them in language is likely to be a function of our familiarity with particular words or grammatical structures. Those for whom *disin-terested* means 'uninterested' find that use perfectly clear and precise. The difference between *She be here* and *She here* is clear and logical to anyone who understands it. Those who find such expressions mud-dled, vague, and illogical have got a problem. But the problem is theirs; it is not one for those who use the expressions. Talk about clarity and logic in language is often an unconscious confession of ignorance and ethnocentrism. What we know, we think logical; what we don't, illogical.

This criterion is often expressed by saying that good writing is the expression of good thinking. Ambrose Bierce, for example, held such a position in his delightfully quirky little book *Write It Right,* subtitled *A Little Blacklist of Literary Faults,* in which he says that good writing "is clear thinking made visible."[13] Bierce is probably best known for his advice to prefer *ruined* to *dilapidated* since the latter—coming from Latin *lapis* 'a stone'—"cannot properly be used of any but a stone structure."[14] That is an example of diaphanous, rather than clear, thinking.

A similar standard was adopted by Richard Mitchell, whose *Underground Grammarian* announced in its first issue: "Clear language engenders clear thought, and clear thought is the most important benefit of education."[15] One may subscribe to the idea that clear thought is the best possible result of education, while finding the proposition that clear language produces clear thought to be muddled. However, one can forgive almost any amount of Mitchell's muddling for the sake of his épée, for example, his palpable hit in saying that "so many [college administrators] seem to be born aluminum-siding salesmen who took a wrong turn somewhere along the line."[16]

The link between good language and clear or exact thinking has been made by many writers on usage. One more example, an older one, will have to suffice. John O'London, who dedicated his book *Is It Good English?* to "Men, Women, and Grammarians," thereby expressing his opinion of our tribe, wrote: "Good English follows clear thinking rather than that system of rules called Grammar which youth loathes and maturity forgets."[17]

A problem with the equivalence of good language and clear thinking is that the latter might be defined as thinking that arrives logically at correct conclusions. T. S. Eliot and John Steinbeck, whom one might suppose to use rather good language, have thought themselves into rather different conclusions. It is hard to see how Eliot and Steinbeck can each be said to be clear thinking on social questions. Or, as Jim Quinn points out, "If good thought made good writing, and good writing made good thought, then Immanuel Kant, Hegel, and Ludwig Wittgenstein are not worth reading."[18]

Personal Criterion

Bernstein's penultimate criterion is the personal preference of the author, of which he asks rhetorically: "And why not? . . . After all, it's my book."[19] Why not, indeed. This is the most honest criterion Bernstein has set forward. By asserting it, he agrees with a cartoon that appeared shortly after the publication of Nancy Mitford's *Noblesse Oblige,* a popular treatment of the difference between U (upper class) and non-U language.[20] In the cartoon, a tweedy, horsy-looking woman says to her companion at the tea table, "I always say, if it's me it's U."

Everyone is certainly entitled to a choice among linguistic options. And if you can get people to buy a book in which you state your choices, why not? First amendment, free enterprise, and all that. Right on, Ted! Let's throw out all that malarkey about communicating unmistakably, reputable writers, linguistic scholars, English teachers, and logic, and just hunker down with good old ipse dixit. If it's me, it's U. As H. L. Mencken said, "No one ever went broke underestimating the intelligence of the American public."

Professional Criterion

Bernstein's last criterion is a letdown from the preceding high point. He cites his experience in working with language as the editor of the *New York Times* and congratulates himself on the newspaper's "precision, accuracy, clarity, and—especially in recent years [under Bernstein's editorship, presumably]—good writing."[21] All this criterion does is to establish Bernstein's credentials for ipse-dixiting. It is a sad anticlimax. How much better to finish off with a glorious burst of egotistic self-assertion. Well, we can't all be perfect.

People who earn their living by the word, particularly the written word, know how to use words effectively. If they did not, they would not earn much of a living. But effective journalism and even great literature are obviously not the same thing as good English. If they were, only effective journalists and great writers would be using good English. That Bernstein spent many years as an editor, worrying about the language of others, explains how he came to write five books on usage; it does not warrant his claiming special authority to determine what is good language.

Stylistic Criterion

Other writers have offered still further criteria for good English. Some have identified the stylistic characteristics of bad writing and thus by inference defined what is good. Richard Mitchell, the Underground Grammarian, for example, focuses on the sins of wordiness, weasel words (*attempt to, may*), passive verbs with no agent, and "needless neologism."[22] Similarly, Edwin Newman castigates cliches, jargon, voguish words, redundancy, and innovations—or what he imagines to be innovations (they frequently are nothing of the kind).

A digression: the subtitle of Newman's first book (*Strictly Speaking: Will America Be the Death of English?*)[23] identifies him as a disciple of the Armageddon school of usageasters. He, like John Simon, whose *Paradigms Lost*[24] is subtitled *Reflections on Literacy and Its Decline,* sees us as living in the time of the end. It is ironic that the demise of English should be predicted at a time when the language is being used by more people for more purposes in more places around the globe than ever before. Thomas Lounsbury expressed an ironic insight that is as applicable today as it was in 1908, when he wrote it:

> There seems to have been in every period of the past, as there is now, a distinct apprehension in the minds of very many worthy persons that the English tongue is always in the condition of approaching collapse, and that arduous efforts must be put forth, and put forth persistently, in order to save it from destruction.[25]

In a generation between Lounsbury and Newman-Simon, the anonymous "Vigilans" was another of the Dying-Declining-Doomsters. In his book *Chamber of Horrors* he castigated jargon, which he characterized as involving circumlocutions; long, abstract, unfamiliar words using classical roots; phrases where single words will do; padding; cautious wording and euphemism; vagueness and woolliness; and esoteric expressions.[26]

Our thoughts and our language are certainly intimately related, if they are not in fact the same thing. And pompous language is fair game. It is great sport to expose and snicker at egregious examples of linguistic bombast and thick-headedness, as the Armageddon usage-asters are wont to do. But such sport is easy to overdo. The cannons of Mitchell-Newman-Simon-"Vigilans" tend to produce, not a bang, but a whimper—kvetching against petty violations of an idiosyncratic standard of style. It is remarkable that so much has been written, so seriously, about such trivia.

Democratic Criterion

A refreshingly different approach to the subject is that of Jim Quinn, whose *American Tongue and Cheek* is a lusty defense of many of the bugbears of contemporary usageasters. Quinn delights in showing that usageasters frequently do not know what they are talking about and that their criteria for defining good language are nonsense. Quinn is straightforward in stating his own criterion: "For me, the only sensible standard of correctness is usage by ordinary people."[27]

And yet Quinn's own usage populism is also nonsense if taken at face value. Ordinary people and extraordinary people alike make mistakes in using language; mistakes are a part of usage. When people notice mistakes—their own or others'—they correct them. Editing language is just as natural as producing it, and so is passing judgment on some forms of language as better than others. The values we attach to our linguistic options are just as much a part of the language as the options themselves. We are value-ridden, judgmental beings. As a piece of rhetoric, a sortie in the Grammar Wars, Quinn's position is great tactics, but it is weak strategy.

Elitist Criterion

In America we have no official aristocracy, whose speechways might provide a standard for the commoners of the realm. So we make do with a less well-defined group: educated, respected, important people in the community. Their usage is sometimes held up as a model for the hoi polloi of the citizenry. Bergen and Cornelia Evans in their *Dictionary of Contemporary American Usage* write: "Respectable English . . . means the kind of English that is used by the most respected people, the sort of English that will make readers or listeners regard you as an educated person."[28] William and Mary Morris echo the theoretical sentiment, if not the practical sensibleness, of the Evanses. The Morrises define *standard* (which is not the same as *good,* but is related) as "word usage occurring in the speech and writing of literate, educated users of the language."[29]

Another digression: the *Harper Dictionary of Contemporary Usage,* which the Morrises edited, deserves special acknowledgment as among the most ignorant usage guides to have made the big time. My favorite lapse is their explanation of the use of the objective case for the subject of an infinitive. Under the heading "infinitive, subject of the," they write:

> The confusion about the use of "I" and "me" is reflected in such statements as "The first thing for somebody like you or I to do. . . ." The *subject of the infinitive* "to do" must be in the accusative or objective case. Since the objective case of the first personal pronoun is "me," the statement should be "The first thing for somebody like you or me to do. . . ."[30]

The Morrises tripped over their own grammatical razzle-dazzle. In the example they cite, the subject of the infinitive is *somebody; you or me* is the object of the preposition *like.* So the example is irrelevant to the point for which it is cited. The Morrises are educated users of the language, but grammatically they are booboisie.

Conclusion

There are other criteria we might identify. But these ten are enough to show what the tendency has been. In deciding what makes good English good, commentators have tried to correlate variation with some outside factor—success in communication, literary excellence, scholarly authority (at least nominally), pedagogical effort, logic, personal authority, professional expertise, esthetic style, a democratic majority, or an elite model. The unspoken assumption is that good English ought to be good for something.

Efforts to correlate goodness in language with something else are all flawed. Good English is simply what English speakers, in a particular situation, agree to regard as good. There are as many kinds of good English as there are situations in which English is used and sorts of participants who use it. Standard English is one sort of good English—good, that is, in the circumstances that call for it—but it is not the only sort.

Robert Pooley says something similar in *The Teaching of English Usage:*

> The English language is full of possible variations. The term "good usage" implies success in making choices in these variations such that the smallest number of persons (and particularly persons held in esteem) are distracted by the choices."[31]

Good English is the cellophane man—you can see right through it. It does not distract because in any given circumstance it is what the participants expect.

To paraphrase Mammy Yokum, "Good English is so much nicer than bad English because it's better." There is no external criterion by which we can judge what is good in language, either standard English or any other kind. Good language is just what the users of the language have decided is good. Their judgments are exasperatingly inconsistent and unpredictable. Moreover, the bounds they assign to the good are disconcertingly fuzzy; those bounds keep changing, as users of the language push this way and that way against them, continually altering the limits of acceptability. Finally, what is good is wholly relative to the circumstances and the speakers. Despite Wilson Follett's asseveration in *Modern American Usage* that "there is a [i.e., one] right way to use words and construct sentences, and many wrong ways,"[32] good in language is multivalent (that's *mul'ti-va'lent* or *mul-tiv'a-lent,* depending on the circumstances).

Because good English is so diverse, to use it in more than a few circumstances requires an equally diverse knowledge and a fine sense of what is appropriate under varying conditions. Charlton Laird made one of the most sensible comments ever written about usage when he observed, in his introductory essay to *Webster's New World Dictionary,* that "good usage requires wide knowledge and tasteful discrimination; it cannot be learned easily."[33] It is appropriate, especially here, for Laird to have the last word.

Notes

1. Joseph Webbe, *An Appeale to Truth, in the Controuersie betweene Art, & Vse; about the Best and Most Expedient Course in Languages* (1622). Reprinted in English Linguistics, 1500–1800, ed. R. C. Alston, no. 42 (Menston, England: Scolar Press, 1967), p. 22.

2. Ibid., p. 46.

3. Thomas L. Clark, "The Usageasters," *American Speech* 55 (1980): 131–36.

4. Theodore M. Bernstein, *The Careful Writer: A Modern Guide to English Usage* (New York: Atheneum, 1965), p. vii.

5. Porter G. Perrin, *Writer's Guide and Index to English,* 4th ed. rev. Karl W. Dykema and Wilma R. Ebbitt (Chicago: Scott Foresman, 1965), p. 27.

6. Bernstein, p. xv.

7. Ibid., p. viii.

8. Thomas R. Lounsbury, *The Standard of Usage in English* (New York: Harper, 1908), p. vi.

9. Bernstein, p. viii.

10. Ibid., p. viii.

11. Martin Joos, *The Five Clocks* (New York: Harcourt, 1967).

12. Bernstein, pp. viii–ix.

13. Ambrose Bierce, *Write It Right: A Little Blacklist of Literary Faults* (New York: Neale, 1909; New York: Union Library Association, 1934), p. 5.

14. Ibid., p. 23.

15. Richard Mitchell, *The Graves of Academe* (Boston: Little, Brown, 1981), p. 27.

16. Ibid., p. 28.

17. John O'London, *Is It Good English?* (New York: Putnam's, 1925), p. xi.

18. Jim Quinn, *American Tongue and Cheek: A Populist Guide to Our Language* (New York: Pantheon, 1980), p. 76.

19. Bernstein, p. ix.

20. Nancy Mitford, ed. *Noblesse Oblige* (New York: Harper & Row, 1956).

21. Bernstein, p. ix.

22. Mitchell, pp. 27, 49.

23. Edwin Newman, *Strictly Speaking: Will America Be the Death of English?* (New York: Warner Books, 1974, 1975).

24. John Simon, *Paradigms Lost: Reflections on Literacy and Its Decline* (New York: Potter, 1980).

25. Lounsbury, p. 2.

26. "Vigilans," *Chamber of Horrors: A Glossary of Official Jargon Both English and American,* intro. Eric Partridge (New York: British Book Centre, 1952).

27. Quinn, p. 11.

28. Bergen and Cornelia Evans, *A Dictionary of Contemporary American Usage* (New York: Random House, 1957), p. v.

29. William and Mary Morris, with the assistance of a panel of 136 distinguished consultants on usage, *Harper Dictionary of Contemporary Usage* (New York: Harper & Row, 1975), p. xxii.

30. Ibid., p. 338.

31. Robert C. Pooley, *The Teaching of English Usage* (Urbana, Ill.: National Council of Teachers of English, 1974), p. 5.

32. Wilson Follett, *Modern American Usage: A Guide* (New York: Hill and Wang, 1966), p. 3.

33. Charlton Laird, "Language and the Dictionary," in *Webster's New World Dictionary of the American Language,* Second College Edition, ed. David B. Guralnik (New York and Cleveland: World, 1970), p. xxv.

Misunderstanding Standards of Usage

Thomas L. Clark

ONCE Bess Truman was entertaining a friend, a proper lady. During the afternoon, the visitor overheard President Truman expounding to an aide that a certain proposal was a "pile of manure." After listening to the phrase several times, the visitor asked Bess if she couldn't reform the president's usage. "Can't you get him to say 'fertilizer,' instead?" Bess regarded her visitor coolly. "It took me twenty years to get him to say 'manure,'" she replied.

What constitutes *appropriate usage* seems to vary from one person to another. The key word here is *appropriate*. *Appropriate* doesn't mean "good." It doesn't mean "bad." *Appropriate* is not a synonym for "incorrect" or "correct." It means "proper to the time and situation." Unfortunately, the determination of what is "proper" requires some judgment. And people may be accused of exercising bad judgment, or praised for their good judgment. Thus, whether a usage is appropriate or inappropriate is often determined by labeling it good or bad. In years past, linguists, grammarians, lexicographers have seen their role as language historians rather than as standard bearers for the language. Dean Richard Chenivex Trench said so in 1857 while describing the function of the *New English Dictionary,* which later became famous as the *Oxford English Dictionary on Historical Principles.*[1] This role has created some misunderstandings and some unfounded accusations by moralists and preachers whose pulpit as often as not is public and well attended, that is, whose pulpit is found in newspapers, in magazines, on late evening talk shows.

The folks who generally bewail the sorry state of English invari-

THOMAS L. CLARK is vice president of the American Dialect Society and is a linguist at the University of Nevada, Las Vegas. Besides the book, *Language: Structure and Use,* he has written on usage and on the problems of teaching usage.

ably attack the nearest standing target (teachers, parents, television, punk rock, communists, the national budget deficit) as lacking in preserving "good grammar." High-frequency phrases such as *like* and *you know* in the language of teenagers are "bad grammar." Mumbling is a sign of "bad grammar." The word *ain't* or any vulgarism (what we used to call four-letter words) is a sign of "bad grammar." Spelling errors, mispronunciations, slips of the tongue, all are "bad grammar."

The first item of business for this article is to determine what these critics mean by the word *grammar.*

It is difficult to believe that the word *grammar* (from the Greek term for 'the art of letters') became, through mutation during the Middle Ages, the word *glamour.* Because grammar was important to the casting of spells and creating of incantations, it was imbued with the mesmerizing appeal we now ascribe to starlets and jet-setters. Through the years, the word *grammar* became many things to many people.

The different meanings of *grammar* have been discussed in many, many places. One recent example will suffice. Patrick Hartwell lists five main perceptions of the words, which can be summarized as follows.[2]

Grammar 1 is the set of formal patterns every human being has with which to communicate, but which has never been completely codified or written down by linguists or grammarians. Our best understanding is that somehow humans have an innate ability to acquire language and the particular language acquired is a circumstance of environment and socialization.

Grammar 2 is a branch of linguistic science which attempts to discover and describe the operations of Grammar 1. Linguists and grammarians spend their time analyzing the sounds, word forms, and meanings used in communicating. And while their body of knowledge is extremely large, as a group they feel they have just scratched the surface of understanding.

Grammar 3 is what these same linguists call *usage,* a sort of linguistic etiquette of word choice and language convention by which people may categorize others as educated, uneducated, boorish, elite, standard, nonstandard, or even substandard. This is what most pop-grammarians mean by *grammar* and most linguists mean by *usage.* Grammar 3 is the source of much of the confusion and misunderstanding between language specialists and nonspecialists.

Grammar 4 is what has come to be known as "school grammar." It is the grammar taught in school, which is partly rules of conduct (don't end a sentence with a preposition), partly misapplied logic (two negatives make a positive), partly a system of patterns in written forms of communication (eight parts of speech, phrases, clauses, and "complete" sentences). In a word, it is what Charlton Laird describes as "the grammar of Latin, ingeniously warped to suggest English."[3]

Grammar 5 is loosely described as "stylistic grammar," the various systems that achieve various degrees of popularity in the ongoing attempt to teach prose style and patterns: Reed and Kellogg diagraming, sentence combining, generative rhetoric, the methods for manipulating written English to achieve clarity, precision, and grace.

Proponents of Grammar 3, the popular conception of usage, are arbitrary in items supported or attacked. There is an essential confusion between speaking and writing as distinct modes of communication. Within the same sentence, one standard-bearer decries the pronunciation of *secretary* and *library* as "sekaterry" and "liberry," and inveighs against leaving out the comma before *and* in a series such as "peanuts, walnuts, *and* cashews." In addition, enthusiastic critics confuse good and bad usage, right and wrong usage, and appropriate and inappropriate usage. When the context of communication is noted at all, it is usually with a long-suffering sigh and the comment that substandard speakers simply don't know any better. The hallmark of books and articles concerning usage written for popular consumption is the listing of individual items and personal preferences. One is reminded of Jonathan Swift clear back in 1714. In his valiant but doomed effort to rid the language of *mob* and *banter,* he said, "I was borne down by sheer numbers, and betrayed by those who promised to assist me."

General alarums have been issued since even before the time of Swift—the scapegoats simply change. More recent than Swift is this statement by Paul Horgan:

> Catering to a huge indiscriminate public, [television] must resort to the lowest vulgate, and even, in effect, invent a new and more debased set of verbal signals, to entertain in order to sell. Like children learning how to speak, the pop audience uncritically repeats what it hears; and, so, popular usage is created and soon has the force to corrupt immediately. . . . I foresee the development of two forms of language: Low English, created by

commercial education, and High English, the survival of evolving tradition based on decent literacy unaffected by the commercial motive.[4]

I can agree with Mr. Horgan to this extent: television has had a stylistic influence on communication, and its message is ubiquitous. The one-liner has become the hallmark of humor, and the repeated phrase has replaced wit and emotion in a variety of social situations. For many social events, whether a large and satisfying meal ("I can't believe I ate the whole thing"), or difficulty in handling a cumbersome object ("It takes two hands to handle a whopper"), or an expression of approval ("It's the real thing"), or disapproval ("Where's the beef"), the commercial tag has replaced the quip and increased the baggage of formula discourse. The frequency of such phrases obviously dulls the senses and voids expression in communication. So pervasive is the commercial that the Popular Culture Association at its annual convention in 1977 featured a seminar on McDonald's. From the flyer: "Preference will be given to those papers which are most likely to provoke serious discussion of McDonald's as an important aspect of the popular culture in America." Already we have witnessed the formation of a productive prefix from this social force. Youngsters in my neighborhood sing the jingled praises of McBurgers, McShakes, and McFries.

My suspicion is that the discussion of usage is a topic that has attracted attention only by default. The number of topics that radio and television hosts have at hand has diminished through the years. One can no longer tell ethnic jokes, for example, without being confronted by this or that antidefamation league. Animal stories? The humane society might take umbrage. Jokes about women drivers? Not if you don't want to be run over by a feminist. There are few traveling salesmen left (they have all gone on local television), which is just as well, since agribusiness has made the farmer's daughter an endangered species. Talk show hosts are reduced to letting guests talk about themselves, a subject which soon wears thin, or sex, conversation about which must be cloaked in leers and chuckling double entendres. Tales and stories about spouses might bring charges of wife abuse (unless you are Henny Youngman), husband abuse, emotional abuse, or mental abuse. About the only abuse left to cuss and discuss is language abuse.

Since language abuse is the topic of discussion by default, two questions must be asked. First, do people really care about written and spoken standards of usage? Second, do people understand what constitutes standards of usage?

The answer to the first question is a resounding *yes*, and easy to quantify. When I was preparing this presentation, I asked for a bibliographic search for articles and books dealing with usage. My purpose was to gauge the importance of the topic based on public interest. My notion was that a large number of articles would indicate a general public and scholarly interest in the topic. The search was conducted on the university's computerized bibliography network. For the five-year period just ending, I was offered more than twelve hundred references to books and articles dealing with usage.

I would say that there is at least a perceived interest on the part of editors and publishers.

The answer to the second question is a resounding *no!* People often do not understand what constitutes standards of usage. By sampling, I found most of the popular articles deal with the sad state of the language, and thereby, through an amazing leap of logic, the decline and fall of western civilization at the tongues of barbarians. In addition, most of these articles catalog individual faux pas, bloopers, misstatements, examples of gobbledygook and doublespeak; or they list examples of bloated, flaccid, impoverished, cliched, overblown, uneducated, or downright godless and unpatriotic drivel. The mixture is haphazard, and I list them here as the adjectives in the titles and subtitles are encountered. If you get the feeling that the overall impression is a hodgepodge, then you have the impression I was left with. Occasionally, the articles deal with misspellings, typing errors, spoonerisms, mispronunciations, slips of the tongue, drawls, accents, or dialects. The point is that there is little to distinguish articles of substance from opinions flung into the wind.

Through all the articles and books written for the general public which I sampled, three common features struck me time and again.

First, there is little or no distinction made between written and spoken standards of usage. Violation of the written standard is understood to mean sometimes spelling errors or even typing errors, sometimes misused vocabulary, sometimes abstract phrasing, sometimes convoluted syntax. More often, violations are seen as a combination of several of these at one time. And examples are often thrown out with little regard as to the category they might represent. The result is a mishmash of condemnations, accusations, and damnations of usage items that may be important, unimportant, or even nonsensical. We will see some examples in a moment.

Second, most of these journalists, editors, and commentators do not seem to understand that elegance in writing has little to do with what constitutes standard usage.

Third, most of these writers seem to have a clear notion about what they mean by good or bad, correct or incorrect usage, but that notion is rarely articulated.

To demonstrate these three points, let me use a single example, better than most, which illustrates. The example I have chosen is from Edwin Newman.

I use Newman for several reasons. I have written unkind things about him in the past, and would like to take this opportunity to recant some of the harsher remarks I made earlier. Recently he spoke at the University of Nevada, Las Vegas. His talk reflected serious concern for the use of English. And it clearly demonstrates the three features I mentioned: lack of distinction between written and spoken standards, confusion of elegance with standard, lack of a clear definition for standard. But the lack of focus in his talk misled the audience into attending to trivial specific items of usage, such as whether *most important* or *most importantly* should be used at the beginning of a sentence. This was one of the more significant questions in the discussion period after Newman's talk. That such questions should result from a talk to more than two thousand people (the total capacity of Artemus Ham Hall) indicates that Newman was not focusing on the more serious problems of attitudes, intentional doublespeak, and duplicity through abstraction. (By the way, he said that *most important* is correct, apparently in keeping with the modern shibboleth, misuse of *hopefully* at the beginning of a sentence.)

This is not to say that Newman did not make any significant statements. He did. Unfortunately, the significant statements, all three of them, were lumped together and came early in his talk, so they were soon forgotten when he began the humorous examples. He said:

I do not advocate freezing the language.
I do not stand in the way of change.
I don't want everybody to speak as I do.

Actually the first two are simply different ways to express the same idea.

Now, these statements reflect an unfortunate set of beliefs held by many of the folk who write about language without having some sense of historical perspective. To announce that one will not freeze the language, will not stop language change, will not make wholesale changes in the way others talk is precisely like my saying that I personally will not do anything to modify or prevent the sun's rising tomorrow. You see how silly that statement is? And how egocentric? And how I ignore the laws of nature, as though I can be personally responsible for the sun's rising, or freezing the language, or making everyone conform to my speech patterns? I suppose it is this attitude, more than any other pronouncement or sweeping generalization, that irks serious students of language who understand the axioms of language change and at least some of the forces responsible for language variation.

Newman went on to voice sentiments held by other usageasters:

I think that slang adds richness and originality to English.
I've heard much colorful, expressive, and economical language from uneducated people.

Then he immediately said, "But if the language declines, we decline with it." The form that such declination takes was not stated. It never is. We are left to extrapolate what that declination must be from the examples provided. The list of examples began with what Newman calls "bloating," that is, what language scholars call "redundancy": such forms as *strangled to death, living survivor, honeymoon for two, married together.* These are sometimes called "baby puppies" by language students: *female cow, single unique event, Jewish synagogue, dead corpse.*

The next set of examples Newman called windy and flabby language, and it is. Educationese is an easy target, as this sample illustrates: "combined cognitive and affective communication skills that utilize experiential functioning of the brain as an input control system."

Then Newman fell into the error that plagues so many usageasters. He lumped together three disparate types of communication. As he began the catalog of sports broadcasters' blunders, particularly Howard Cosell's nuggets, Newman said, "This may be too easy." It was. What Newman neglected to say was that blunders delivered orally are quite different from those found in writing. Many of his examples are slips of the tongue, or spoonerisms. You know, the "President Hoobert Heever" type. Since he targets sportscasters caught up in the frenzy of a game, most of the examples can be simply humorous. He missed my two favorites, however. The "New Yank Yorkees," and one from a recent World Series, the "San Piedro Doggies."

His next category was the misuse of language by corporations. He meant, I suppose, the misuse of syntactic patterns and word formation on the part of the advertising firms which write copy for corporations. An example of this type of "error" is the advertisement for Underalls, in which the model ducks into camera view with a look that depicts cute sex play and says that Underalls make her look like she is "not wearing nothing." Newman neglects to point out that most such obvious violations of traditional rules are purposeful. Copywriters know that if their syntax is outrageous enough, people will note it and comment on it; witness the flap about the "Winston tastes good" campaign of several years ago. Furthermore, copywriters know that should they make the big time, people like Edwin Newman will provide all sorts of free advertising by repeating the phrase time and again all over the country. As the reader, you have just been subjected to a free plug from the Underalls and Winston people.

The third type of "error" Newman lumped into this section dealt with misspellings, mainly from newspapers. Never mind that many of these were typographical errors. They were all condemned by Newman. It is fine that Newman can announce demanding standards. But he again lost sight of a fundamental point. The people he wanted to castigate were not the writers, but the proofreaders at these newspapers.

Hopefully, we will try to educate our students to the appropriate use of *hopefully* and *importantly* at the beginning of a sentence. Hopefully, we can look forward to that time when writers in the popular press distinguish between important matters of bloated language and doublespeak, and unimportant oral slips, misstatements, misfires, and spoonerisms. Hopefully, we will teach our students to distinguish between important and unimportant advertisers' usage, separating the obvious pleas for attention from the red herrings which hide the truth about products. Hopefully, we will continue to read and listen to Newman and note when he does make those distinctions.

Ultimately, Newman's major crime is his devotion to equality. From his comments, one must conclude that every example of language abuse is equally bad in his judgment, from the tiniest superficial error to the gravest semantic distortion. And this lack of focus distorts his message.

At the very least, he might distinguish among politicians in public meetings, frenzied sportscasters, advertisements with designed fracturing of traditional grammar, and those types of semantic distortion designed to hinder communication, as William Lutz describes in his essay.

At the same time, Mr. Newman's finest accomplishment is that he keeps public attention focused on language use. If it weren't for him, people like me would rarely be heard in public, rarely be given the opportunity to urge the general public to pick up fine, readable books such as *Famous Last Words* by Harvey A. Daniels or *American Tongue and Cheek* by Jim Quinn, both of which are enlightening, entertaining, and serious but not oppressive.

Newman's talk was representative of most of the twelve hundred articles I mentioned earlier. The irony in all of this is that many studies through the years demonstrate that the list of objectionable usage errors is surprisingly small and surprisingly consistent, though the question of which form of an item is "correct" is surprisingly inconsistent.

Thomas Creswell's 1975 study continues to enlighten and surprise people who believe that questions of usage are settled and unchanging.[5] For example, he lists ten words and points out that one dictionary calls the first five slang, but not the second five. Then he reveals that another dictionary does just the reverse. In fact, Creswell examined more than three hundred disputed usage items in nine dictionaries. He found only one word that all nine seemed to agree on: the use of *ain't*. The lack of consistency among dictionaries led Creswell to conclude: "As there is no well developed external criterion or bench mark currently available to evaluate dictionary judgements on usage, the dictionaries' claims of objectivity and authoritativeness in the treatment of usage must be rejected" (p. 85).

Creswell is even less enthusiastic about usage guides, as opposed to dictionaries. Such guides are so inconsistent that he throws up his hands in exasperation. "This study," he writes, "has become a problem in the orderly documentation of chaos." Perhaps because of his frustration, he quotes even less complimentary students of language. He reports Robert A. Hall's comment about folks who believe there is a pure English out there somewhere: "There are only three psychological bases for purism; sadism, masochism, and desire for personal aggrandizement" (p. 130). Only half-facetiously, I once offered a suggestion for a way out of the quagmire:

> Lists of usage items are strings of shibboleths that serve as labels of social class, education, and parentage. The solution to the entire problem might be to compile a list of about 500 controversial items, then drill students until the items are memorized and regularly avoided. Our spelling drills already operate in such a fashion.[6]

Ironically, most usage "errors" are damned when found in print, but condemnation varies when they are used orally. Creswell's point, that readers of usage guides too often take them as gospel truth, inviolate and unassailable, has been demonstrated time and again. The following example is illustrative of most. Mary Vaiana Taylor, in "The Folklore of Usage," relates the experiences of her students who made a study of usage among parents and acquaintances, educated people all:

> The reactions of my students and of their informants to the oral-written distinction also support the hypothesis that the standards for the language of the classroom have been established as absolute and inflexible. The informants to whom the questionnaire was given orally did not display acute Questionnaire Neurosis and were willing to give their opinions about the appropriateness of various usages; they were also far less prescriptive in their judgements. It is apparent that spoken language was not, in the view of these informants, subject to classroom standards; therefore, an oral questionnaire was not cause for terror. Even more striking was the surprise my students expressed at the discrepancy between the oral and written results. This surprise suggests that these students certainly did not recognize that oral and written standards of usage should vary; if they had been exposed to the distinction at some time in their formal education, they had no confirmed commitment to it.[7]

Despite a variety of judgments about the acceptability of any given usage item, the list of "most objectionable usage errors" was surprisingly small and surprisingly consistent (p. 760).

Even writers of usage books admit there is inconsistency, but sometimes have different explanations for it. In the *Harper Diction-*

ary of Contemporary Usage, William and Mary Morris used a usage panel to find answers to sticky questions. "The lack of unanimity by the one hundred and thirty six panelists," they wrote, "is proof that language is no static thing to be fixed by rules [agreed, I said]. Rather it is ever growing, ever changing [bravo, I agreed], and the often expressed hope of the panelists as well as of the editors is that the changes may be influenced for the better."[8] But what is *better?* All I could discern was that *better* meant what was better for the 136 panelists, who, of course, lacked unanimity. So it goes.

The Morrises' confession bothered me for two reasons. First, no panel has ever had much influence on language modification. The long history of failure by the French Academy to keep English words out of Parisian mouths is proof of that. The second reason is more serious, because it reflects an elitist attitude that somewhere there exists a group of people who know the most effective means of communication for the rest of the speakers of a language. Such an attitude is not deplorable because it is elitist. In fact, most of us favor elitism. Rather, it is disconcerting because it reflects a lack of understanding, by people who should know better, about the processes that cause language change.

This inconsistency of agreement about specific items among usage-asters should not be quite so surprising, however. These people don't realize the difficulty of the general questions.

The hard questions are not those which might be supposed to be hard: For example, is this a hard question or an easy question?: "What is the distribution and force of operation in phonological split and merger of low-back vowels in the United States?" This is an easy question. It is clear, precise, and we have the methods to collect information through fieldwork to answer it. It may be time-consuming, but we should never confuse time requirements with difficulty. After all, the gestation period of an elephant is two years, but there is nothing particularly difficult about it, as long as you are an elephant.

No, the hard quesions are usually the basic questions, such as: "What is the meaning of life?" Or: "How can I afford automobile insurance for my three teenage drivers?" (I let them buy their own.) In our studies of language the hardest question seems to be: "What is Standard English?" Others are: "Who uses it? Who determines it? Who legislates it?" Only slightly easier is the question: "What is standard *written* English?" For this, at least, we have a long tradition of editors, writers, spellers, printers who have set most of the written standards in English, from country to country, though the standard shifts slightly from England to the United States to Australia.

I have been searching for answers to these questions for twenty-five years. Some of the people who contributed to this volume have been searching even longer. In spite of yeoman efforts by scholars like Albert Marckwardt and Sterling Leonard, we still have a devilish time trying to describe standard spoken English.

Unfortunately, English teachers play a role that is at once abstract and an easy target. English teachers as a group are damned for not upholding standards, yet they are individually as intimidating as any nightmarish memory of the fourth-grade teacher who ridiculed our lack of control over *aluninum, limoleum, hangruber,* and so on. Also unfortunately, English teachers have helped to instill deeply ingrained attitudes of language insecurity in generations of students. And most of those attitudes are linked directly to teaching this or that unimportant form while neglecting to teach processes of thought. There cannot be an English teacher alive who has not heard "I'd better watch my language" from a new acquaintance. But few have ever heard "Thank you for teaching me to use appropriate language to express myself."

Sometimes it helps to put the entire matter into perspective. In 1970, when I first moved to Nevada, Charlton Laird gave a talk in Las Vegas titled "Language: Relevance and Irrelevance, or How to Suffer from Hallucination." The talk has since been published in his book *And Gladly Teche.* At that time, Laird gave me a bit of advice I have never forgotten. He said:

> Basically, my belief is that language should be taught on the broadest practicable bases and at all levels, and that on the whole we have been too narrow and too limited in our teaching. We have tended to teach the minutiae like spelling and usage—which are of course desirable within limits—but we have mainly neglected teaching language as mind, language as thought, language as a means of society.[9]

Beside that notion, the question of whether to begin a sentence with *most important* or *most importantly* is pale. Pale, indeed.

Notes

1. Richard Chenivex Trench, "On Some Deficiencies in Our English Dictionaries," *Transactions of the Philological Society* 9 (1857): 4.

2. Patrick Hartwell, "Grammar, Grammars, and the Teaching of Grammar," *College English* 47 (February 1985): 109ff.

3. Charlton Laird, *Language in America* (Englewood Cliffs, N.J.: Prentice-Hall, 1970), p. 294.

4. Paul Horgan, in William Morris and Mary Morris, *Harper Dictionary of Contemporary Usage* (New York: Harper and Row, 1975), p. 36.

5. Thomas Creswell, *Usage in Dictionaries and Dictionaries of Usage* (University, Ala.: University of Alabama Press, 1975).

6. Thomas L. Clark, "The Usageasters," *American Speech,* 55:2 (1980): 135.

7. Mary Vaiana Taylor, "The Folklore of Usage," *College English* 35:7 (1974): 756–68; quotation on p. 761.

8. William and Mary Morris, *Harper Dictionary of Contemporary Usage.*

9. Charlton Laird, "Language: Relevance and Irrelevance, or How to Suffer from Hallucination," *And Gladly Teche* (Englewood Cliffs, N.J.: Prentice-Hall, 1970), p. 18.

On the Linguistic Forms of Prestige
Snobs and Slobs Using English

Edward Finegan

W H E N scholars upon occasion give thought to an ideal language, the preferred ones tend to have a one-to-one correspondence between form and meaning. Such an idealized language would possess a unique expression for each nuance of thought and a one-to-one mapping between thought and expression. For each expression, there would be but a single thought; for each thought, a unique expression. Ideal languages of this kind would lack both ambiguity and synonymy, and doublespeak would be ruled out.

We can imagine a different kind of idealized communication—a language in which to express all the richness of thought there would be but a single expression—presumably *uh* [ə], the simplest vocalization. With each utterance of *uh,* a speaker's thought would be uniquely conveyed to addressees, and no misunderstanding could arise in this most efficient form of communication. Fortunately, such efficiency is beyond human capacity—fortunately, for such telepathy, while stimulating to imagine, would make for dull novels, poems, puns, and other forms of word play and verbal art. The entire process of communicating through a medium would be short-circuited; we would possess a direct, medium-free language. (And many of us would be out of work, needless to add.)

In reality, existing varieties of natural language fall between these extremes of expression. The two idealizations represent opposing communicative strategies, ideals in a tug of war between the forces of clear communication and those of efficient communication. For the advantage of hearers and readers, one force propels language in the direction of full—and therefore unique—expression for each mean-

---

E D W A R D F I N E G A N of the University of Southern California is the author of the book, *Attitudes toward English Usage: The History of a War of Words,* and of many essays in linguistics.

ing, while for the advantage of speakers and writers, the forces of efficient communication tug in the direction of minimal voice for any meaning, thereby fostering simple, homophonous expression.

To invoke an analogy from the physical world, language use is governed by both a centrifugal force that teases out expression and a centripetal force tending to collapse it. The centrifugal force attends to the needs of addressee and audience, the centripetal force to the needs of speaker and writer.[1] In the interplay of these opposing forces we derive much of our pleasure in reading and writing and our challenge as teachers, critics, and linguists.

It was to this centripetal force, the force to collapse expression, that Dr. Johnson referred when he said that "tongues, like governments, have a natural tendency to degeneration." Such "degeneration" is the inevitable result of a natural bent to communicate efficiently. For the sake of efficiency, we abbreviate, blend, use homonyms and structurally ambiguous sentences, reduce certain sounds or skip them altogether, eliminate entire words, and so on. "Said 'e'd be 'ere" for "He said that he would be here" and [jit yɛt] for "Did you eat yet?" are the workaday products of this centripetal force.

Otto Jespersen and Dwight Bolinger have both described the benefits of this centripetal force. Though chiefly concerned with lexical matters, their insights apply equally well to syntax and phonology. Jespersen writes:

> Language is only attending to its proper business when it comprehends a multitude of like things under the same appelation: it is just this which makes the communication of thought possible. Synonyms are all very well, but only within reasonable bounds. One has to remember . . . that words are not obtained without cost. Every word that is to be used or understood must be first learnt. We have therefore to weigh against one another the advantage of having accurately shaded expressions, and the inconvenience of learning and remembering them.[2]

Bolinger more tersely concedes that:

> We cannot say explicitly all we need to say—it would take forever, and there would not be enough words to go around. Much has to be taken on trust, and that leaves nicks and crannies that vermin can use as hideouts.[3]

In richly contextualized circumstances such as face-to-face communication between intimates, the degree of abbreviation tends to be affordably great. In less contextualized circumstances, or where the degrees of contextualization are not balanced between addresser and addressee, linguistic elaboration must be greater if communication is to succeed. In writing, the centrifugal force must predominate, and considerable effort is expended coaching students to make explicit in that medium what can remain implicit in their conversation with people of similar background and shared assumptions. More than a mere convention of the English essay, explicit expression is a communicative requirement of expository prose—the chief object of native language instruction.

To return to our analogy, English language instruction aims in part to exercise the centrifugal force in language use, helping to insure adequate expression for communication. This doubtless is what Gorrell and Laird have in mind in quoting Richard Brinsley Sheridan's perceptive comment, "But easy writing's curst hard reading,"[4] for teaching must counteract the robust centripetal force that dominates young conversation and intimate talk, the force that is the natural ally of *homo loquens* in a rush.

Into the perpetual tug of war between centripetal and centrifugal linguistic forces have ventured the prescriptive grammarians. While linguists are persuaded that the two forces operating on language are balanced by the nature of things—that the need for clear communication adequately balances the urge to be efficient—prescriptivists fear that centripetal efficiency will overpower the need for articulated expression, especially in writing. Although explicitness is negotiable in the course of conversation, readers have very limited bargaining potential; hence, the traditionalists' phobia about the triumph of the forces centripetal. Recognizing the nature of centripetal pressures in language use, traditionalists rally around Dr. Johnson's challenge to hold the line: "If the changes that we fear be thus irresistible, it remains that we retard what we cannot repel, that we palliate what we cannot cure."

In the discussion to follow, I want to suggest that—however obliquely and however haltingly—prescriptivists exercise the centrifugal force in language use and that their prescriptions have the potential to sensitize language users to the communicative value of this centrifugal force. I do not believe that the pop-grammarians (as they have recently been called) are fully aware of what they are doing, and I concede that their rigidity and absolutism betray ignorance of much that sociolinguists and rhetoricians take for granted about linguistic variation and its functions. I concede further that the pop-grammarians have done more harm than good. But I also recognize that linguists have not afforded the guardians a fair hearing and that this imbalance is exacerbated by the bad press the guardians have in turn inflicted on linguists, a bad press that has bruised the credibility of the linguistics profession and drawn linguists into certain vulnerable positions. My intention is to invite a more open-minded approach to questions of linguistic prestige in the hope of contributing to such understanding of the battle between prescriptivism and descriptivism as has hitherto evaded us and whose absence has insinuated a damaging discordancy between humanistic and linguistic approaches to language, a discordancy no more necessary than it is desirable.

Linguists have argued that the forms sanctioned by prescriptivists differ from dispreferred locutions in arbitrary ways. The argument is premised upon the assumption that all dialects are linguistically equal; thus, since any expression can serve as well as any other, the forms sanctioned by the prescriptivists can be preferred only because of their *association* with educated users or users of higher socioeconomic status. Chambers and Trudgill exemplify the almost universal view of linguists toward variation and prestige; discussing the socially stratified pronunciations [il] and [i] for Montreal French *il*, they write that the "difference in social status stems from the relationship between this variable and social class membership."[5] The same view is echoed in Hudson's generalization that "linguists would claim that if they were simply shown the grammars of two different varieties, one with high and the other with low prestige, they could not tell which was which, any more than they could predict the skin colour of those who speak the two varieties."[6] It is my contention that at least as these and similar statements are commonly interpreted they appear more definitive than the data warrant (and they may be inaccurate). Dell Hymes comes nearer the truth when he concedes that "we hardly know in any systematic way what communities have made of language."[7]

What is insufficiently recognized is that there is a pattern to the prescriptions: they tend to sanction a one-to-one relationship between form and meaning and to minimize the telescoping of expression. Where there are two forms, as in *imply/infer, shall/will, lie/lay,* and *like/as,* prescriptivists urge two meanings and rail at the collapsing of expression and the indiscriminate distribution of two forms over two meanings. Where a form exists, as in *regardless,* the preference of the prescriptivists is to exclude a second form for the same content; thus, because *irregardless* duplicates *regardless,* it is dispreferred. True, the prescriptivists have objected to *irregardless* for its redundancy, but redundancy may have been unwittingly invoked because the transparency of its argument is more persuasive even to the prescriptivists. (The tendency to want different meanings for different forms, incidentally, is not limited to the guardians of the language: when Labov inquired of a New York City informant about her two pronunciations of *vase,* she volunteered that "vahses" were larger than "vases.")

We might also mention *hopefully,* dubbed by *Time* magazine the watershed issue in twentieth-century usage. Used as a speaker-oriented sentence adverbial to comment on the content of a proposition, as in "Hopefully, the rain is finished," this disjunct exercises Edwin Newman, John Simon, and most of their cohorts (though not William Safire, the record should show). Regrettably, Surprisingly, Unfortunately, and Lamentably, Simon and Newman are not the grammarians they lay claim to being; certainly, they are not sharp at observing the patterns of English. Still, they fret about *hopefully* because it could conceivably be ambiguous, yielding two meanings for one form. Where its use is unambiguous, we have two forms for one meaning. Either way, according to them, we lose.

Consider another claim regarding the preferences of the guardians. It is alleged that one important motivating factor for conservers of the language is the creation and maintenance of social distinctions. As in clothes, neighborhoods, schools, restaurants, automobiles, and modes of travel, the argument goes, the middle classes also have linguistic preferences that serve in part to distance them from groups of lower socioeconomic status. As we have already seen, most linguists would claim that what sets value on prestige variants is mere association with socioeconomic advantage but that the forms used by lower socioeconomic status groups are as inherently suitable as the forms of any group.

This claim may be correct, but at present there is insufficient knowledge to prove it, for we know very little about how prestige and nonprestige forms differ, about whether the differences are arbitrary or systematic, and, if the latter, in what ways and to what ends.

Alluding to the possibility of unexpected findings should objective investigation of these questions be undertaken, Hymes warns in unmistakable terms:

> From the standpoint of scientific understanding, and social change based on scientific understanding, the treacherous facts of interdependence between linguistic means and the social ends they have evolved to serve must also be addressed. Our discipline is somewhat schizophrenic in this regard. When differences are presented as favorable to the underdog, . . . we can rejoice. . . . When differences might reflect unfavorably on the underdog, we retreat to the equality of all languages in the eyes of science. Yet it is inconsistent to approve of Hopi being "rapierlike" (Whorf's word) in some respects in comparison to English, yet not to recognize the opposite of "rapierlike" as a fact of language as well. The marvelous accounts of the continuity of expansion in content and function of Tok Pisin . . . have as their implicit counterpart contraction in content and function in other language varieties in other situations.[8]

I want to suggest that the linguistic forms of the educated and other elite classes do not, in fact, differ arbitrarily from those of other classes but do so in systematic ways. In particular, the linguistic forms of prestige tend to conform more to the one-to-one idealization described above and to exhibit lesser contraction in form. To draw on the earlier analogy, prestige varieties are more strongly governed by the centrifugal force, whereas the centripetal force dominates less prestigious varieties. In saying that language varieties are not randomly distributed socially, I recognize that they are also not randomly distributed as to function and that the social and functional development patterns are not independent of one another.

Looking at the evidence, we find considerably more data in phonology than in syntax. Investigations reported in Labov (1966, 1972), Sankoff (1980), Trudgill (1974, 1978, 1984), and elsewhere reveal that the forms of pronunciation characteristic of higher socioeconomic status groups tend to be fuller in their consonantal shape than those of lower socioeconomic status groups.[9] Thus, among lower socioeconomic status groups in New York City, we find less /d/ in phrases like *wild oats,* less /r/ postvocalically in words like *car* and *barn,* less *thin* [θ] and *then* [ð] and more "tin" and "den." Similar examples from Montreal French, Panamanian Spanish, and Brazilian Portuguese have been cited in the literature,[10] and similar patterns have been described for the English of England, Ireland, and Scotland.

In equivalent contextual circumstances, speakers of lower socioeconomic status tend to telescope the phonetic manifestations of words to a greater degree than speakers of higher socioeconomic status. As Kroch puts it:

> Aside from the specific consonant changes documented by Labov and others, there is a more general tendency towards simplifying consonantal articulation that is favored by non-prestige dialects—that is, a tendency to favor the articulatory reductions of rapid speech.[11]

The sociolinguistic literature further suggests a general tendency for informal pronunciations to be less full than formal ones for all social groups, while each successively higher social group uses higher percentages of fuller forms in equivalent styles. If the matter were indeed arbitrary, we should expect that more formal circumstances would exhibit the telescoped forms instead of the fuller ones in perhaps half the instances. This is not the case.

With respect to vowels, the speech of lower socioeconomic groups shows "a greater tendency to undergo 'natural' vowel shifts," according to Kroch. While vowel shifting is less well understood than consonant cluster simplification, the point is that the "natural" and common tendency to raise vowels is exhibited to a greater degree among lower socioeconomic status groups. In New York City, for example, there is more *bad* [bæ:d] and *off* [ɔ:f] among higher socioeconomic groups and more *bad* [bɪːᵊd] and *off* [ʊːᵊf] among lower socioeconomic groups.[12]

From such evidence as consonant cluster simplification and vowel raising, Kroch infers that

> prestige dialects resist phonologically motivated change and inherent variation because prestige speakers seek to mark themselves off as distinct from the common people and because inhibiting phonetic processes is an obvious way to do this, . . . there is particular ideological motivation at the origin of social dialect variation. This ideology causes the prestige dialect user to expend more energy in speaking than does the user of the popular vernacular. . . . These dialects are maintained by social elites and such elites are by and large conservative. The use of

conservative linguistic forms is for them a symbol of their whole value system.[13]

The conclusion that it is concern for social status that maintains the prestige dialect is tantalizing, and it would please egalitarians if it could be confirmed. In any case, the argument is based on phonology, the chief concern of neither prescriptive grammarians nor the schools that propagate their doctrines.[14]

To investigate syntactic variation, Kroch and Small examined radio talk show discussions. They sorted speakers into two groups, assuming show hosts and studio guests to be speakers of "a more standard English than the caller group." Two linguistic variables were tallied: *particle movement* and *that-deletion* (*particle movement* refers to pairings like "She put out the fire" and "She put the fire out"; *that-deletion* refers to sentence pairs like "She thinks that he's reliable" and "She thinks he's reliable"). From the fact that callers deleted *that* and separated particles from verbs more frequently than hosts and studio guests, Kroch and Small hypothesize "a grammatical ideology" at work by which "the guardians of the standard language impose their linguistic norms on people who have perfectly serviceable norms of their own."[15]

Again, however, it is sobering to reflect on the data, for neither particle movement nor that-deletion figure prominently in the prescriptivists' canon of shibboleths. There is no mention of either in Strunk and White, while Fowler, who ignores particle movement, is sensible and balanced about that-deletion, observing simply that more formal verbs occur with *that* more frequently than do the informal verbs of saying, believing, and so on.

The explanation for the differences between the linguistic forms of prestige must be sought elsewhere than in grammatical ideology, I believe. To test an alternative hypothesis about the relationship between sociolinguistic variation and the degrees of form/meaning correspondence and fullness of expression in surface form, a colleague and I measured frequency of occurrence of several linguistic variables in seven text types.[16] We selected texts from written and spoken samples representing varying degrees of formality. Two text types were extracted from the Brown University Corpus of Present-day Edited American English, the other five from the London-Lund Corpus of Spoken English. Writing is represented by academic journals as a highly formal text type and by newspaper sports pages and society pages as a less formal type. For the spoken samples, three kinds of telephone conversation serve as informal text types, while public speeches and broadcast commentaries represent more formal exemplars. In all, 108 texts were examined, more than 129,000 words selected systematically from two corpora containing more than a million and a half words.[17]

It was expected (a) that the written samples would display more fullness of expression and a stronger isomorphism between form and meaning than the spoken genres, and (b) that the texts would display parallel differences in accordance with their degree of formality. Thus form/meaning correspondence and fullness of expression were expected to be greater in the written texts and in the more formal genres (like public speeches and academic writing) than in less formal genres (like telephone conversation).

Two linguistic variables were selected to represent fullness of expression: *that-deletion* from subordinate clauses and everyday *contractions*. Thus, within the limits of the corpora, one measure each for syntactic and phonological expression was included. To represent the isomorphism between meaning and surface form, *preposition stranding* and the disruption of verbs and infinitives by *-ly* adverbs were counted. *Preposition stranding* is better known as "final prepositions" (what we are advised not to end sentences with); disruption of verbs and infinitives includes the familiar shibboleth of split infinitives.[18]

Table 1 presents the mean scores per 2,000 words for contractions, one of the linguistic variables chosen to measure fullness of expression.

TABLE 1.
*Mean Number of Contractions per 2,000 Words
in Seven Text Types*

Personal telephone	121	
Business telephone	118	
Distal telephone	112	Spoken Texts
Broadcast	56	
Speeches	34	
Press	23	Written Texts
Academic journals	4	

TABLE 2.
*Mean Percentages for Stranded Prepositions
in Seven Text Types*

Personal telephone	27.0	
Distal telephone	26.6	
Speeches	26.4	Spoken Texts
Business telephone	24.4	
Broadcast	21.6	
Academic journals	0.6	Written Texts
Press	0.4	

The values for contractions reveal that the highest mean score is 121 for personal telephone conversations, followed by telephone conversations between business associates, and distals; then come broadcast speech, speeches, press, and academic journals in that order. This ranking reflects a systematic decline from less formal to more formal text types and a correlated decrease in the degree of contraction. Note, too, that although the two written genres exhibit less contraction than the five spoken text types, no major distinction exists between speech and writing on this count.

Table 2 presents the counts of stranded prepositions as a percent of total prepositions for each genre. While the ranking of the genres differs somewhat from that for contractions, the only statistically significant difference among the means in table 2 is that between spoken and written text types. The fact that contractions are distributed differentially across all text types, while preposition stranding differentiates essentially only between spoken and written genres, suggests that these two variables may be functions of distinct sociolinguistic or communicative parameters that do not function equivalently, a hypothesis that is confirmed by Biber.[19]

It is useful to recognize that *particle movement*—which is sometimes obligatory in English, as in "I tore it up"—has the effect of separating semantically linked units, thus reducing the degree of correspondence between surface form and underlying (i.e., semantic) structure. The same can be said for that-deletion. *That* serves to mark the onset of a subordinate clause, and its absence can be viewed as reducing the match between form and meaning. That-deletion is a syntactic parallel to the phonetic truncations discussed above. Thus if we were to predict whether that-deletion would be more characteristic of formal or informal speech, of upper or lower socioeconomic status groups, of speech or writing, and so on, it is clear what our predictions would be, and if these predictions are correct—as they appear to be—it is also clear that the prescriptivists do not deserve credit for the characteristic distribution.

The observations and findings above suggest that in more formal styles there is a marked tendency for speakers and writers to use fuller forms and to match form and semantics more closely. This is apparently true of all socioeconomic groups. Further, a closer correspondence between form and meaning is exhibited in the usage of higher socioeconomic status groups, though the reasons for this correlation remain obscure. While the work of Bernstein[20] and his collaborators may help unravel this mystery, the long and short of it is that this matching of form and content marks situations and language users alike. Further, it is clear that it enhances (or at least can enhance) communication, and to that extent should characterize writing more than speech.

What the language guardians may have been providing, then, are prescriptions to counteract the centripetal force operating on language—prescriptions for fuller expression, for one-to-one correspondence between form and meaning—prescriptions for expression that favors a closer matching of syntax and lexicon with semantics. Whether and to what degree various prescriptions accomplish this aim is an empirical question. That it remains uninvestigated is tribute to the entrenched position of unexamined dogma both prescriptive and descriptive (or liberal and conservative if the politics of the situation frames the discussion). That there has been little recognition of the macroscopic patterns in the use of language by different groups and in different circumstances is tribute to the vitality of the creed that all varieties are linguistically equal.

For centuries now, prescriptivists and descriptivists have been hurling obscenities at each other while their treatises dismiss all opposing claims. We have seen distinguished conservers of the language, including Dr. Johnson, George Campbell, and Noah Webster, and we have seen informed and ingenious defenders of usage, including Joseph Priestley, George Philip Krapp, Albert Marckwardt, Charlton Laird, and James Sledd. Still lacking, though, are successful attempts to get beneath the surface of the accusations and defenses, although Sledd has perceptively suggested that the situation is by no means as simple as it appears.[21]

Regrettably, as the linguists' views have become entrenched, the description of the language has fallen into the inkwells of those reluctant to describe contexts of usage. Recall Sledd's criticism of *Webster's Third,* a supposed bastion of liberalism. He asked how the 200,000 citations in the *Third* "will enable the inexpert reader to do what 10,000,000 quotations did not make possible for the expert lexicographers" who had access to Merriam-Webster's files in compiling the mammoth dictionary.[22] On the other hand, the guardianship of the language is in worse straits. However appealing to some the clever criticisms of Newman or the snobbery of Simon, we have fallen a long way from Campbell and Johnson and Fowler, as Nunberg has pointed out.[23]

The findings outlined above, if confirmed by larger samples of texts and a wider selection of linguistic features, suggest, of course, not that any variety of English is better than others but that systematic relationships exist between linguistic form and communicative function. Doubtless, these relationships have evolved in response to psycholinguistic factors, to varying constraints on the need to be expressive in different situations, to the cooperative principle articulated by Grice,[24] to the different processing strategies deployed in speech and writing, and to the nature of language acquisition and language change.

From a sociolinguistic point of view, it would appear that positive valuation generally attaches to forms resulting from the centrifugal force that enables language to follow what Slobin has called the maxim to "Be Clear,"[25] while the centripetal force, addressing the maxim to "Be Quick and Easy," creates forms that are socially dispreferred.[26] The prestige of a variety tends to correlate with the degree to which its linguistic forms are "clear" rather than "quick and easy."

In 1964, the Linguistic Society of America reported to the National Commission on the Humanities that "the impact which the recent advances in linguistics have had upon the general public [is] essentially zero" and that "a fair portion of highly educated laymen see in linguistics the great enemy of all they hold dear."[27] We can contrast this view—an accurate and persistent one—with another one expressed by Nunberg: "From Dr. Johnson to the Fowlers, the great grammarians have acquired their stature only because they spoke eloquently and sensibly to the linguistic concerns of the literate public."[28] It is becoming clearer that we do not adequately understand what chords were struck by the great grammarians nor in what their sensibility lay.

John Simon has betrayed an odious belief that the explanation for the poor use of English today is that "most people—92 percent, perhaps—are not intelligent enough to be human beings."[29] Other remarks—by both linguists and language guardians—similarly suggest that lack of intelligence accounts for the obstinate refusal of the other side to grasp their arguments and to capitulate. Clearly, the arguments have been unpersuasive on both sides, and capitulation is as unlikely now as ever.

As linguists examine the surface structure of sentences for clues to underlying structure, and as ethnographers seek the patterns underlying behavior, so those who lament the chasm between C. P. Snow's two cultures—cultures in the narrower sense of humanistic and scientific approaches to language use—must examine both conservers and linguists for what underlies their views and motivates the condemnations of one another's *raisons d'être*. Until the intellectual grounds of the combatants are better understood, the invocation of linguistic ideologies should be barred, for such ideology advances neither scientific nor humanistic understanding.

A first step in the direction of reconciling the mutually hostile views is to ascertain the distribution of linguistic variants throughout the linguistic repertoire of English speakers, seeking a basis on which to understand the relationship between the psycholinguistic and sociolinguistic explanations of such distribution. "Why in the world are you doing that?" asked R. B. Lees in 1962 when W. Nelson Francis reported that he had a grant to compile a million-word corpus of American English. "That is a complete waste of your time and the government's money. You are a native speaker of English; in ten minutes you can produce more illustrations of any point in English grammar than you will find in many millions of words of random text."[30] A quarter of a century later, an adequate response to Lees's legitimate question is emerging, for, at the intersection of social and psychological aspects of language use, the study of actual texts and the distribution of linguistic features therein can help provide answers to those questions about correctness and prestige that have troubled English speakers since publication of the first grammars of English.

Notes

1. Charlton Laird used the terms *centrifugal* and *centripetal* to capture another but related fact about language variation. In "Language and the Dictionary" (*Webster's New World Dictionary of the American Language,* Second College Edition, ed. David B. Guralnik (New York and Cleveland: World, 1970, "*Languages are at once centrifugal and centripetal.* Languages tend to break into dialects and at the same time to pull together."

2. Otto Jespersen, *Mankind, Nation and Individual* (Bloomington: Indiana Univ. Press, 1964), p. 79.

3. Dwight Bolinger, "Fire in a Wooden Stove: On Being Aware in Language," in *The State of the Language,* eds. L. Michaels and C. Ricks (Berkeley: Univ. of California Press, 1980), p. 384.

4. Robert Gorrell and Charlton Laird, *Modern English Handbook,* 4th ed. (Englewood Cliffs, N.J.: Prentice-Hall, 1967), p. v.

5. J. K. Chambers and P. Trudgill, *Dialectology* (Cambridge: Cambridge Univ. Press, 1980), p. 73.

6. R. A. Hudson, *Sociolinguistics* (Cambridge: Cambridge Univ. Press, 1980), p. 191.

7. Dell Hymes, *Foundations in Sociolinguistics: An Ethnographic Approach* (Philadelphia: Univ. of Pennsylvania Press, 1974), p. 204. Other linguists have expressed the linguistic relativity hypothesis more cautiously, perhaps none better than Gillian Sankoff in *The Social Life of Language* (Philadelphia: Univ. of Pennsylvania Press, 1980), pp. 6–7:

> The basic tenet of linguistic relativity is that all natural languages are on an equal footing in terms of their capacities for human communication. There is no denying, of course, that some languages are used in cultural contexts and for purposes for which other languages are not, and that they are to some extent adapted or specialized to these purposes and contexts. This adaptation is, however, largely a matter of lexical proliferation and stylistic elaboration; there is no evidence that in terms of the basic machinery of a language considered as a code for transmitting messages, i.e., the phonology, morphology, syntax, or even the overall semantic organization, any one language is inherently superior, more logical, accurate or efficient, or in any way preferable to any other language.

Sankoff adds that "extreme linguistic relativism needs a good deal of qualification. . . . Situations of prolonged bilingualism, . . . situations of language contact, of the use of *lingue franche* and especially of pidgins seem to lead to certain types of reduction in surface complexities of the languages used. . . ."

8. Dell Hymes, foreword to Sankoff, *Social Life,* p. xix.

9. William Labov, *The Social Stratification of English in New York City*

(Washington, D.C.: Center for Applied Linguistics, 1966); Labov, *Socio-linguistic Patterns* (Philadelphia: Univ. of Pennsylvania Press, 1972); Sankoff, *Social Life;* Peter Trudgill, *The Social Differentiation of English in Norwich* (Cambridge: Cambridge Univ. Press, 1974); Trudgill, ed., *Sociolinguistic Patterns in British English* (London: Edward Arnold, 1978); and Trudgill, ed., *Language in the British Isles* (Cambridge: Cambridge Univ. Press, 1984).

10. Anthony Kroch, "Toward a Theory of Social Dialect Variation," *Language in Society* 7 (1978): 17–36.

11. Ibid., p. 27.

12. Labov, *Patterns,* pp. 127–29.

13. Kroch, "Social Dialect Variation," p. 30.

14. Another explanation for the differences between forms of phonological prestige could be related to degrees of literacy, for the fuller pronunciations generally conform more closely to standard spellings. This argument is considerably weakened, however, by the fact that the fuller forms occur at all social levels, though to different degrees (i.e., with different frequencies). This fact demonstrates that the underlying (psychological) phonological forms generally match the orthography for all speakers equally and thus vitiates the force of the argument from literacy.

15. Anthony Kroch and Cathy Small, "Grammatical Ideology and Its Effect on Speech," in *Linguistic Variation: Models and Methods,* ed. David Sankoff (New York: Academic Press, 1978), pp. 45–55.

16. Edward Finegan and Douglas Biber, "Toward a Unified Model of Sociolinguistic Prestige," in *Diversity and Diachrony,* ed. David Sankoff (Amsterdam: Benjamins, forthcoming).

17. Henry Kučera and W. N. Francis, *Computational Analysis of Present-Day American English* (Providence, R.I.: Brown Univ. Press, 1967); Jan Svartvik and Randolph Quirk, eds., *A Corpus of English Conversation* (Lund: Liber, 1980).

18. The details of selection, extraction, and measurement of these variables are discussed in Biber, *Textual Relations in Speech and Writing* (Cambridge: Cambridge Univ. Press, forthcoming). The procedures did not allow for an exhaustive counting of *that-deletion* in the texts.

19. Douglas Biber, "Spoken and Written Textual Dimensions in English: Resolving the Contradictory Findings," *Language* 62:2 (June 1986): 384–414.

20. Basil Bernstein, *Theoretical Studies Towards a Sociology of Language,* vol. 1 of *Class, Codes and Control* (London: Routledge and Kegan Paul, 1971).

21. James Sledd, "Linguistic Relativism: The Divorce of Word from Work," in *Studies in English Linguistics,* eds. Sidney Greenbaum, Geoffrey Leech, and Jan Svartvik (London and New York: Longman, 1979), pp. 228–36.

22. James Sledd, "The Lexicographer's Uneasy Chair," in *Dictionaries and*

THAT Dictionary, eds. J. Sledd and W. R. Ebbitt (Chicago: Scott, Foresman, 1962), p. 232.

23. Geoffrey Nunberg, "The Decline of Grammar," *The Atlantic Monthly,* December 1983, pp. 31–46.

24. H. P. Grice, "Logic and Conversation," in *Speech Acts,* vol. 3 of *Syntax and Semantics,* eds. Peter Cole and Jerry Morgan (New York: Academic Press, 1975), pp. 41–58.

25. Dan I. Slobin, *Psycholinguistics,* 2nd ed. (Glenview, Ill.: Scott, Foresman, 1979).

26. Generally, though not always, for there are a few cases where the need to be clear has produced in less prestigious varieties usages that exhibit greater form-meaning correspondence than the parallel usages in the more prestigious varieties. New Yorkers, Western Pennsylvanians, and Southerners, for example, say *yous, y'uns,* and *y'all,* respectively, thereby repairing an apparent deficiency in the pronominal system of standard English. The same might be said for invariant *be* in Black English Vernacular, which does not have a parallel in standard English. Language systems evolve to meet needs and are by no means arbitrary in their developmental patterns.

27. Linguistic Society of America, *Report of the Commission on the Humanities* (New York: The American Council of Learned Societies, 1964), pp. 155–56.

28. Nunberg, "The Case for Prescriptive Grammar," a preliminary version of "The Decline of Grammar."

29. Quoted in Flora Johnson, "Making the Mother Safe from Democracy," *TWA Ambassador* (June 1980), pp. 53–58.

30. W. Nelson Francis, "Problems of Assembling and Computerizing Large Corpora," in *Computer Corpora in English Language Research,* ed. Stig Johansson (Bergen: Norwegian Computing Center for the Humanities, 1982), pp. 7–8.

Usage and Style
1984 and 1066

Walker Gibson

UNLIKE just about every other participant in the "Miracle of Language" symposium, I never knew Charlton Laird at all well personally. We were at best nodding acquaintances at meetings of English teachers. When the symposium was first being planned, I looked forward to becoming better acquainted with Laird and to seeking his advice and counsel. So I was particularly grieved to learn of his death. I would have liked to share with him some questions of usage and style (as my advertised title promises), and in reference to two particular dates that seem to be on my mind these days. One of these dates is of course 1984, and the other is 1066.

As to 1984, leaving Orwell aside for once, let's ask what Mr. Laird might have said about the language of the 1984 political campaign. I'm sure he would have found that language alternately entertaining, monotonous, and frightening—as we all have—and I know, too, that he would have been enlightening about some of the linguistic events we were exposed to in the last national election. As always in an election year, we English teachers can take note of language going by that we are particularly trained to appreciate. At the same time, with our familiar ruefulness, we recognize that our special concern about language is not invariably what wins elections, and I will comment later on what apparently *does* win elections. Meanwhile let me tick off a few examples of election-year word use in which we English teachers might have a sort of professional interest. We will have to imagine how Laird might have footnoted and refined these observations.

First, I recall to your minds the comma flap of August 1984 in Dallas. It turned out during the writing of the platform at the Republican Convention that the presence or absence of a single comma

WALKER GIBSON of the University of Massachusetts, Amherst, is a poet and writer and past president of the National Council of Teachers of English. His writings include *Tough, Sweet and Stuffy,* a well-known discussion of writing style, *The Reckless Spenders,* and *The Limits of Language.*

made a big difference in the plank about taxes—made a big difference in what the plank actually promised. Here is the way the plank read before the hard-line conservatives got hold of it and amended it: "We therefore oppose any attempt to increase taxes which would harm the recovery and reverse the trend toward restoring control of the economy to individual Americans." Now we know what that sentence means. It means the Republicans are put on record as opposing those taxes—and only those taxes—which would harm the recovery. Quite conceivably, according to this plank, the Republicans could *approve* certain taxes if they were considered as *not* harmful to the recovery. The hard-line conservatives didn't like that possibility. They were against *any* taxes. So what did they do? They inserted one little comma, in the right place, and the whole sentence changed meaning: "We therefore oppose any attempt to increase taxes, which would harm the recovery and reverse the trend . . ." and so on. Now they're on record as opposing any tax at all, because all taxes (almost by definition) harm the recovery.

We recognize a distinction beloved among English teachers between the restrictive and nonrestrictive clause. We have all confused our students for generations with that distinction and its pedantic nomenclature. Might it not be helpful to show them, just once, that here is a case where the distinction made a real difference in very practical affairs?

Another entertaining aspect of language behavior that emerged during the 1984 election year is the coinage of new words. Coinage of new words is a serious business, as Laird often observed, essential to the growth and health of any language, and it's going on all the time. Bright people are constantly inventing new words or new combinations of words, and once in a thousand times these new words stick around a while. (I recall from one of Laird's works his delight in "sandwich words," found apparently especially in Britain, where a long word is split up and an intensifier inserted in the middle. One of his examples was *abso-bloody-lutely*.) I'm going to give you three examples of new words that surfaced during the election year, and I doubt if any one of them is going to stick around for long—though you never know. The first of these dates from the Democrats' convention in July 1984 in San Francisco, and its creator was Gary Hart. Hart was upset at what he felt was the aggressive politics of the Mondale supporters in San Francisco, and he complained about what he called the *Mondalization* of the convention. You see what Hart did.

First he took a noun, *Mondale,* and made a verb out of it with a familiar Greek ending, *Mondalize,* and then he made another noun out of the verb by adding the latinate suffix, *Mondalization.* (I don't mean that Hart thought all that out in those English teacher terms—he just went ahead, as we all do from time to time, and strung together his new word.) The process he used, though, is a clear and traditional one by which words are added to in order to change the part of speech.

(To old-timers like me, the notorious example of *final—finalize* comes to mind. Students today simply cannot believe that the word *finalize* could possibly irritate anybody, as it certainly did back in the sixties during the brouhaha over *Webster's Third.* Yet to this day, in the corridors where English professors are quartered, you will not hear that word uttered by anybody, except perhaps with an ironic lift of the eyebrow, as if to say: we all know what a vulgar term it is that I find myself using. A hundred yards away, at the School of Management, *finalize* is used every minute of every day, without the slightest awareness of anything amiss. Who is right? Rather ask, who is winning, or who has already won?)

My second instance of a word coinage comes from New York's Governor Cuomo, also at the San Francisco convention. Cuomo was quoted as saying that some people he didn't approve of were making an unfair argument by using—and here's his new word—*insinuendo.* Here again we have a familiar and traditional process at work, and the technical name for his particular coinage is a *portmanteau word.* The governor took two quite different words, *insinuation* and *innuendo,* and chopped them up and put the pieces together into a single receptacle, just as you might throw socks and shirts into two compartments of a traveling bag. (A portmanteau is, or was, a collapsible bag with a divider down the middle.) I don't expect *insinuendo* to hang around very long, any more than *Mondalization,* but at least the bemused student of language can applaud the governor's wit as the word fades away into the blue yonder.[1]

My third example of a nice coinage in the 1984 election year comes from Anne Burford. As you remember, she held a high office in the Reagan administration as protector of the environment, until it developed that under her direction, her agency wasn't protecting the environment at all—and she was forced to resign. Some time later Mr. Reagan, always loyal to his friends, asked her back to chair some committee or other that was supposed to oversee environmental affairs. And there was hell to pay, and once again she was forced to back out. She got in the last word, though, even if it has a sour-grapes sound: she referred to the committee she was to chair as a *Nothingburger*. This is another portmanteau, I suppose, and a familiar one. Laird remarks somewhere that you can put anything at all ahead of *-burger* except *ham*.

These observations on some current usage—interesting, I hope, to us professionals—are peripheral to an election, to say the least. Are there other activities that linguists and English teachers might engage in that might point to more telling comments on the election? One can study politicians' choices of words and the way they put sentences together, and sometimes one can learn something from such an analysis. Or one can speak of regional dialects, and speculate on the effect on voters of Ms. Ferraro's brassy Queens style. (Since 1976, with Carter's election, the question of regional dialect can in my judgment no longer be a central issue, just as, it is to be hoped, after Ferraro's nomination, the question of gender may be permanently diminished as an issue.) I confess, though, that the results of studies such as these—in style and sentence structure, or in regional dialect—might well be pretty limited. The fact is that in the 1984 election, as in all elections but especially in that one, there was a lot going on that defied traditional English teacher approaches. It seems to be clear that people were not listening to the candidates' language, as language is traditionally defined; rather, people were sensitive to some other kind of language that is variously referred to as *personality* or *TV image* or *charisma*. Take the fact that millions of people who opposed Reagan on important issues—defense, Grenada, abortion, environment, care for the poor, supply-side economics—nevertheless said that they were going to vote for him. What the Great Communicator was communicating is not the sort of message that we customarily think of as resulting from rational statements expressed in English. Again, this wordless message of his has been variously referred to: a macho image, an ambience of confidence, an upbeat character. Whatever it is, we recognize that Mondale didn't have it. Many heard, in Mondale's voice and manner, a kind of whine, a vague complaint. Reagan's macho image, and particularly its apparent appeal to male voters, cries out for explanation. There are a lot of things in the 1984 election we don't understand very well, and machismo is one of them. The appeal has been documented with statistics: in the 18-to-29-year-old group, men favored Reagan almost two to one, whereas women favored the Democrats.

Some remarks from professional politicians on this subject are interesting. "It's the perfect gentleman versus the cowboy. Reagan is a healthy dose of macho, and Mondale is part of the Brie-and-Chablis crowd. The Mondale people need to toughen their boy up." Another critic of Mondale's allegedly "feminine" style was quoted as saying, "Above all he must look, feel, and smell as if he would not be taken to the cleaners in a poker game." Notice that to look, feel, and smell is to do something or other that is quite explicitly wordless.

In that election, then, we recognize, perhaps as never before, that voters' decisions were based on much more than issues communicated in the English language. A 1984 piece by a *New York Times* writer cautiously makes the familiar point:

> With polls showing that many voters prefer Mr. Reagan despite their sharp differences with him on issues, some Democratic leaders and political analysts are beginning to question whether issues are any longer relevant to this campaign. Some of them suggest that the election may be turning instead on perceptions of the candidates and the feelings they have engendered in the electorate.

If issues are not relevant, what is? Perceptions, feelings, as dramatized (and that's the word!) on television, in the debates, and elsewhere. We are reminded of Marshall McLuhan's famous and exaggerated *mot,* The Medium is the Message, a dictum that has turned out to be true in many respects.

In the future the study of persuasive language is going to have to attend to a lot more than words. If I were starting a career all over again—and on the whole I'm glad I'm not—and if I wanted to set myself up as a student of persuasive communication, I think I would try to address myself to all those nonverbal ways in which we impress ourselves on other people, especially via television. There is, for example, the young area of investigation known as *kinesics,* or body language. The public's perception that Mondale was more "comfortable" in the first debate, and that Reagan was not, is a perception that emerged more from observation of gesture than from anything that was said. Mondale's hands were waving happily in the air while his opponent gripped his podium as if desperately. This is the kind of thing we need to know more about. We *do* know a lot, in traditional English teacher terms, about how to expose an illogical argument or a faulty choice of words. Is it possible that someday we may know enough about nonverbal persuasion so as to be equally on our guard against being conned?

Now, more briefly, let me turn to the other date that's on my mind these days—1066, and all that. You know the familiar story. William the Conqueror moved in with his lords and ladies, all speaking Norman French. Anybody who was anybody and had serious business to do did it in French or in Latin; these were the languages of royalty, of the law courts, of the church, of education. English, Old English, Anglo-Saxon endured as a kind of blue-collar tongue, a peasant tongue, and it evidently persevered largely as an oral tongue. We have all seen those lists of animals that had two names, one in English on the hoof and one in French for the noble's table. It was an English *deer* that was shot with the peasant's trusty crossbow, but when it was served at the banquet it became a French *venison*.

Mr. Laird has a characteristic passage on this double-language situation in *The Miracle*:

> Most Englishmen must have gone right on talking Anglo-Saxon while they wrote in French. [I would add, if they wrote at all.] Or at least their wives went on talking Anglo-Saxon, and little Athewold learned Anglo-Saxon as he learned to toddle. Little Athewold's daddy, if he had to sue his neighbor, may have sued him in French, and he prayed to the Virgin Mary in Latin; but when he spanked little Athewold he spanked him in Anglo-Saxon, and the evidence that he did is all over the language. The words *bottom, buttocks, butt,* and *rump* are all from Germanic roots, along with some other terms now considered vulgar.[2]

Now what happened to this English tongue during the next couple of hundred years? How had the language changed by the time Chaucer and others got round to using it in writing three centuries later? Well, most obviously, English had picked up thousands of French words, especially in the later centuries, words for government processes and ecclesiastical terms, borrowed from their more sophisticated conquerors to fill in gaps in our plain old English. And, of course, we are grateful to all that borrowing for the enormous richness of choice in vocabulary that our modern language provides. But what interests me even more is what happened to grammar and syntax during that period when English was almost an underground language. Deprived of English-speaking bureaucrats, priests, or professors of English, those English-speaking peasants, most of them surely illiterate, brought about more sweeping changes in the grammar of the language than ever happened before or since. For one thing, they got rid of most of the inflected endings in nouns and adjectives. (This is the "telescoping" process Mr. Finegan mentions in his essay.) As a result, word order became dominant to compensate for the loss of inflection, and English became a distributive language. Demonstrative pronouns were reduced from eighteen to five. Many strong verbs became regularized, and all new verbs introduced in the language were conjugated on the weak pattern—a process still going on today. And here's another wonder: grammatical gender disappeared entirely, and all that was left was the natural gender we use today for people and animals, and maybe your favorite car.

As you look at the list of the changes in English brought about by a crude and uneducated populace, it is hard to conclude that these changes were anything but magnificent! Those second-class citizens were able to bring about such worthy reforms, as I understand it, precisely because they were unencumbered by educated superiors who would have resisted such sloppy goings-on. As long as little or nothing gets written down, it would appear, possibilities for change, for better or worse, are there for the taking. (It wasn't until 1450 that the town laws in Britain were written down in English.) Surely this is very sobering. The most profound reform movement in our language took place without benefit of professionals, writers, scholars, professors—who in any case would have opposed it. It was a folk operation.

That English syntax was virtually "modern" by the time of Chaucer was dramatized for us during Harry Brent's readings from the Clerk's Tale at the Laird symposium. Brent went back and forth during his reading between Middle English and Modern English, and in doing so all he had to manage was change in pronunciation. Vocabulary was not incomprehensible; word order was much like our own. Things would have been very different if Brent had been dealing with an Old English text.

Back in 1960 the linguist Robert Hall wrote a book called *Leave Your Language Alone!* Actually none of us wants to leave the language alone. We are in the business of *not* leaving our language alone, and what sobers me a little about our business is to recognize how fundamentally conservative our influence is, no matter how free-swinging we may think we are. In many ways this is all to the good. At the same time we ought to remember, with wondering gratitude, that period after 1066 when for a considerable time the language really was left alone, to our great benefit.

I would have dearly liked to share this little historical irony with Charlton Laird, and I glanced through some of his work wondering if he had commented on it. All I found was a remark about change in grammar, worth repeating here:

> At least some changes in grammar are obvious; Anglo-Saxon words are thick with inflectional endings, in some instances with rather long ones. Anyone can see them, and anyone can see also that modern English does very well without them, and that when he compares an ending-language with a no or few-ending language he has grammar visible, right there before his eyes.[3]

Change, of course, is as always the issue. As language professionals, we recognize that we are inevitably conservative in our influence upon others, and in many respects, no doubt, that is all to the good. If at the same time we can keep a reasonably open mind about change, we will perhaps have done something to compensate for that built-in conservatism. *Finalize* is here to stay. Laird was always very good on this question, and I'll end with another small quotation in which he attacks the notion that "the correct meaning of a word is whatever it used to be." He writes:

> The opposite is true; the "correct" use or uses of a word—if such a concept as correctness has much pertinence in a subject so fluid—are whatever the modern users of a term need from it. This is probably the best way for languages to work, but whether we like it or not, that is the way they do work, and probably the only way they can work.[4]

Notes

1. After my luncheon talk at the symposium, I was gently informed by Professor Allen Walker Read, who is a real linguist and not an amateur like me, that in fact *insinuendo* has been around since at least 1904! So much for the governor's wit, and I stand corrected.

2. Charlton Laird, *The Miracle of Language* (New York and Cleveland: World Publishing Company, 1953), p. 46.

3. Laird, *And Gladly Teche* (Englewood Cliffs, N.J.: Prentice-Hall, 1970), p. 89.

4. Laird, *The Word* (New York: Simon and Schuster, 1981), p. xii.

Selected Publications of Charlton Laird

Compiled by Anne K. Phillips

And Gladly Teche: Notes on Instructing the Natives in the Native Tongue. Englewood Cliffs, N.J.: Prentice-Hall, 1970.

"Aristotle's Katharsis in an Impersonal World." *College English* 3 : 3 (December 1941): 215–25.

A Basic Course in Modern English (with Robert M. Gorrell and Raymond J. Pflug). Englewood Cliffs, N.J.: Prentice-Hall, 1963.

"Character and Growth of the Manuel des Pechiez." *Traditio* 4 (1946): 253–306.

"Comparative Literature." In *Contemporary Literary Scholarship,* edited by Lewis Leary. New York: Appleton Century Crofts, 1958, pp. 339–68.

Course in Modern English (with Robert M. Gorrell). Englewood Cliffs, N.J.: Prentice-Hall, 1960.

"Diversions of *The Diversions of Parley* in the New World." *Rendezvous* (Idaho State University) 1 : 1 (Spring 1966): 1–11.

English as Language (with Robert M. Gorrell). New York: Harcourt, 1961.

"Etymology, Anglo-Saxon, and Noah Webster." *American Speech* 21 : 1 (February 1946): 3–15.

"Five New Gretham Sermons and the Middle English *Mirrur.*" *PMLA* 57 : 3 (September 1942): 628–37.

"A Footnote to the Footnote: Science, Linguistics, and the Kwakiutl Grammarian." *College English* 19 : 8 (May 1958): 354–57.

"Freshman English during the Flood." *Phi Delta Kappan* 38 : 5 (February 1957): 204–10.

"The Future of American English." *California English Journal* 1 : 1 (Winter 1965): 6–19.

ANNE K. PHILLIPS has experience in theater, public speaking, and debate. With a master's degree from the University of Nevada, Reno, she is currently pursuing Ph.D. studies in English at the University of Arizona.

Ginn Casebook Series (editor). Boston: Ginn, 1964.

Laird's Promptory. New York: Holt Publishing, 1948.

"Language." *Baltimore Bulletin of Education* 43:2–4 (1966–67): 2–25.

"Language and the Dictionary." In *Webster's New World Dictionary of the American Language,* Second College Edition, edited by David B. Guralnik. New York and Cleveland: World, 1970.

Language in America: The Influence of Man on Language and of Language on Man. New York and Cleveland: World, 1970.

"Language—Not Entirely Confounded." *Paths to International Understanding* 35:8 (May 1954): 321–29.

"Language: Second Phase of the Rocket." In *Reflections on High School English: NDEA Institute Lectures 1965.* Tulsa, Oklahoma: University of Tulsa, 1966, pp. 158–76.

"The *Literati* at Iowa in the Twenties." *Books at Iowa* 37 (1982): 16–37.

The Miracle of Language. New York: World Publishing, 1953.

Modern English Handbook (with Robert M. Gorrell). Englewood Cliffs, N.J.: Prentice-Hall, 1953.

Modern English Reader (with Robert M. Gorrell and Ronald S. Freeman). Englewood Cliffs, N.J.: Prentice-Hall, 1970.

Modern English Workbook (with Robert M. Gorrell). Englewood Cliffs, N.J.: Prentice-Hall, 1963.

"New Thoughts on the Same Old Language." *Forum* 1:1 (Spring 1960): 17–27.

"A Nonhuman Being Can Learn Language." *College Composition and Communication* 23:2 (May 1972): 142–54.

"The Parts, or Vestigial Remnants, of Speech." *College English* 18:7 (1957): 335–41.

Pickett at Gettysburg. Boston: Ginn, 1965.

Reading about Language (with Robert M. Gorrell). New York: Harcourt Brace Jovanovich, 1972.

Revising and Re-editing a Guide for Comparative Literature. Washington, D.C.: United States Office of Education, Bureau of Research, 1966.

"Seen But Not Heard: Language Teaching and Language Learning." In *The Range of English.* Urbana, Ill.: National Council of Teachers of English, 1968, pp. 75–104.

"Sufficient unto the Day Is the Propaganda Thereof." *School and Society* 51 (June 29, 1940): 769–73.

Thinking about Language: New York: Holt, Rinehart, and Winston, 1959.

Thunder on the River. New York: Atlantic Monthly/Little, Brown, 1949.

The Tree of Language (with Helene Laird). New York: World Publishing, 1955.

Webster's New World Thesaurus. New York: World Publishing, 1971.

West of the River. New York: Atlantic Monthly/Little, Brown, 1953.

"What Is the Matter That You Read?" In *The Meaning of Accountability in Reading,* edited by Adrian B. Sanford. Educational Development Corporation, 1977, pp. 25–39.

The Word: A Look at the Vocabulary of English. New York: Simon and Schuster, 1981.

Words, Words, Words. New York: Harcourt Brace Jovanovich, 1972.

The World through Literature (editor). New York: Appleton Century Crofts, 1951.

A Writer's Handbook. Boston: Ginn, 1965.

Writing Modern English (with Robert M. Gorrell). Englewood Cliffs, N.J.: Prentice-Hall, 1973.

You and Your Language. Englewood Cliffs, N.J.: Prentice-Hall, 1973.

Bibliography

Barnhart, Clarence L. "American Lexicography, 1945–1973." *American Speech* 53 (1978): 83–140.

Bentley, Robert H., and Samuel D. Crawford, eds. *Black Language Reader.* Glenview, Ill.: Scott, Foresman, 1973.

Bereiter, C., and S. Englemann. *Teaching Disadvantaged Children in the Pre-school.* Englewood Cliffs, N.J.: Prentice-Hall, 1966.

Bernstein, Basil. "Elaborated and Restricted Codes: Their Social Origins and Some Consequences." In *Communications and Culture,* edited by A. G. Smith, pp. 427–41. New York: Holt, Rinehart and Winston, 1966.

———. *Theoretical Studies towards a Sociology of Language.* Vol. 1 of *Class, Codes and Control.* London: Routledge and Kegan Paul, 1971.

Bernstein, Theodore M. *The Careful Writer: A Modern Guide to English Usage.* New York: Atheneum, 1965.

Biber, Douglas. "Spoken and Written Textual Dimensions in English: Resolving the Contradictory Findings." *Language* 62 (1986): 384–414.

———. Forthcoming. *Textual Relations in Speech and Writing.* Cambridge: Cambridge University Press, forthcoming.

Bierce, Ambrose. *Write It Right: A Little Blacklist of Literary Faults.* 1909. Reprint. New York: Union Library Association, 1934.

Blake, N. F. *Non-standard Language in English Literature.* London: André Deutsch, 1981.

Boardman, Phillip C. "'Beware the Semantic Trap': Language and Propaganda." *Etc.* 35 (1978): 78–85.

Bolinger, Dwight. "Fire in a Wooden Stove: On Being Aware in Language." In *The State of the Language,* edited by Leonard Michaels and Christopher Ricks, pp. 379–88. Berkeley: University of California Press, 1980.

———. *Language—The Loaded Weapon.* London: Longman, 1980.

Bush, Douglas. "Polluting Our Language." *American Scholar* (Spring 1972): 238–47.

Carroll, John B., ed. *Language, Thought and Reality: Selected Writings of Benjamin Lee Whorf.* Cambridge: MIT Press, 1956.

Chambers, J. K., and P. Trudgill. *Dialectology.* Cambridge: Cambridge University Press, 1980.

Clark, Thomas L. "The Usageasters." *American Speech* 55 (1980): 131–36.

Corbett, Edward P. J. "Public Doublespeak: If I Speak with Forked Tongue." *English Journal* 65:4 (April 1976): 16–17.

Creswell, Thomas. *Usage in Dictionaries and Dictionaries of Usage.* University, Ala.: University of Alabama Press, 1975.

Daniels, Harvey A. *Famous Last Words: The American Language Crisis Reconsidered.* Carbondale: Southern Illinois University Press, 1983.

Davies, Peter. *Roots: Family Histories of Familiar Words.* New York: McGraw-Hill, 1981.

Dillard, J. L. *Black English.* New York: Random House, 1972.

Dobson, E. J. "Early Modern Standard English." *Transactions of the Philological Society.* 1955. Reprinted in *Approaches to English Historical Linguistics,* edited by Roger Lass, pp. 419–39. New York: Holt, Rinehart and Winston, 1969.

Drysdale, Patrick. "Dictionary Etymologies: What? Why? and for Whom?" In *Papers of the Dictionary Society of North America 1979,* edited by Gillian Michell, pp. 39–50. London, Ont.: School of Library and Information Science, University of Western Ontario, 1981.

Durkacz, Victor Edward. *The Decline of the Celtic Languages.* Edinburgh: John Donald Publishers, Ltd., 1983.

Evans, Bergen, and Cornelia Evans. *A Dictionary of Contemporary American Usage.* New York: Random House, 1957.

Farrell, Thomas J. "IQ and Standard English." *College Composition and Communication* 34 (December 1983): 470–84.

Finegan, Edward. *Attitudes toward English Usage: The History of a War of Words.* New York: Teachers College Press, Columbia University, 1980.

Finegan, Edward, and Douglas Biber. "Toward a Unified Model of Sociolinguistic Prestige." In *Diversity and Diachrony,* edited by David Sankoff. Amsterdam: Benjamins, forthcoming.

Fisher, John H. "Chancery and the Emergence of Standard Written English in the Fifteenth Century." *Speculum* 52 (1977): 870–99.

Fisher, John H., Malcolm Richardson II, and Jane L. Fisher. *An Anthology of Chancery English.* Knoxville: University of Tennessee Press, 1984.

Follett, Wilson. *Modern American Usage: A Guide.* New York: Hill and Wang, 1966.

Fowler, Roger, Bob Hodge, Gunther Kress, and Tony Trew. *Language and Control.* London: Routledge and Kegan Paul, 1979.

Francis, W. Nelson. "Problems of Assembling and Computerizing Large Corpora." In *Computer Corpora in English Language Research,* edited by Stig Johansson, pp. 7–24. Bergen: Norwegian Computing Centre for the Humanities, 1982.

Fries, Charles Carpenter. *American English Grammar.* New York: Appleton-Century, 1940.

Fussell, Paul. *Caste Marks: Style and Status in the U.S.A.* London: Heinemann, 1984.

Goodman, Kenneth S., and C. Buck. "Dialect Barriers to Reading Comprehension Revisited." *Reading Teacher* 27 (1973): 6–12.

Goodman, Kenneth S., and Yetta Goodman. "Learning about Psycholinguistic Processes by Analyzing Oral Reading." *Harvard Educational Review* 47 (1977): 317–33.

Gorrell, Robert M., and Charlton Laird. *Modern English Handbook.* 4th ed. Englewood Cliffs, N.J.: Prentice-Hall, 1967.

Gove, Philip B. "Etymology in *Webster's Third New International Dictionary.*" *Word* 22 (1966): 7–82.

Greenough, James Bradstreet, and George Lyman Kittredge. *Words and Their Ways in English Speech.* New York: Macmillan, 1901.

Grice, H. P. "Logic and Conversation." In *Speech Acts.* Vol. 3 of *Syntax and Semantics,* edited by Peter Cole and Jerry L. Morgan, pp. 41–58. New York: Academic Press, 1975.

Haas, W. "On the Normative Character of Language." In *Standard Languages Spoken and Written,* edited by W. Haas. Manchester: Manchester University Press, 1982.

Hall, Robert A., Jr. *Leave Your Language Alone!* Ithaca, N.Y.: Linguistica, 1950. (Later retitled *Linguistics and Your Language.*)

Hartmann, R. R. K., ed. *Lexicography: Principles and Practice.* London: Academic Press, 1983.

Hartwell, Patrick. "Dialect Interference in Writing: A Critical View." *Research in the Teaching of English* 14 (1980): 101–18.

———. "Grammar, Grammars, and the Teaching of Grammar." *College English* 47 (1985): 105–27.

Haugen, Einar. "National and International Languages." In *The Ecology of Language: Essays by Einar Haugen,* edited by Anwar S. Dil. Stanford: Stanford University Press, 1972.

Heller, Louis G. "Lexicographic Etymology: Practice versus Theory." *American Speech* 40 (1965): 113–19.

Hess, David. "Reagan's Language on Benefits Confused, Angered Many." *Philadelphia Enquirer,* July 31, 1981, p. 6-a.

Hirsch, Jr., E. D. *Philosophy of Composition.* Chicago: University of Chicago Press, 1977.

Hockett, Charles F. "Distinguished Lecture: F." *American Anthropologist* 87 (1985): 263–81.

Hudson, R. A. *Sociolinguistics.* Cambridge: Cambridge University Press, 1980.

Hymes, Dell. *Foundations in Sociolinguistics: An Ethnographic Approach.* Philadelphia: University of Pennsylvania Press, 1974.

———. Foreword to *The Social Life of Language,* by Gillian Sankoff. Philadelphia: University of Pennsylvania Press, 1980.

Jespersen, Otto. *Mankind, Nation and Individual from a Linguistic Point of View.* 1925. Bloomington: Indiana University Press, 1964.

Johnson, Flora. "Making the Mother Tongue Safe from Democracy." *TWA Ambassador* (June 1980): 53–58.

Joos, Martin. *The Five Clocks.* New York: Harcourt, 1967.

Kiparsky, V. "Über etymologische Wörterbücher." *Neuphilologische Mitteilungen* 60 (1959): 209–30.

Kochman, Thomas. "Social Factors in the Teaching of Standard English." *Florida FL Reporter* (Spring/Summer 1969): 87–88, 157.

Kroch, Anthony S. "Toward a Theory of Social Dialect Variation." *Language in Society* 7 (1978): 17–36.

Kroch, Anthony S., and Cathy Small. "Grammatical Ideology and Its Effect on Speech." In *Linguistic Variation: Models and Methods,* edited by David Sankoff, pp. 45–55. New York: Academic Press, 1978.

Kučera, Henry, and W. Nelson Francis. *Computational Analysis of Present-Day American English.* Providence, R.I.: Brown University Press, 1967.

Labov, William. *The Social Stratification of English in New York City.* Washington, D.C.: Center for Applied Linguistics, 1966.

———. "The Logic of Nonstandard English." In *Report of the Twentieth Annual Roundtable Meeting on Linguistics and Language Studies,* edited by James E. Alatis, pp. 1–43 (widely reprinted). Washington, D.C.: Georgetown University Press, 1970.

———. *Sociolinguistic Patterns.* Philadelphia: University of Pennsylvania Press, 1972.

———. "Language Characteristics: Blacks." In *Black Language Reader,* edited by Robert H. Bentley and Samuel Crawford, pp. 96–116. Glenview, Ill.: Scott, Foresman, 1973. Reprinted from *Reading for the Disadvantaged,* edited by Thomas D. Horn, pp. 258–70. New York: Macmillan, 1973.

Landau, Sidney I. *Dictionaries: The Art and Craft of Lexicography.* New York: Charles Scribner's Sons, 1984.

Lehmann, Winfred P. *Proto-Indo-European Phonology.* Austin: University of Texas Press and Linguistic Society of America, 1952.

Lord, Robert. *Comparative Linguistics.* Teach Yourself Books. London: English Universities Press, 1966.

Lounsbury, Thomas R. *The Standard of Usage in English.* New York, Harper, 1908.

Macaulay, R. K. S. *Language, Social Class, and Education.* Edinburgh: Edinburgh University Press, 1977.

Malkiel, Yakov. *Etymological Dictionaries: A Tentative Typology.* Chicago and London: University of Chicago Press, 1976.

Mandelbaum, D. G., ed. *Selected Writings of Edward Sapir.* Los Angeles: University of California Press, 1949.

Mathews, M. M. *Words: How to Know Them.* New York: Henry Holt, 1956.

Meillet, Antoine. *The Indo-European Dialects.* Translated by Samuel N. Rosenberg. Alabama Linguistic and Philological Series, no. 15. University, Ala.: University of Alabama Press, 1967. French original, 1908.

Michaels, Leonard, and Christopher Ricks, eds. *The State of the Language.* Berkeley and Los Angeles: University of California Press, 1980.

Mitchell, Richard. *The Graves of Academe.* Boston: Little, Brown, 1981.

Mitford, Nancy, ed. *Noblesse Oblige.* New York: Harper and Row, 1956.

Morris, William. "The Making of a Dictionary—1969." *College Composition and Communication* 20 (1969): 198–203.

Morris, William, and Mary Morris. With the assistance of a panel of 136 distinguished consultants on usage. *Harper Dictionary of Contemporary Usage.* New York: Harper and Row, 1975.

Newman, Edwin. *Strictly Speaking: Will America Be the Death of English?* New York: Warner Books, 1974.

Nunberg, Geoffrey. "The Decline of Grammar." *Atlantic Monthly* (December 1983): 31–46.

O'London, John. *Is It Good English?* New York: Putnam's, 1925.

Orwell, George. *1984.* New York: New American Library, 1961.

Orwell, Sonia, and Ian Angus, eds. *The Collected Essays, Journalism and Letters of George Orwell.* 4 vols. Berkeley: University of California Press, 1976.

Partridge, Eric. *The Gentle Art of Lexicography as Pursued and Experienced by an Addict.* New York: Macmillan, 1963.

Pei, Mario. *The Families of Words.* New York: Harper and Brothers, 1962.

Perrin, Porter G. *Writer's Guide and Index to English.* 4th ed. Revised by Karl W. Dykema and Wilma R. Ebbitt. Chicago: Scott, Foresman, 1965.

Pooley, Robert C. *The Teaching of English Usage.* Urbana, Ill.: National Council of Teachers of English, 1974.

Price, Glanville. *The Languages of Britain.* London: Edward Arnold, 1984.

Quinn, Jim. *American Tongue and Cheek: A Populist Guide to Our Language.* New York: Pantheon, 1980.

Rank, Hugh, ed. *Language and Public Policy.* Urbana, Ill.: National Council of Teachers of English, 1974.

Richardson, Malcolm. "Henry V, the English Chancery, and Chancery English." *Speculum* 55 (1980): 726–50.

Ross, Alan S. C. *Etymology: With Especial Reference to English.* Language Library. London: André Deutsch, 1958.

Rubin, Donald L. "The Myth of Dialect Interference in Written Composition." *Arizona English Bulletin* 22:3 (1980): 55–67.

Samuels, M. L. "Some Applications of Middle English Dialectology." In

Approaches to English Historical Linguistics, edited by Roger Lass. New York: Holt, Rinehart and Winston, 1969.

———. *Linguistic Evolution.* Cambridge: Cambridge University Press, 1972.

Sankoff, Gillian. *The Social Life of Language.* Philadephia: University of Pennsylvania Press, 1980.

Schwartz, Judith I. "Dialect Interference in the Attainment of Literacy." *Journal of Reading* 25 (1982): 440–46.

Shaklee, Margaret. "The Rise of Standard English." In *Standards and Dialects in English.* Edited by Timothy Shopen and Joseph M. Williams. Cambridge, Mass.: Winthrop, 1980.

Shaughnessy, Mina. *Errors and Expectations.* New York: Oxford University Press, 1977.

Simon, John. *Paradigms Lost: Reflections on Literacy and Its Decline.* New York: Potter, 1980.

Sledd, James. "The Lexicographer's Uneasy Chair." *College English* 23 (1962): 682–87. Reprinted in *Dictionaries and THAT Dictionary,* edited by James Sledd and W. R. Ebbitt, pp. 228–36. Chicago: Scott, Foresman, 1962.

———. "Doublespeak: Dialectology in the Service of Big Brother." *College English* 33 (1972): 439–56.

———. "Linguistic Relativism: The Divorce of Word from Work." In *Studies in English Linguistics,* edited by Sidney Greenbaum, Geoffrey Leech, and Jan Svartvik, pp. 256–63. London and New York: Longman, 1979.

———. "Like Gag Me with a Spoon!" In *Test Your Word Power.* Edited by Jerome E. Agel. New York: Ballantine Books, 1984.

Slobin, Dan I. *Psycholinguistics.* 2d ed. Glenview, Ill.: Scott, Foresman, 1979.

Smitherman, Geneva, ed. *Black English and the Education of Black Children and Youth: Proceedings of the National Invitational Symposium on the King Decision.* Detroit: Wayne State University, 1981.

Svartvik, Jan, and Randolph Quirk, eds. *A Corpus of English Conversation.* Lund: Liber, 1980.

Taylor, Mary Vaiana. "The Folklore of Usage." *College English* 35:7 (1974): 756–68.

Trench, Richard Chenivex. "On Some Deficiencies in Our English Dictionaries." *Transactions of the Philological Society* 9 (1857): 3–8.

Trudgill, Peter. *The Social Differentiation of English in Norwich.* Cambridge: Cambridge University Press, 1974.

———, ed. *Sociolinguistic Patterns in British English.* London: Edward Arnold, 1978.

———, ed. *Language in the British Isles.* Cambridge: Cambridge University Press, 1984.

"Vigilans." *Chamber of Horrors: A Glossary of Official Jargon Both English and American*. Introduction by Eric Partridge. New York: British Book Centre, 1952.

Webbe, Joseph. *An Appeale to Truth, in the Controuersie betweene Art, & Vse; about the Best and Most Expedient Course in Languages*. 1622. Reprinted in English Linguistics, 1500–1800, edited by R. C. Alston, no. 42. Menston, England: Scolar Press, 1967.

Wilson, Kenneth G., R. H. Hendrickson, and Peter Alan Taylor. *Harbrace Guide to Dictionaries*. New York and Burlingame: Harcourt, Brace and World, 1963.

Wolfram, Walter A., and Ralph W. Fasold. "Toward Reading Materials for Speakers of Black English: Three Linguistically Appropriate Passages." In *Teaching Black Children to Read*, edited by Joan Baratz and Roger W. Shuy, pp. 138–55. Washington, D.C.: Center for Applied Linguistics, 1969.

Zgusta, Ladislav. *Manual of Lexicography*. Janua Linguarum, series maior 39. The Hague/Paris: Mouton, 1971.

Index